ADVANCE PRAISE

"Sweeton distills neuroscience into engaging, comprehensible information for the everyday clinical psychologist, making it significantly easier to incorporate it into our therapeutic work. I've used this with my toughest trauma clients with measurable success."

—**Gricelda Fragoso, Psy.D.**, Clinical Psychologist, Owner of Mind Body Soul Psychology

"Sweeton adeptly and singularly identifies and addresses the gap in translational science between neuroscience and mental health treatments. She moves neuroscience from an abstract, oblique idea to a comprehensible framework for clinicians and provides them with important and useful information about the vessel, the brain, through which they work. Her writing is clear and accessible; and the content goes above and beyond what most clinicians know about the brain and mental health and illness."

—**Christa Watson Pereira, Psy.D.**, Assistant Professor, University of California, San Francisco; Affiliate, University of California, Berkeley

"Sweeton has written a wonderful, well-written and insightful description of the way in which mental health and neuroscience connect."

—**Emma Seppälä, Ph.D.**, Yale School of Management, CCARE, Stanford University, author of *The Happiness Track*

Eight Key Brain Areas of Mental Health and Illness

Eight Key Brain Areas of Mental Health and Illness

JENNIFER SWEETON

W. W. NORTON & COMPANY
Independent Publishers Since 1923

Note to Readers: Standards of clinical practice and protocol change over time, and no technique or recommendation is guaranteed to be safe or effective in all circumstances. This volume is intended as a general information resource for professionals practicing in the field of psychotherapy and mental health; it is not a substitute for appropriate training, peer review, and/or clinical supervision. Neither the publisher nor the author(s) can guarantee the complete accuracy, efficacy, or appropriateness of any particular recommendation in every respect. As of press time, the URLs displayed in this book link or refer to existing sites. The publisher and author are not responsible for any content that appears on third-party websites.

For information about permission to reproduce selections from this book, write to Permissions, W. W. Norton & Company, Inc., 500 Fifth Avenue, New York, NY 10110

For information about special discounts for bulk purchases, please contact W. W. Norton Special Sales at specialsales@wwnorton.com or 800-233-4830

Manufacturing by Versa Press
Book design by Vicki Fischman
Production manager: Katelyn MacKenzie

Library of Congress Cataloging-in-Publication Data

Names: Sweeton, Jennifer, author.
Title: Eight key brain areas of mental health and illness / Jennifer Sweeton.
Description: First edition. | New York : W.W. Norton & Company, [2021] |
   Series: A Norton professional book | Includes bibliographical references and index.
Identifiers: LCCN 2021037037 | ISBN 9780393714135 (paperback) |
   ISBN 9780393714142 (epub)
Subjects: LCSH: Mental health. | Mental illness--Treatment. | Neuroscience.
Classification: LCC RC460 .S94 2021 | DDC 362.2--dc23
LC record available at https://lccn.loc.gov/2021037037

W. W. Norton & Company, Inc., 500 Fifth Avenue, New York, N.Y. 10110
www.wwnorton.com

W. W. Norton & Company Ltd., 15 Carlisle Street, London W1D 3BS

1 2 3 4 5 6 7 8 9 0

FOR MY CURIOUS AND BRIGHT DAUGHTER, ANNALIESE,
WHO IS THE INSPIRATION FOR ALL OF THE WORK I DO!

CONTENTS

CHAPTER 8
The Ventromedial Prefrontal Cortex

CHAPTER 9
The Dorsolateral Prefrontal Cortex

CHAPTER 10
Synthesis

ACKNOWLEDGMENTS

Thank you to all of my family, friends, and everyone at Norton for helping me write this book. I could not have made it through this process without your support! All books are difficult to write, but this one was especially challenging, as brain science is rarely straightforward and often difficult to synthesize. Reflecting on this journey, I am especially grateful for the unrelenting support of my husband, Tim, over these past few years. Thank you for all of the ways you've bolstered me, and for always believing in me and encouraging me to keep going! Additionally, I am thankful for Annaliese, my daughter, who keeps me grounded and motivates me to be the best possible version of myself. I'd also like to thank my parents for instilling in me the values of hard work and perseverance, and for cheering me on even when I've felt discouraged.

Finally, a huge thank you to the Norton team, and Deborah Malmud in particular, for their kindness and flexibility. This is a time-consuming and difficult process and everyone at Norton did a fantastic job at making it go as smoothly as possible. Thank you so much!

Eight Key Brain Areas of Mental Health and Illness

CHAPTER 1

Introduction

THE PURPOSE OF THIS HANDBOOK

I was originally trained as a neuroscientist, before becoming a clinical and forensic psychologist. In graduate school I studied affective neuroscience, which is essentially how emotion and mental health are represented in the brain, and I loved participating in neuroimaging research. I found brain science to be fascinating because it provided me with an inside view (literally!) of the brain and how it functions when people experience depression, anxiety, PTSD, or other mental health conditions. However, as time passed, I found myself becoming increasingly more interested in how we can *apply* neuroscience to treatment, in order to better understand and help those experiencing mental illness. I often completed research projects asking, "Now what? How can we use this information about the brain to help people?" This prompted me to pursue a doctorate in clinical psychology, so that I could focus more on translational research and treatment, though I still have a place in my heart for basic science.

Since my time in graduate school, a lot of progress has been made in the field of affective neuroscience (and in other types of neuroscience), but one thing has not changed: It is still difficult to know how to translate brain science into practice. In fact, given the depth and complexity of neuroscience research, it is arguably harder than ever to make sense of the research. This is especially true for mental health professionals without a neuroscience background who, like me, want to integrate up-to-date neuroscience data into their practice so they can take a brain-informed approach to treatment planning. If you've wanted to learn about the neuroscience of mental health and illness and how it can be applied to psychotherapy but have found some neuroscience courses or books to be overly detailed, technical, or too laborious to digest, this book is for you.

The good news is that you don't have to be a neuroscientist to learn the neuroscience of mental illness and to begin applying it to your practice. In fact, if you learn about just a few brain regions, you'll quickly be able to understand how several different mental health conditions may change the brain and how these brain changes show up in the therapy room as behaviors or symptoms. Moreover, when you learn which types of psychotherapeutic techniques alter brain functioning in the direction of health, you'll be able to take a client-centered, strategic, brain-based approach to treatment planning, that is, you can select therapeutic approaches based on the brain changes you hope to help your clients achieve.

With this book, I aim to provide you with that knowledge. Specifically, this handbook will help mental health clinicians:

Master the Neuroscience Basics Learn about the top eight brain regions that are most commonly involved in mental health and illness.

Link Brain Changes to Symptoms Discover how brain changes associated with mental illness may present in clients, as symptoms or behaviors.

Bridge (neuro)Science and Practice Identify the psychotherapeutic and psychopharmacological approaches that neuroscientific research indicates may repair or regulate specific brain regions.

HOW TO USE THIS HANDBOOK

The main content chapters of this handbook include Chapters 2–9; each chapter focuses on one specific brain region involved in mental health and illness. The brain areas are presented from the "bottom up"; that is, beginning with the lowest parts of the brain and working upward. The lower areas of the brain, such as the thalamus and amygdala, are subcortical regions involved in survival and some emotional functions. The midrange structures, such as the insula, are limbic structures involved in functions such as reward, body awareness, and emotional processing. The upper areas of the brain, such as the ventromedial cortex, are cortical structures and, as such, tend to focus mainly on cognitive functions, self-regulation, rational thought, and the integration of cognition and emotion.

While many readers will find it most helpful to read each chapter in full, and in order, the handbook chapters do not build on or rely on each other. Thus, each chapter stands on its own and can be read or referenced as needed, in no particular order.

Chapter 10 summarizes the content of Chapters 2–9 and organizes several key take-home points in its informational charts. A short synopsis of each content chapter is included for readers who want a quick refresher on a particular brain area or who seek a straightforward overview of the brain regions before reading the detailed content chapters. Thus, Chapter 10 can be thought of as a quick reference guide that helps readers consolidate and reinforce what they learned in earlier chapters or as an introduction to the content chapters. It is my hope that this handbook will help you feel excited about and confident in your knowledge about the neuroscience of mental health and how brain science can be applied to clinical practice.

CHAPTER 2

The Thalamus

THE THALAMUS'S LOCATION

The thalamus is an egg-shaped brain structure located above the brain stem, between the midbrain and the cerebral cortex (Franklin, 2017). It forms a large portion of the diencephalon (Snell, 2010), and is named after the Greek word "thalamos," meaning "inner-most room" (Jones, 2007). This is a fitting description, as the thalamus is found deep within the center of the brain (Figure 2.1).

The thalamus is comprised of more than 20 subsections (not pictured here; Herrero et al., 2002) within three main sections: anterior thalamus, medial thalamus, and lateral thalamus. Additionally, the thalamus contains three types of nuclei: sensory relay nuclei (which relay sensory information to the cortex), association nuclei (which receive input from the cortex), and nonspecific nuclei (which relay sensory information to, and receive it from, the cortex). The functions of the thalamus's main sections and nuclei are described in the following section.

THE THALAMUS'S FUNCTIONS
In a Nutshell

The thalamus has sometimes been referred to as the relay station for sensory information, because one function of this brain structure is to reroute incoming sensory information (except for smell, which projects directly to the amygdala) coming from the body to other brain regions for processing. Specifically, when the thalamus receives sensory input, it reroutes this information in two general directions: one route projects directly to

THALAMUS

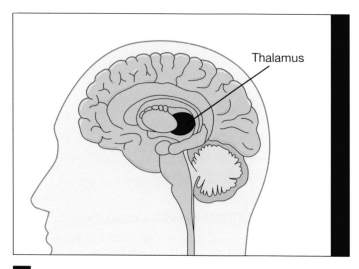

■ FIGURE 2.1: **THALAMUS**

the amygdala (involved in threat detection) and the other projects to the neocortex (the upper areas of the brain involved in executive functioning), and this information flows from the neocortex to the hippocampus (long-term memory center) and then down to the amygdala. Notably, the sensory information that is routed to the amygdala reaches this structure in about half the time it takes for the sensory information to arrive at cortical structures (12 and 25 milliseconds, respectively; LeDoux, 1996), meaning that the amygdala always processes information long before it reaches cortical areas. In other words, because of how the thalamus routes sensory information to these two areas of the brain, we always evaluate information in terms of its potential danger (amygdala processing) first, before "thinking" about the situation (cortical processing).

However, asserting that the thalamus simply reroutes sensory information is an oversimplification, as it is involved in several additional functions. For example, the thalamus serves as a relay station for some motor information and is believed to help keep the cortex updated on motor commands (Guillery & Sherman, 2011). Additionally, the thalamus is involved in sustaining short-term memory (Guo et al., 2017) and helps you keep your train of thought (Halassa et al., 2011). The following sections describe the thalamus's functions in additional specific domains.

~~~~~~

SLEEP

The thalamus plays a critical role in sleep, especially non-rapid eye movement (NREM) and slow wave sleep (Sforza et al., 1995; Jan et al., 2009). In particular, the thalamus has been found to produce slow wave sleep oscillations and sleep spindles (Coulon et al., 2012), which substantially affect sleep onset and quality.

Specifically, sleep spindles, which facilitate the transfer of neural signals between the prefrontal cortex (the site of working memory) and hippocampus (the site of long-term memory), are critical for long-term memory consolidation, learning, and sensory processing (de Gennaro & Ferrara, 2003; Gais et al., 2002; Maingret et al., 2016; see next section on the thalamus and memory). In other words, the thalamus, through the production of sleep spindles, helps to shift new information from working memory (which is short-term) to long-term memory, promoting learning and the strengthening long-term memory. This is why sleep spindle frequency dramatically increases right after an individual has had a novel experience or learned something new (Fogel & Smith, 2011). When sleep spindles are shorter, individuals experience poor sleep and insomnia (Normand et al., 2016) and may have difficulty performing well on cognitive and memory tasks.

~~~~~~

MEMORY

It is well-established that the prefrontal cortex is the main brain region involved in working memory (Goldman-Rakic, 1995). The thalamus, however, may also contribute to short-term memory. According to recent research, thalamic involvement may be essential for successful working memory. Specifically, during working memory the thalamus serves as a partner to the cortex, repeatedly communicating with the prefrontal cortex through strong connections with this region (Guo et al., 2017). In order to keep information in working memory, as you might do while rehearsing a phone number, both thalamic and prefrontal cortex activation may be required (Bolkan et al., 2017), and evidence suggests that thalamic activation during working memory tasks facilitates the prefrontal cortex activation needed to hold information in mind (Schmitt et al., 2017).

Additionally, the anterior nucleus of the thalamus may be involved in episodic memory, as it contributes to reciprocal hippocampal–prefrontal communications, thereby facilitating the maintenance of episodic memories. Damage to this area of the thalamus has been linked to episodic memory deficits, including those observed in thalamic strokes and Wernicke-Korsakoff syndrome (Child & Benarroch, 2013).

THE THALAMUS: MENTAL HEALTH CONDITIONS AND TREATMENT IMPLICATIONS

The thalamus is rarely thought of as a key area of the brain involved in mental health and illness, but it is involved in several mental health conditions. However, more often than not its role is to collaborate with other areas of the brain or to facilitate collaboration between different regions. Thus, it is rarely the case that the thalamus alone is responsible for symptoms of mental illness, and psychotherapy neuroscience research rarely discusses how therapies impact the activation or functioning of the thalamus. Below are some examples of how the thalamus is involved in mental health conditions and how it might contribute (with the help of other brain areas) to the efficacy of psychotherapy.

TRAUMA
Trauma and the Thalamus: What Happens?

A key neuroscience finding about the thalamus is that it tends to be less activated in individuals with PTSD when compared to healthy controls (Etkin & Wager, 2007; Kim et al., 2007; Yan et al., 2013). Hypoactivation of this area is apparent at rest; that is, when spontaneous brain activity is observed (Yan et al., 2013), as well as when some re-experiencing symptoms occur. Under some circumstances, however, individuals experiencing PTSD symptoms may exhibit *increased* thalamic activation (Kim et al., 2007). Specifically, this is most likely to occur when individuals experience dissociation and flashbacks (Liberzon et al., 1996), as opposed to when there is intentional trauma memory recall (see next section). Additionally, research has found weaker connectivity between the thalamus and the amygdala in trauma-exposed individuals with strong PTSD symptoms (Zhu et al., 2018); a decrease in PTSD symptom severity has been associated with an increase in thalamus–amygdala connectivity (Yoon et al., 2017).

Trauma and the Thalamus: How It Presents

The thalamus appears to be most involved in the re-experiencing symptoms of PTSD. In particular, the intentional recall of traumatic memories and some other re-experiencing symptoms, such as traumatic sensory reenactments, are associated with thalamic hypoactivation (Kim et al., 2007) and reduced connectivity with the amygdala (Yoon et al., 2017). In general, lower activation of the thalamus is believed to result in less filtering of sensory information (which is its main role as a sensory gatekeeper). More specifically, reduced connectivity between the amygdala and thalamus may indicate a disruption in the relaying of sensory information traveling from the thalamus to the amygdala (Lanius et al., 2006). It has been hypothesized that when individuals with PTSD are faced with trauma reminders, they are not able to filter, and thereby reduce the salience of, the sounds, smells, images, and other sensory components of these traumatic memories. This lack of sensory filtering makes trauma memories feel especially intense, and it can seem as though these events are happening in the present, not the past. Kim et al. (2007) added that when experiencing the re-experiencing symptoms of PTSD, individuals may shift their attention away from external stimuli toward internal sensory experiences. This in turn may further intensify re-experiencing symptoms and make them feel all-consuming to the person.

Conversely, it has been suggested that a sudden *increase* in thalamic activity may contribute to dissociative experiences (Lanius et al., 2001). As briefly alluded to above, the thalamus is believed to be involved in the shifting of attention between internal sensory experiences and external environmental stimuli. It has been posited that the thalamus helps integrate these internal and external experiences, creating one "reality" that takes both into consideration (Lanius et al., 2005). During dissociation, thalamic activity increases, and as with re-experiencing symptoms, this results in the individual withdrawing from the external world (Huber at al., 2001). To an outside observer, the individual may appear to be spacey and disconnected, and this is because the individual has become immersed in their own internal experiences. However, while re-experiencing symptoms produce strong sensory experiences, presumably due to low thalamic activation that results in lowered filtering of sensory information, dissociation creates a different experience. In the case of dissociation there is thalamic hyperactivation that may lead to an overfiltering of sensory information, creating a feeling of numbness or nothingness.

Treatment Implications

Unlike some other areas of the brain, such as the insula, prefrontal cortex, or amygdala, ways to directly alter thalamic functioning with psychotherapy are unclear. This is partly due to the thalamus's intimate connections with other brain areas. First and foremost, the thalamus is a relay station for sensory information; connecting various brain regions is its main function, making it difficult to know exactly how to change thalamic functioning in isolation.

However, some treatment implications can be gleaned from an increased understanding of the thalamus. For example, Eye Movement Desensitization and Reprocessing (EMDR) is an evidence-based therapy for PTSD that may alter thalamic functioning so that individuals with PTSD can better integrate the components of a traumatic experience (Bergmann, 2008), while staying rooted in present moment awareness, when reminders of these memories arise. Specifically, the bilateral movement/stimulation that characterizes EMDR has been proposed to activate multiple areas of the thalamus (Bergmann, 2008), resulting in better filtering of sensory information, integration of multiple components of a traumatic experience (including somatosensory, cognitive, and memorial components), and improved inhibition of amygdala activation (Bermann, 2008; Peres et al., 2007). These, in turn, reduce the intensity of re-experiencing symptoms. This may not be surprising, given that the thalamus activates during eye movements (Huber et al., 2001). It has also been proposed that the eye movements that characterize EMDR activate the thalamus and orient the individual to their external world (through focus on an external stimulus) while simultaneously allowing the individual to access their internal world (including the sensations associated with the traumatic memory; Bergmann, 2008). In this way, EMDR helps the client attend to their internal and external worlds at the same time and prevents the individual from becoming too immersed in their internal experiences. Interestingly, cognitive behavioral therapy (CBT) has also been shown to activate the thalamus, with a corresponding reduction in re-experiencing symptoms (Peres et al., 2007).

ANXIETY

Anxiety and the Thalamus: What Happens?

Thalamic activation has consistently been associated with fear conditioning, worry, and anticipatory anxiety, especially in specific regions of the thalamus. For example, the paraventricular nucleus of the thalamus (PVT), which receives input from pain-sensing brain structures, activates in response to psychological stressors (Spencer et al., 2004) and appears to facilitate and regulate fear processing that subsequently occurs in the amygdala (Wilensky et al., 2006). In other words, the thalamus is involved in fear acquisition (Dunsmoor & Paz, 2015). In fact, when the PVT is prevented from projecting neurons to the amygdala, fear conditioning does not occur, and fear memory is not stored (Penzo et al., 2015).

Additionally, the thalamus activates during anticipatory anxiety and worry. In one fMRI study, increased thalamic activation was observed when individuals with phobias anticipated phobia-relevant stimuli (Straube et al., 2007), and several additional studies have shown the thalamus to activate in response to threat expectancy in general (Nitschke et al., 2006; Yoshimura et al., 2014). Similarly, worry has been associated with an increase in cerebral blood flow in the thalamus, especially in those who meet criteria for generalized anxiety disorder (GAD; Karim et al., 2017).

Anxiety and the Thalamus: How It Presents

Thalamic activation, in the context of anxiety, may present as a sensitivity to threat or danger. The individual may appear jumpy or vigilant and may experience a vague feeling that something bad might happen. This anticipatory anxiety may have a specific target, as in the case of a specific phobia, or may be more generalized, as with generalized anxiety disorder, wherein the individual experiences worry about a variety of situations and topics. Also, because thalamic activation (especially in the PVT) facilitates fear conditioning, anxious individuals may become afraid of situations, people, or circumstances faster and more intensely than nonanxious individuals. One way to think about this is that anxious individuals, partly due to thalamic activation, are primed to learn fear, which may in part explain the high comorbidity between various anxiety disorders.

Treatment Implications

To date, there has been a paucity of research showing the impact of anxiety treatment on the thalamus, specifically. However, psychopharmacological treatment has shown promising results, as has CBT. For instance, paroxetine has been shown to decrease thalamic activation (Duval et al., 2015) and may weaken the functional connectivity between the thalamus, insula, and anterior cingulate cortex (Gimenez et al., 2014). These changes have been associated with lowered anxiety and a reduction in reactivity/sensitivity to anxiety cues. Previously, similar results had been demonstrated with the use of fluoxetine (Baxter et al., 1992) and citalopram (Furmark et al., 2002) for anxiety treatment.

While the mechanisms of change are not clear, CBT has also been associated with lowered thalamic activation in anxious individuals. Some research showing this finding examined the effects of CBT, medication, and placebo groups. For instance, Furmark et al. (2002) found that individuals with social anxiety during public speaking exhibited reduced thalamic blood flow after completing CBT. These individuals reported feeling less anxious about public speaking than they felt prior to CBT. Also, Baxter et al. (1992) found CBT was associated with reduced connectivity between the thalamus and other brain regions, such as the orbitofrontal cortex, after CBT, suggesting a reduction in reactivity and sensitivity to anxiety cues. Finally, Schwartz et al. (1996) found that behavior modification therapy alone reduced functional connectivity between the thalamus and other regions, and this reduction was associated with reduced OCD symptoms. In some studies, CBT consisted of techniques such as breath control, psychoeducation, progressive muscle relaxation, cognitive restructuring, and in vivo exposure (Porto et al., 2009). Thus, it is reasonable to conclude that a combination of medication and cognitive behavioral techniques may be helpful in treating anxiety and for helping to reduce thalamic activation and connectivity.

ADDICTION

Addiction and the Thalamus: What Happens?

The paraventricular nucleus of the thalamus (PVT), described in the last section, is one of the main regions of the thalamus believed to be involved in the neurocircuitry of addiction, as it is part of the cortico-striatal-thalamo-cortical circuit (Huang et al., 2018). While the thalamus alone may not play a large role in the development or maintenance of addiction, the brain circuits it is involved in have been found to regulate motivation and reward (Haber & Calzavara, 2009), control goal-directed behavior (Parnaudeau et al., 2015) and may influence drug-seeking behavior (Zhou & Zhu, 2019).

Specifically, the PVT is part of a drug-seeking circuitry that includes the nucleus accumbens, prefrontal cortex, and amygdala (Vertes & Hoover, 2008), and it can influence all of these structures (Otake & Nakamura, 1998), which are known to be key players in addiction. Moreover, stimulation of this area of the thalamus produces dopamine in the nucleus accumbens, often referred to as the addiction center of the brain (Parsons et al., 2007), and is believed to promote drug-seeking behaviors (Millan et al., 2017). Thus, it is possible that the PVT is partially responsible for the activation of the nucleus accumbens and the dopamine increase in this area when individuals think about, or engage in, drug-seeking behavior. Interestingly, lesions in the PVT are associated with a suppression of drug-seeking behavior (James & Dayas, 2013), providing further evidence of the PVT's role in motivation and goal-directed behavior.

Addiction and the Thalamus: How It Presents

Activation of the PVT in individuals with a history of addiction can indicate a heightened reactivity, or sensitivity, to drug-related reward cues (Wolter et al., 2019), making it difficult to divert focus from stimuli such as beer commercials, drug-related smells, etc. Sustained focus on these types of stimuli can lead to the release of anticipatory dopamine (presumably in the nucleus accumbens), which predicts subsequent relapse (Witteman et al., 2015). Thus, addicted individuals may feel particularly drawn to drug and alcohol cues and reminders of usage, more so than individuals who have no history of addiction. While it might be possible for nonaddicted individuals to resist, or orient away from, drug or alcohol-related reward cues, the PVT appears to make this especially difficult for addicted individuals, especially when under stress (Watson et al., 2019).

Treatment Implications

As stated before, it can be difficult to isolate the role of the thalamus in mental disorders, as it functions mainly as a relay station that connects several brain regions. This makes thalamus-specific treatment implications difficult to identify. However, some broad recommendations have been proposed that may help those experiencing addiction recover and heal. One suggestion from Watson et al. (2019) is to train individuals to strengthen executive control abilities so that individuals become able to override or suppress attention toward drug-related reward signals. If this strategy were successful, addicted individuals might be able to attend away from drug or alcohol reminders, such as a beer commercial, and focus instead on a target of their choosing.

In order to develop this ability, concentrated effort needs to be spent on strengthening the prefrontal cortex, the site of executive functioning and control. Notably, the prefrontal cortex is connected to the thalamus and under some circumstances may be capable of downregulating the activation of the thalamus, resulting in greater executive control. For instance, Watson et al. (2019) note that executive control training, which strengthens the prefrontal cortex, can reduce alcohol consumption and even relapse in individuals diagnosed with alcohol use disorder.

The processes by which executive control can be trained are not clear; however, it has been proposed that the skills taught in some cognitive behavioral therapies may help strengthen executive control. These therapies, which often include skills such as thought-stopping or cognitive restructuring, have also been associated with increased prefrontal cortex activation (Mohlman & Gorman, 2005) and volume (De Lange et al., 2008). Additionally, it has been suggested that cognitive behavioral therapies may help addicted individuals learn how to anticipate and desire nonalcohol or nondrug-related rewards, in addition to reacting less intensely to substance-related cues. In one study, cocaine-dependent individuals who began CBT one year prior showed increased activation in the thalamus when anticipating a monetary reward as compared to their baseline activation the previous year (Balodis et al., 2016). The authors concluded that these individuals were able to learn how to anticipate nondrug rewards, as evidenced by thalamic activation, with the help of CBT.

OTHER MENTAL HEALTH CONDITIONS

The thalamus is likely involved in several additional mental health conditions or challenges, two of which are depression and insomnia. Further research is needed to better understand the thalamus's role in these conditions and in treatment implications, but some basic patterns of activation and connectivity have been identified. For instance, compared to healthy controls, thalamic volume in depressed individuals tends to be lower (Du et al., 2012; Li et al., 2010) and connectivity between the thalamus and other regions, such as the medial prefrontal cortex, orbitofrontal cortex, and ventral striatum, tends to be weaker (Jia et al., 2014; Satterthwaite et al., 2015). It has been posited that these thalamic structural and functional patterns contribute to mood regulation difficulties.

As discussed earlier in this chapter, a main function of the thalamus is to regulate NREM sleep, in part through sleep spindles. Thus, it is perhaps not surprising that the thalamus also plays a role in insomnia and conditions related to insomnia and/or sleep spindle disruption more broadly. Specifically, insomnia has been associated with reduced thalamic volume and connectivity with other brain regions (Li et al., 2019; Liu et al., 2016), much like in depression. Individuals with this thalamic profile tend to experience early morning awakenings in addition to difficulty falling asleep, which are also common in depressive disorders. While research does not yet provide guidance for how to shift thalamic activity directly, the altered thalamic activation and functioning observed in various disorders might eventually help clinicians identify brain markers for different conditions, and future research may help clinicians discover ways to change thalamic activations and networks in the direction of health.

CHAPTER 3

The Amygdala

THE AMYGDALA'S LOCATION

The word "amygdala" comes from the Greek word for "almond" due to the almond-like shape of this structure (LeDoux, 2007), which is found deep in the temporal lobes of the brain (see Figure 3.1 for a side, or sagittal, view of this region). The amygdala is comprised of several nuclei clusters, which will not be detailed here. Together, these amygdala clusters are considered part of the limbic (emotion) system (Amunts et al., 2005), though the medial and central nuclei have also been considered a part of the basal ganglia (Swanson & Petrovich, 1998). The amygdala, which a critical component of the emotional brain, is positioned near the anterior (front) border of the hippocampus (Rajmohan & Mohandas, 2007), which is involved in memory storage (see Chapter 4 for information on the hippocampus). Technically, humans and other vertebrates have two amygdalae (plural), one in each hemisphere of the brain, and each is involved in slightly different functions (see following sections for more details).

THE AMYGDALA'S FUNCTIONS
In a Nutshell

The amygdala is perhaps best known as the fear processing center of the brain (see next section for more details). Sometimes considered the "fear center" of the brain, the amygdala plays an important role in aggression, fear learning, stress, anxiety, and emotional memory (Abuhasan & Siddiqui, 2018). However, the amygdala is not simply a fear center; research has shown the left and right amygdalae may each be involved in process-

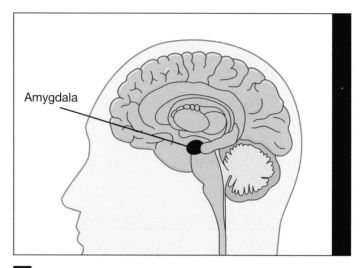

Amygdala

FIGURE 3.1: AMYGDALA

ing different emotions. For example, when electrically stimulated, the right amygdala tends to induce the experience of negative emotions (including fear), whereas stimulating the left amygdala has been found to produce aversive *or* pleasant emotions, such as happiness (Lanteaume et al., 2007).

The left amygdala also plays a role in positive reinforcement (Murray et al., 2009), connecting to the reward circuit in the brain. This may explain why the amygdala is involved in libido (Salamon et al., 2005) and sexual activity (Baird et al., 2004) as well as risk-taking behaviors. For instance, lesions in this region of the brain, which can lead to reduced activation, have been associated with increased risk-taking and reduced loss aversion (De Martino et al., 2010), even when risk-taking is not logical or likely to be of benefit to the individual. Also, amygdalar volume decreases with age (Walhovd et al., 2005), often leading to less activation. When this occurs, individuals tend to become less loss-averse.

Increased amygdalar volume, conversely, has been linked to rage, fear (Blair, 2012), and negative emotions more broadly (Gerritsen et al., 2012; Holmes et al., 2012), in addition to binge drinking and alcoholism (Cozzoli et al., 2016; Hill et al., 2001). Larger amygdalae have also been observed in individuals who experienced adverse experiences in childhood, such as abuse or neglect (Tottenham et al., 2010). However, larger amygdalae are also associated with strong social skills; individuals with large amygdalae tend to have more friends and active social circles (Dunbar, 2012). Increased activation in this region may also facilitate the encoding of emotional memories, especially fear memories (Schafe et al., 2000).

The following sections describe the amygdala's functions in specific domains.

FEAR

When mental health professionals think about the amygdala, fear is often the first thing that comes to mind. Often dubbed the "smoke detector" of the brain (Van der Kolk, 2015), the amygdala is perhaps best known for its role in producing and processing fear through threat detection. Specifically, when threat is perceived, the amygdala activates, and it deactivates when no danger is detected. Research has shown that electrical stimulation of this area of the brain induces fear, while amygdalar lesions can reduce one's ability to experience fear (Amuhasan & Siddiqui, 2018).

The amygdala is considered a survival brain structure and is one of the first areas of the brain to process incoming sensory information from the body. All of our interactions with the external world come into the body through one or more of the senses and are then routed to the spinal cord. From there, sensory information travels upward to the brain for processing. The thalamus receives most of this sensory information, which is then routed to other areas of the brain, including the amygdala. Smell, however, bypasses the thalamus and goes directly to the amygdala (see Chapter 2 for more details on the thalamus), which is likely why our experience of smell is so emotional (Arshamian et al., 2013).

After sensory information is processed by the thalamus, it travels to two locations: the cortex and the amygdala (Garrido et al., 2012). Notably, the amygdala receives this sensory information in about half the time it takes for the information to reach the cortex. This means that the amygdala, this subcortical area outside of conscious awareness and conscious control, always processes sensory information long before the rational, logical, conscious areas of your brain (Pessoa & Adolphs, 2010; see Chapters 7–9 for more information about specific areas of the prefrontal cortex and anterior cingulate cortex).

When sensory information reaches the amygdala, this "smoke detector" of the brain then asks the question, "Is this dangerous?" If the amygdala determines that a threat is present, it activates in proportion to the perceived level of danger. If not, baseline activation is maintained. When a threat is perceived and the amygdala activates (as measured by blood flow), fear may be experienced. When this occurs, the amygdala sends threat signals up to the cortical areas of the brain, dulling their activation, while also sending threat signals down to the hypothalamus, which activates the fear pathway of the brain and body (Davis et al., 2010). Thus, amygdala activation, which produces fear, can make it difficult to think rationally (because the thinking areas of the brain get shut down), and puts the body into the fight-or-flight response via activation of the HPA axis (hypothalamus-pituitary-adrenals pathway). It is believed that this enhances survival; when faced with an acute threat, we feel afraid and the amygdala prepares us to manage the threat (through fighting, fleeing, or freezing) in order to stay alive. The dulling of the thinking center of the brain is also advantageous in moments of intense fear and threat, as it's rarely intelligent to deeply analyze something or someone who is about to kill you!

MEMORY

The amygdala also plays roles in implicit memory formation (and to a limited extent, explicit memory consolidation; Phelps & LeDoux, 2005). Implicit memories, by definition, are ones we cannot consciously remember. Implicit memories are housed in lower, more subcortical areas of the brain, including the amygdala, cerebellum, and basal ganglia (Baars & Gage, 2010). These memories are not experienced as thoughts, but rather as sensory experiences (Payne et al., 2015) and emotions. Most often, implicit memories are formed in response to situations, people, or events that were threatening and produced fear.

A famous example that demonstrates how implicit memory functions comes from a neurologist's case study of a woman who had lost the ability to form new explicit memories. This woman's implicit memory system was intact, but brain damage prevented her from forming new explicit memories, which are memories that can be consciously recalled. The neurologist examining this woman met with her frequently, and every time he presented himself, she greeted him as a stranger, with no conscious recollection of having ever met him. Week after week the two met, and the woman was never able to form an explicit memory of the doctor. One day, the neurologist greeted the patient and tried something different, placing a sharp pin between his fingers and pricking her as he shook her hand when they greeted one another. The patient immediately pulled her hand back in response to the sharp prick and refused to speak with the doctor further. After this, when the neurologist returned to see the patient days later, the patient did not have any explicit memory of the pin incident and greeted the doctor with a smile. However, when the doctor reached out to shake the woman's hand, she refused to, but could not provide an explanation for this. It simply didn't *feel right* (Draaisma, 2000). This is a great example of implicit memory, wherein the amygdala remembers a threat or danger even when the explicit memory center (hippocampus) did not encode them.

EMOTIONAL/AFFECTIVE EMPATHY

In addition to playing a role in fear processing, the amygdala is more broadly involved in emotion recognition, social information processing, and social behavior (Becker et al., 2012). For example, research has demonstrated social judgment and emotion recognition impairment in individuals with amygdala lesions (Adolphs et al., 2005), indicating the importance of the amygdala in these domains. It has been hypothesized that the amygdala's ability to recognize, reconstruct, and perhaps even predict the emotional states of others may be possible thanks to mirror neurons in this brain region.

Mirror neurons (or simulation neurons) may help individuals read and understand the mental and emotional states of other people (Grabenhorst et al., 2019). It has also been suggested that these neurons, when activated, may help individuals *experience* and effectively respond to the emotions of others (Pfeifer et al., 2008). In other words, the mirror neurons in the amygdala (and other brain regions) may promote empathy, which is considered a key function of the amygdala. Interestingly, the absence of mirror (simulation) neurons in the amygdala has been associated with reduced social cognition and empathy (Grabenhorst et al., 2019), whereas overactivation of these neurons in the amygdala has been linked hypersensitivity to others' emotions and social anxiety (Amaral, 2002). Similarly, amygdalar damage resulting from Urbach-Wiethe disease was associated with impaired affective empathy (Stone et al., 2003), and individuals with psychopathic traits showed amygdala underactivation during an empathy task (Marsh et al., 2013).

To summarize, lower amygdala activation is associated with lower empathy; higher amygdala activation is associated with higher empathy. Moreover, amygdala volume has also been linked to the experience of empathy. Specifically, high empathy is associated with larger left amygdalae, whereas alexithymia (wherein an individual has a difficult time experiencing emotion) is associated with smaller left amygdala volume (Goerlich-Dobre et al., 2015). Thus, both amygdala activation and size appear to correlate with the experience of affective/emotional empathy.

It has been proposed that the amygdala is part of a larger neural system of emotional empathy that may include other brain regions, such as the insula, inferior frontal gyrus, superior temporal gyrus, anterior cingulate cortex, prefrontal cortex, and other areas (Carr et al., 2003; Stone et al., 2003). Together, these areas help the brain recognize and experience the emotions of others through facial expressions, body language, tone of voice, etc. (Gorno-Tempini et al., 2001). Thus, the amygdala likely does not function in isolation, but rather as part of a larger neural network involved in emotional/affective empathy (Leigh et al., 2013). Cognitive empathy, which involves higher level perspective-taking, involves some of the same areas of the brain as emotional empathy but is not believed to involve the amygdala (Decety & Jackson, 2004; Shamay-Tsoory et al., 2003; see Chapter 9 for more information on cognitive empathy).

THE AMYGDALA: MENTAL HEALTH CONDITIONS
AND TREATMENT IMPLICATIONS

The amygdala, more than most other brain structures, is implicated in many mental health conditions. In particular, the amygdala plays a large role in the development and maintenance of anxiety disorders, PTSD, and depressive disorders (Forster et al., 2012; Perlman et al., 2004) as well as personality disorders. Below, the role of the amygdala in some of these disorders is detailed, and clinical implications are explored.

ANXIETY

Anxiety and the Amygdala: What Happens?

Anxiety is a broad term that encompasses several mental health conditions, including (but not limited to) social anxiety disorder (SAD), generalized anxiety disorder (GAD), panic disorder (PD), and specific phobia (SP). Though OCD is no longer categorized as an anxiety disorder by the DSM-5, much of the research still considers OCD to be a type of anxiety. While the functioning and volume size of the amygdala may vary in each of these disorders, some patterns can be identified. For example, the amygdala has consistently been found to be hyperactive, or hyperreactive, in PD, SP, and SAD. While this has also been found to be true in GAD and OCD at times, these latter two disorders may be partially characterized by activation in a connecting brain region, called the "extended amygdala" (described later in this section).

Some research has found no difference in amygdala activation at rest, both in SAD (Stein & Leslie, 1996) and PD (Eren et al., 2003). However, when presented with stressful social situations, such as public speaking, the amygdala's activation was found to be higher in those with SAD than in healthy controls (Tillfors et al., 2001). Similarly, the amygdala (especially the right amygdala) has been shown to activate during panic attacks (Dresler et al., 2011; Pfleiderer et al., 2007) and in SP when individuals are presented with stimuli related to their phobia(s) (Åhs et al., 2009; Dilger et al., 2003; File et al., 1998). Interestingly, in SAD, the amygdala's activation was substantially higher even when presented with aversive stimuli that had nothing to do with social interaction or performance (Schneider et al., 1999). This has also been found to be the case with those experiencing OCD (Breiter & Rauch, 1996), meaning that the amygdalae of those with SAD, OCD, and perhaps other anxiety disorders may be especially reactive to distressing stimuli, regardless of what the stimuli are. This is especially pronounced when, as is often the case in anxiety disorders, high amygdala activation is paired with low activation in some areas of the prefrontal cortex, such as the ventromedial prefrontal cortex (Adhikari et al., 2015; for more information on the ventromedial prefrontal cortex, refer to Chapter 8).

Additionally, amygdala volume has been found to be smaller in OCD (Szeszko et al., 1999) and PD (Hayano et al., 2009), suggesting that increased amygdala activation does not necessarily imply a larger amygdala. In fact, the opposite might be true; it has been proposed that hyperreactivity of the amygdala may lead to atrophy or smaller amygdalae may be prone to overactivation (McEwen, 2003). But regardless the reason, it has been found that smaller amygdalae is sometimes associated with higher amygdala activation.

Thus, while some generalizations can be drawn from the research about amygdala activation and size in anxiety disorders, there is also some complexity worth noting, as a deeper understanding can help clinicians better select treatments that may be effective for treating anxiety. In particular, the amygdala may not be responsible for the sustained anxiety experienced in disorders such as GAD and OCD. A lesser-known area, the bed nucleus of the stria terminalis (BNST), has been found to be involved in worry, chronic anxiety, and dread, whereas the amygdala is more associated with acute, short-term experiences of threat and fear (Yassa et al., 2012). The BNST, sometimes referred to as the extended amygdala (Daldrup et al., 2016), may have evolved after the amygdala, as a sort of extension to this structure (Buckley et al., 2018). The BNST appears to play a strong role in disorders such as OCD and GAD (Kohl et al., 2016; Winter et al., 2019) and is believed to collaborate with the amygdala to mediate anxiety in these disorders (Lesting et al., 2011).

Anxiety and the Amygdala: How It Presents

In anxiety disorders it is common for the amygdala to hyperactivate in response to distressing stimuli, which are experienced as acute, "in the moment" fear and threat. This is especially common in those individuals suffering from SP and PD. Additionally, in some anxiety disorders the extended amygdala, the BNST, is hyperactive, leading to feelings of worry and/or sustained anxiety. This type of activation has been observed in OCD, GAD, and SAD. Thus, the amygdala may contribute to short-term, acute fear and panic (including panic attacks), whereas the BNST may help induce feelings of prolonged anxiety, including dread. Of course, it is possible that some individuals with anxiety experience activation of both the amygdala and BNST and thus report feeling panic *and* dread or worry.

Amygdala activation can present in anxious clients as physical correlates of stress, such as muscle tension, rapid breathing, gastrointestinal discomfort, shakiness, increased heart rate, etc. Clients with high amygdala activation may also feel hypervigilant, easily startled, distracted, and panicked. In session, these individuals may appear, or report feeling, overwhelmed and out of their "window of tolerance." When this occurs, clients may have a difficult time staying present and focusing and may feel overwhelmed and distracted by intense, distressing physical sensations, such as the ones described above.

Extended amygdala (BNST) activation may present a bit differently in session. Often, activation in this brain region is associated with worry, dread, and sustained anxiety that is a bit less intense than the amygdala activation described above, which is linked to more acute panic and emotional overwhelm. While clients with BNST activation will experience similar physical correlates of stress, they are less likely to be so overwhelmed by these sensations that they cannot attend to what is being discussed or practiced during psychotherapy. In fact, these clients often seem to intellectualize, focusing on talking themselves in and out of worries. They may even report that they are not experiencing strong anxiety as they ruminate, though usually they can recognize that some level of stress or anxiety is attached to the worries. In a psychotherapy session, clients with BNST may appear talkative and engaged with their ruminative thoughts. They often spend time in sessions focusing on the situations, people, or things they fear or worry about. They may also repeatedly seek comfort and assurance from the therapist.

Additionally, amygdala and BNST activations can co-occur, producing a hybrid of what is described above. This is commonly the case in clients who experience both acute, intense anxiety reactions (such as panic) and also the slightly less intense but prolonged anxiety that is associated with worry and dread.

Treatment Implications

The amygdala is one of the most studied brain regions involved in mental health and illness, making it a focus of neuroscientific psychotherapy research. While it can be difficult to discern why evidence-based therapies for various disorders work so well, an abundance of research suggests that treatment efficacy may be linked in part to changes elicited in the amygdala (in addition to other brain regions). Moreover, various types of techniques and approaches have been linked to amygdala (and BNST) deactivation, providing a variety of options for clinicians who treat anxiety disorders.

Exposure-based therapies are commonly utilized when treating PD, SP, OCD, and SAD, and their effectiveness has been well-established (Abramowitz et al., 2019; McNally, 2007; Mineka & Thomas, 1999). While these therapeutic approaches and techniques, including Exposure and Response Prevention, other in vivo exposure techniques, imaginal exposure techniques, systematic desensitization, and EMDR, have been associated with brain change in several areas, a key finding is that they have been linked to reduced amygdala activation (Hauner et al., 2012; DeRaedt, 2006; Pagani et al., 2013; Simon et al., 2014). One theory for this association is that repeated exposure calms the amygdala by pairing the feared stimulus (or situation, etc.) with a neutral (or even positive) outcome, thereby teaching the amygdala that activation in response to that stimulus is not needed. For example, if a client has a phobia of driving over bridges, then in exposure therapy the client may be gradually exposed to this fear, eventually driving repeatedly over bridges. So long as driving over the bridges does not result in some catastrophic outcome, eventually the client's amygdala will habituate to this behavior and will no longer activate so strongly when faced with the prospect of driving over a bridge. In other words, the amygdala is able to learn, through experience, that driving over bridges is not as dangerous as once experienced.

In addition to exposure therapies, somatic-based, or "bottom-up," approaches to therapy have been associated with amygdala deactivation (to varying degrees). These techniques, which are often considered relaxation exercises, can include progressive muscle relaxation, autogenic training, diaphragmatic breathing exercises, and body-focused mindfulness practices, such as a body scan (Kim et al., 2014; Leung et al., 2018; Marchand, 2014). For instance, mindful attention to one's breath has been associated with a reduction in amygdala activation and increased connectivity between the amygdala and prefrontal cortex (PFC), an area of the brain involved in rational thought and executive functioning (Doll et al., 2016). This improved connectivity between the PFC and amygdala better enables the PFC to downregulate the amygdala. Similarly, mindfulness-based stress reduction, an eight-week protocol that has been found to reduce stress and anxiety, largely focuses on somatic techniques and has been linked to reduced amygdala activation (Gotink et al., 2016).

Moreover, some cognitive approaches, such as meditation and cognitive restructuring, have been associated with lowered amygdala and/or BNST activation (Hölzel et al., 2013; Straube, 2016; Taren et al., 2015; Weng et al., 2018; Winter et al., 2019). Whereas exposure-based approaches tend to be recommended for anxiety conditions such as PD and SP, classic cognitive techniques are often selected for the more prolonged anxiety observed in GAD and SAD. A possible explanation for this is that cognitive-intensive techniques tend to strengthen areas of the PFC (see Chapters 8 and 9 for more information about the PFC), which in turn can downregulate the activation of the amygdala. For example, specific areas of the prefrontal cortex, such as the ventromedial prefrontal cortex and medial prefrontal cortex, have been found to downregulate the basolateral section of the amygdala through top-down control (Adhikari et al., 2015; Likhtik et al.,

AMYGDALA

2014). This, in turn, can help facilitate fear extinction (Greenberg et al., 2013) and improve emotion regulation (Narayanan et al., 2006).

Thus, techniques that require clients to engage in cognitive reframing, restructuring, and reappraisal, along with exercises that train clients how to direct, redirect, and focus attention, can be helpful for reducing amygdala and BNST activation. These skills are often taught in cognitive or cognitive behavioral therapies, in meditation, and in other mindfulness-based interventions. For instance, Hölzel et al. (2013) found that mindfulness training was associated with improved emotion regulation, increased ventrolateral prefrontal cortex activation, reduced amygdala activation, and improved connectivity between the prefrontal cortex and amygdala. Similarly, Weng et al. (2018) showed that amygdala activation decreased after compassion meditation training, and Desbordes et al. (2012) demonstrated an association between mindfulness meditation training and lowered amygdala response to aversive stimuli in SAD. Moreover, therapies that incorporate traditional cognitive restructuring or reframing techniques, such as metacognitive therapy, may help reduce BNST activation in anxiety disorders such as OCD (Straube, 2016; Winter et al., 2019).

Finally, psychiatric medications may be helpful in the treatment of anxiety. In particular, anxiolytics may help reduce amygdala activation (Davis et al., 2010). Also, antidepressants have been associated with both amygdala (Harmer et al., 2006) and BNST reduction (Cadeddu et al., 2014), though some research has not found lowered amygdala activation (Pelrine et al., 2016). An antibiotic called D-cycloserine may reduce amygdala activation and has sometimes been found to facilitate extinction/habituation in exposure therapy (Schade & Paulus, 2016).

TRAUMA

Trauma and the Amygdala: What Happens?

Amygdala activity trends after trauma, broadly, and in PTSD more specifically can be difficult to decipher due to inconsistencies in neuroimaging findings (Forster et al., 2017). One common finding is that the amygdala tends to be hyperreactive in response to threatening cues in individuals who have experienced psychological trauma (Badura-Brack et al., 2018; El Khoury-Malhame et al., 2011; McLaughlin et al., 2014). In fact, the amygdala exhibit hyperreactivity to any emotional stimuli in these individuals (Etkin & Wager., 2007; Morey et al., 2009; Murrough et al., 2011). Similar results have been found in the BNST (Brinkmann et al., 2017). Interestingly, this amygdalar hyperreactivity in traumatized individuals has also been found in response to neutral cues (Brunetti et al., 2010; Hendler et al., 2003). But finding seems to be unique to those with a PTSD diagnosis; of course, reactivity in response to danger/threat cues usually occurs in individuals with and without a history of trauma.

It has been proposed that hyperactivation of the amygdala in PTSD may be related to underactivation of other cortical brain areas, such as the anterior cingulate cortex or ventromedial prefrontal cortex (see Chapters 7 and 8 for more information about these brain regions; Etkin & Wager, 2007; Lanius et al., 2010). According to some PTSD models, amygdalar hyperactivation/hyperreactivity is associated with the underactivation of these cortical brain regions, which are believed to downregulate amygdala activation. This is supported by research indicating weakened connectivity between the anterior cingulate cortex and the amygdala (Milad et al., 2008; Wessa & Flor, 2007). In PTSD, however, cortical structures fail to fully activate and thus cannot inhibit amygdala activation (Brashers-Krug & Jorge, 2015; Hayes et al., 2012).

While this explanation for amygdala hyperactivation seems intuitively reasonable, some studies have reported findings inconsistent with the above research. Specifically, a small number of studies have found amygdala *hypoactivation* in response to threatening cues and trauma-related stimuli (Hayes et al., 2011; Tuescher et al., 2011). While it can be difficult to resolve contradictory neuroimaging findings, a couple of explanations have been posited. First, because the amygdala is a small structure, it is especially susceptible to artifact (Brabec et al., 2010), which can lead to inconsistent findings. Second, hypoactivation of the amygdala in response to emotional stimuli may indicate emotional numbing (Felmingham et al., 2014) or dissociation (Phan et al., 2006), which are common symptoms of PTSD.

Trauma and the Amygdala: How It Presents

In PTSD and other trauma- or stressor-related disorders, a hyperreactive amygdala may present as a sensitive startle response, hypervigilance, or strong emotional reactions to nonthreatening (or mildly distressing) situations or stimuli. Traumatized individuals often report feeling on-guard and reactive to their environment, especially when in unfamiliar, unpredictable, or crowded situations. To those around them, these individuals may appear distracted, jumpy, and reactive. This can also be the case in the context of therapy, where the therapeutic setting may provoke anxiety in clients. These individuals may spend substantial time scanning the room during sessions, and they often seem to have difficulty concentrating during therapy. Conversely, dissociation or emotional numbing may indicate a hypoactive amygdala. Clients with a hypoactive amygdala may seem disconnected or detached from their traumas as they discuss them and may report feeling lethargic and depressed.

Treatment Implications

The "Treatment Implications" in the anxiety section earlier in this chapter details several therapeutic approaches associated with amygdala activation reduction, several of which are also included in treatment for trauma. In particular, exposure-based therapies, such as prolonged exposure and EMDR, have been associated with therapeutic brain change, including amygdala deactivation (Laugharne et al., 2016; Roy et al., 2014; Zhu et al., 2018). Furthermore, the application of repetitive sensory stimulation, such as tapping or other types of bilateral stimulation applied in EMDR, has been found to facilitate the extinction of fear memory networks, resulting in lowered amygdala activation (Harper, 2012). Interestingly, this seems to be the case regardless of whether the stimulation is applied unilaterally or bilaterally, supporting the hypothesis that distraction, broadly, may reduce amygdala activation (Simon et al., 2014). Additionally, cognitive behavioral therapies have also shown promise for PTSD treatment, as these treatment approaches are linked to improved connectivity between the amygdala and prefrontal regions of the brain in those with a PTSD diagnosis (Shou et al., 2017).

DEPRESSION

Depression and the Amygdala: What Happens?

There are several types of depression, each of which is associated with different brain "profiles." However, there are some trends that can be gleaned from the neuroscience data on depression and amygdala function and structure. For instance, depression symptoms have been associated with increased limbic activity in general and amygdala activation in particular (Siegle et al., 2007). However, amygdala hyperactivation does not appear to occur at rest in depression, in comparison to healthy controls. Instead, amygdala hyperactivation in depression may reflect it is a strong reaction to negative information, whether from a recollection of negative past events (Young et al., 2016), in response to aversive stimuli outside of conscious awareness (Suslow et al., 2010), or in anticipation of negative information or events (Abler et al., 2007). This increased activation in the amygdala, especially the right amygdala, in response to anticipated negative information may explain the tendency for depressed individuals to assume a pessimistic view of the future.

As with PTSD, it has been hypothesized that amygdala activation observed in depression may be related to decreased activation in prefrontal areas, including the dorsolateral prefrontal cortex (Siegle et al., 2007). A finding of weakened connectivity between the amygdala and several other areas of the brain, including the dorsolateral prefrontal cortex and ventromedial prefrontal cortex, has been replicated several times (Cheng et al., 2018; Connolly et al., 2017; Dichter et al., 2015; Jalbrzikowski et al., 2017; Wackerhagen et al., 2019). In fact, reduced amygdalar connectivity may be more characteristic of depression than increased amygdalar activation in response to negative stimuli and may explain why those experiencing depressive disorders struggle with emotion regulation. Without strong connectivity to the amygdala, it may be difficult for the "rational" cortical areas of the brain to downregulate amygdalar activation, which would otherwise allow for better regulation of thoughts and emotions.

Depression and the Amygdala: How It Presents

Amygdala activation in depression often presents similarly to such activation in anxiety and trauma, wherein individuals appear to be nervous, distracted, and on-edge. In therapy, these clients may never quite seem at ease while in session, and while they may be low-energy, they also usually seem a bit anxious. In depression, amygdala activation may be apparent when individuals discuss past events or possible future events. In depressed individuals, past events are often recalled with strong negative emotion, even when those events are not traumatic. When thinking about future possibilities, amygdala activation in depression may present as negative predictions and an inability to envision a future with positive outcomes.

Treatment Implications

The treatment approaches and medications described in the "Treatment Implications" of the anxiety section of this chapter apply to depression as well. However, whereas a main goal of anxiety and trauma treatment is to decrease amygdalar activation, a primary objective in depression treatment is to increase amygdalar connectivity with other brain areas, including cortical regions. Thus, while trauma and anxiety treatment may emphasize exposure and relaxation techniques, depression treatment may focus more on strengthening connectivity with cortical areas of the brain, thereby allowing those areas to downregulate amygdala activity. This may promote better emotion regulation, thought regulation, and rumination management.

Cognitive and mindfulness techniques have been shown to improve amygdala connectivity with cortical regions (Hölzel et al., 2013; Weng et al., 2018). Specifically, interventions that teach clients how to restructure unhelpful thoughts and generate alternative thoughts, such as cognitive therapy for depression, have shown promise for improving connectivity between the amygdala and prefrontal cortex (Connolly et al., 2017; Shou et al., 2017; Young & Craske, 2018), leading to better thought and emotion regulation. Thus, cognitive therapy may be considered the gold standard for depression treatment partly due to the therapeutic brain changes it may elicit, such as improved neural connectivity. However, other therapeutic approaches may also strengthen connectivity between the amygdala and cortical areas. For example, one study found improved connectivity between the amygdala and cingulate cortex after participants completed a combination acupuncture and antidepressant treatment (Wang et al., 2016). Additionally, neuromodulation has been associated with improved connectivity and fewer depression symptoms (Liu et al., 2016), as has neurofeedback (Zotev et al., 2016) and even electroconvulsive therapy (Redlich et al., 2017).

OTHER MENTAL HEALTH CONDITIONS

Given that most psychiatric disorders involve a stress component, it is perhaps not surprising that the amygdala is implicated in many mental health conditions (Abuhasan & Siddiqui, 2018; Blair, 2006), including (but not limited to) neurodevelopmental disorders (Schumann et al., 2011), bipolar disorder (Li et al., 2018), psychosis (Watson et al., 2012), addiction (Stamatakis et al., 2014), autism (Swartz et al., 2013), and personality disorders (Baczkowski et al., 2017; Fulwiler et al., 2012; Hyde et al., 2014). Though the amygdala's function and structure vary across disorders, neuroimaging research has concluded that the amygdala tends to be hyperactive, or hyperreactive, in many psychiatric disorders. The main exception to this finding is antisocial personality disorder, wherein the amygdala tends to be underreactive to typically distressing stimuli and underactive in general (Birbaumer et al., 2005). This finding suggests that individuals with antisocial traits may experience less empathy and less regard for the well-being of others and may not consider possible aversive consequences to their actions.

Additionally, in mental illness the amygdala is often weakly connected to cortical areas of the brain and/or too strongly connected to other limbic areas, such as the insula. This may explain why most psychiatric disorders contain a stress component (usually resulting in distress) and are characterized by emotion regulation difficulties (which can contribute to functional impairment). In several disorders, it is likely that the amygdala is either hyperactive or hyperreactive in response to different stimuli or situations.

And, unfortunately, the amygdala cannot rely on cortical structures (such as the prefrontal cortex or cingulate cortex) to help downregulate its activation due to a weak connection with cortical structures. Without strong connectivity to cortical areas, the prefrontal cortex and surrounding areas cannot easily influence the amygdala's functioning.

CHAPTER 4

The Hippocampus

THE HIPPOCAMPUS'S LOCATION

The hippocampus is a limbic structure, located at the bottom of the temporal horn of the brain (Duvernoy, 2013; see Figure 4.1) in the medial region of the temporal lobe, very close to the amygdala (Amaral and Lavenex, 2007; Giap et al., 2000). It has been described as having an S-shaped, ram's horn-shaped, or seahorse-shaped structure (Amaral & Lavenex, 2007) that contains millions of densely packed neurons. Together, these neurons form a fairly distinct neural network (Giap et al., 2000) that is reciprocally connected to several other structures, including the amygdala (Saunders et al., 1988).

The hippocampus, though considered a distinct structure, can be further divided into multiple subregions, each of which plays a role in memory and other functions. Specifically, subregions of the hippocampus include the hippocampus proper, the dentate gyrus, and the subiculum (Teyler & Discenna, 1984; see Figure 4.2). The hippocampus proper is further divided into three subfields: the CA1, CA2, and CA3. Together, these subfields of the hippocampus proper form the trilaminar loop, which is largely involved in encoding long-term, episodic memories (Meeter et al., 2005). The dentate gyrus, located at the tip of the S-shape (or, backward S-shape), is believed to integrate incoming information from all five senses, thereby facilitating the encoding of memories that are rich in sensory detail (Hamilton & Rhodes, 2015). On the other end of the hippocampus, near the bottom of the S-shape, is the subiculum. This subregion is posited to be

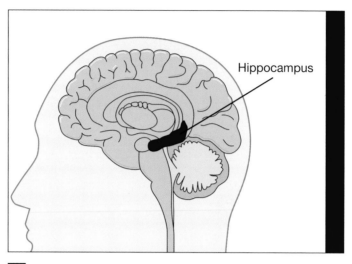

FIGURE 4.1: HIPPOCAMPUS

most strongly involved in spatial navigation and the regulation of the stress response (O'Mara, 2005). More information about the functions of the hippocampus as a whole is provided in the next section.

THE HIPPOCAMPUS'S FUNCTIONS
In a Nutshell

Perhaps best known for its involvement in memory encoding and consolidation, the hippocampus is a fairly large brain structure that is involved in a variety of functions. Aside from memory, the hippocampus has been found to play a role in spatial navigation (Stoianov et al., 2018), learning (Khodagholy et al., 2017), goal-directed behavior (Le Merre et al., 2018), emotion/information processing (Zheng et al., 2017), sleep (Sawangjit et al., 2018), and stress management (Kim et al., 2015). This chapter will detail the hippocampus's role in three specific domains: spatial navigation, memory, and stress regulation.

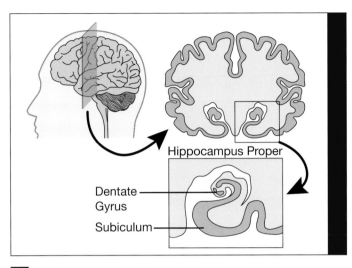

Hippocampus Proper

Dentate Gyrus

Subiculum

■ FIGURE 4.2: **HIPPOCAMPAL SUBREGIONS**

SPATIAL NAVIGATION

A few decades ago, early hippocampus research indicated that rat hippocampi might be involved in spatial navigation. Specifically, it was proposed that the hippocampus played a role in the development of cognitive maps of locations, which aid in spatial navigation (O'Keefe & Dostrovsky, 1971). By the late 1970s this research on the hippocampus's role in rodent cognitive mapping had been widely published and accepted and culminated in a book, "The Hippocampus as a Cognitive Map" (O'Keefe & Nadel, 1978). In fact, some studies showed that without a fully functioning hippocampus, spatial memory tasks became impossible for some animals (Morris et al., 1982).

Hippocampus research eventually extended to humans, and by the early 2000s it became generally accepted that the hippocampus tends to be involved in human cognitive mapping and spatial coding as well (Moser et al., 2008). The cognitive map hypothesis asserts that the hippocampus helps the brain create an integrated representation of the external environment that facilitates memory. The hippocampus's functions are enhanced by the prefrontal cortex, which uses this information to plan spatial navigation. The spatial navigation is then largely executed by the hippocampus (Epstein et al., 2017). Thus, not surprisingly, research has shown that the hippocampus activates (meaning, blood flow to this area increases) when attempting to navigate in a computer-simulated navigation task (Maguire et al., 1998). Additionally, the hippocampi of navigation experts, such as taxi drivers, tend to be larger than those in the general population (Maguire et al., 2000).

MEMORY AND TIME-KEEPING

It has been proposed that the role of the hippocampus in spatial navigation is memory (Eichenbaum, 2017), which is perhaps the most well-known function of this brain region. Specifically, it has been well-established that the hippocampus is involved the formation of long-term, autobiographical, episodic, and declarative memories (Eichenbaum & Cohen, 1993; Squire, 1992; Squire and Schacter, 2002). Thus, the hippocampus is believed to help encode and store memories that can be consciously recalled, including memories of events and facts that have been learned (Bird & Burgess, 2008; Steinvorth et al., 2005). Consistent with findings that the hippocampus plays a role in memory, research has shown that hippocampal damage can result in anterograde amnesia, wherein an individual cannot form new memories (Postle, 2016). Such damage can also result in retrograde amnesia, in which some memories encoded before the damage are impacted, dulled, or lost (Squire & Schacter, 2002).

The hippocampus is also sometimes referred to as the "timekeeper" of the brain, along with the dorsolateral prefrontal cortex (van der Kolk, 2015). The hippocampus keeps track of sequences of events and includes a sort of time stamp on long-term memories (Brown et al., 2010; Tubridy & Davachi, 2011), and the dorsolateral prefrontal cortex keeps track of when an event happened and approximately how long ago (van der Kolk, 2014). Together, these brain structures help individuals remember events in sequence and experience them as further in the past over time.

STRESS MANAGEMENT

In addition to being a critical memory center of the brain, the hippocampus is also involved in stress management. This little-known fact has clinical implications that many mental health professionals are unaware of. Specifically, the hippocampus has been shown to help regulate cortisol, a stress hormone that is released when a person is faced with a threat or danger (Sheline, 2000). While the presence of cortisol can be adaptive in life-threatening situations because it helps our bodies and brains go into survival mode (sympathetic nervous system arousal), too much or prolonged cortisol circulating can be damaging to both the brain and body. One major role of the hippocampus is to reduce the stress response (sympathetic nervous system arousal) by downregulating cortisol (Kolb & Whishaw, 2009). One way to think of the hippocampus is as your internal air conditioner; it turns down the heat (stress) that was cranked up when the amygdala (fear center) activated. In other words, your amygdala turns up the heat and prepares you to handle danger, while the hippocampus cools everything back down so you can relax!

However, with chronic stress, anxiety, trauma, or danger, the hippocampus can become overwhelmed by cortisol and unable to regulate the stress response. Over time this overwhelming of the hippocampus, due to the presence of too much cortisol in this area, can lead to damage and atrophy of the hippocampus (Kolb & Whishaw, 2009). As a result, this weakens the hippocampus so that the internal "air conditioner" of the brain becomes broken. At that point, the person is no longer able to internally regulate stress and may feel emotionally dysregulated (Sheline, 2000). Also, as hippocampal damage occurs, individuals will also often experience memory impairment, as the hippocampus may no longer be able to help encode and retrieve memories as well (Henckens et al. 2009; Roozendaal, 2002; Tollenaar et al., 2009). This is why memory is impacted by severe or chronic stress.

HIPPOCAMPUS

THE HIPPOCAMPUS: MENTAL HEALTH CONDITIONS AND TREATMENT IMPLICATIONS

The hippocampus is impacted by and may contribute to the development or exacerbation of several mental health conditions. This is perhaps not surprising given the hippocampus's role in stress management and its strong connections to other key brain regions involved in mental health and illness, such as the amygdala, insula, and prefrontal cortex. The following sections detail the hippocampus's role in trauma and anxiety, depression, and addiction and how it may contribute to some of the common symptoms experienced in those conditions.

DEPRESSION AND ANXIETY

Depression and Anxiety and the Hippocampus: What Happens?

This section combines depression and anxiety because neuroscience research indicates the hippocampus functions similarly in these conditions. When an intense, prolonged stress response progresses to anxiety or depression symptoms, it is common for the hippocampus to become underactivated and atrophied (McEwen & Magarinos, 2001; Sala et al., 2004). As described in the Stress Management section earlier in this chapter, one job of the hippocampus is to downregulate cortisol, a stress hormone, to help reduce stress naturally and effortlessly. However, the hippocampus's ability to manage stress becomes compromised when the stress is severe or chronic, such as when an individual develops an anxiety or depressive disorder. This is because the cortisol can overwhelm the hippocampus, making it increasingly difficult for the hippocampus to downregulate this stress hormone and contributing to hippocampal atrophy (Dedovic et al., 2009).

In depression research, two consistent neuroscience findings are that the hippocampus tends to be less activated and smaller in individuals who meet criteria for those disorders compared to healthy controls (Campbell & MacQueen, 2004; Milne et al., 2012; Roddy et al., 2019; Sapolsky, 2001). Some research on anxiety and the hippocampus has drawn similar conclusions; various anxiety disorders are associated with hippocampal underactivation and atrophy (Cha et al., 2016; Mah et al., 2016; Shin &

Liberzon, 2010). The explanations for these findings are fairly straightforward. In these disorders (as well as trauma, discussed in the next section), stress dysregulation is a key feature, and cortisol levels tend to be high. When stressed, the amygdala activates, sending signals to the hypothalamus to begin activating the HPA axis (stress pathway). The stress signals are then communicated to the pituitary and the adrenals, thereby activating the entire HPA axis, where "H" is the hypothalamus, "P" is for pituitary, and "A" is for adrenals. Once the HPA axis activates, the body enters a stress response, called sympathetic nervous system arousal, which results in more than 1,400 biochemical and psychophysiological reactions. One important component of the stress response is the release of cortisol into the body and brain (Dedovic et al., 2009). The more severe the stress, the more cortisol gets released into a person's system.

If the hippocampus did not contain cortisol receptors, the release of cortisol during stress would not impact this structure directly. However, the hippocampus contains a large number of glucocorticoid receptors (Joëls, 2008), which essentially function as magnets for cortisol. Thus, when under stress, cortisol quickly binds to the hippocampus's glucocorticoid receptors, saturating the hippocampus with cortisol. Unfortunately, a high level of cortisol in the hippocampus is toxic and leads to the underactivation and eventual atrophy of this structure, especially if the anxiety or depression symptoms remain untreated over time. When stress is mild or moderate, the hippocampus can remain activated enough to downregulate cortisol. However, when overwhelmed by cortisol, the hippocampus cannot function well and subsequently cannot help lower cortisol. Thus, those who suffer from severe, chronic stress and mental health challenges often experience emotion dysregulation and allostatic load, which is the wear and tear that occurs to the body when stress is not well-managed (McEwen & Stellar, 1993).

Depression and Anxiety and the Hippocampus: How It Presents

Hippocampal underactivation and atrophy often presents as memory impairment and/or stress dysregulation. It is not uncommon for a new client to initiate therapy due (in part) to concerns about memory deficits. In particular, clients may express fear about developing Alzheimer's Disease or dementia, or they may have concerns about not retaining information they are trying to learn in a classroom (or other) setting. While a neuro-psychological evaluation may be helpful for clarifying and better under-standing the client's deficits, it is often the case that these individuals meet criteria for an anxiety or depressive disorder. In these cases, the client has often experienced many months, or years, of overwhelming stress and anx-iety that has contributed to the progressive atrophy and underactivation of the hippocampus. This hippocampal damage explains why the client may have difficulty encoding and/or retrieving memories and learning new information.

Additionally, individuals with hippocampal atrophy and/or underac-tivation may experience difficulty with stress management and emotion regulation more broadly. While someone who is depressed or anxious may want to simply stop feeling bad and stop having the thoughts that nega-tively impact their mood, they may find it hard to gain a sense control over their thoughts and emotions. Deficits in several brain regions play a role in these experiences, but a main contributor is the hippocampus; if the brain's "air conditioner" is broken, the individual's internal stress management system malfunctions. This means that the person has to exert much more effort to effectively manage their stress and anxiety, and they may appear to struggle to "just calm down."

Treatment Implications

Thankfully, the hippocampus is one of the few areas of the brain that has shown to be capable of neurogenesis, and this is true even for depressed (Sahay& Hen, 2007) and aging individuals (Boldrini et al., 2018). This means that neurons—usually those that were damaged or obliterated by cortisol—can be regenerated in this area of the brain. Neuronal regener-ation helps repair and strengthen the hippocampus, and the main mech-anism involves protein called brain-derived neurotrophic factor (BDNF; Noble et al., 2011). BDNF is a protein that, when there are high amounts of it, can promote neurogenesis in the brain. Thus, a main goal of depres-sion and anxiety treatment is to increase BDNF, which then rebuilds the hippocampus (Foltran & Diaz, 2016). This, in turn, aids individuals in managing stress and downregulating cortisol and can help with memory and learning impairment.

Thankfully, there are several ways to increase BDNF in the brain. One way is to take antidepressants (both SSRIs and SNRIs), which have been shown to halt hippocampal atrophy even when individuals report no depression symptom improvement (i.e., when they do not notice mood changes; Campbell & MacQueen, 2004). Other ways to increase BDNF are to take omega-3 supplements daily and meditate daily (Xiong & Doraiswamy, 2009; Wu et al., 2008), as both have been shown to boost BDNF in the brain. Finally, and perhaps most important, BDNF is increased through exercise (Loprinzi & Frith, 2019). Becoming a marathoner is not required, but elevating heart rate is; the recommendation is to exercise 3–4 times per week, for 20 or more minutes each time. If the exercise can include novel movement, even better, though a brisk walk may be sufficient.

Interestingly, while CBT is established as an evidence-based therapy for both depression and anxiety, it likely does not contribute to BDNF increases in the hippocampus (da Silva et al., 2018). However, CBT has been found to increase hippocampal activation (Ritchey et al., 2011). This implies that while CBT may not help the hippocampus regenerate neurons, it can still promote activation of this brain region, thereby enhancing its functioning. Thus, the main ways to repair and strengthen the hippocampus are to consider medication management of symptoms and/or engage in CBT. That, along with the maintenance of a healthy diet and regular exercise, can strengthen the hippocampus. In fact, research has shown that clinical outcomes are better when psychotherapy is combined with medication *and* exercise (Gourgouvelis et al., 2018)!

TRAUMA

Trauma and the Hippocampus: What Happens?

The impact of trauma on the hippocampus is very similar to that of depression and anxiety, likely because trauma- and stressor-related disorders are associated with high cortisol levels and stress (Dedovic et al., 2009; McEwen & Magarinos, 2001; Sala et al., 2004). Given the similarities between trauma- and stressor-related disorders, anxiety disorders, and depressive disorders, the information and treatment implications detailed in the last section also apply to this section. In PTSD, the hippocampus has been found to be underactive and atrophied (Bremner et al., 2000; Gurvits et al., 1996; Hayes et al., 2011; Szeszko et al., 2018). Moreover, there are some additional ways that the hippocampus can be impacted by traumatic events, and these are discussed below.

As discussed, the hippocampus's functioning and structure are affected by chronic stress, which research has shown deactivates and atrophies this brain structure. Additionally, the hippocampus is often immediately impacted when an individual experiences an acute traumatic event, and this affects how trauma memories are encoded, consolidated, and retrieved in the brain (Wingenfeld & Wolf, 2014). During a traumatic event, cortisol floods the hippocampus (Lindauer et al., 2006), which can affect memory encoding and retrieval. Increased cortisol (due to acute stress) is associated with less activation in several limbic areas, including the hippocampus (Pruessner et al., 2008).

When the hippocampus is working well and is able to fully activate, it encodes memories in a predictable way. First, the hippocampus prioritizes emotional information; if a situation does not elicit any sort of emotional reaction, it is unlikely to be encoded and kept as a memory. Second, the hippocampus encodes the memory *in context*. Instead of taking snapshots of various fragments of a situation, the hippocampus encodes the entire event, almost like it is a camera taking a panoramic picture of an entire scene. Third, the hippocampus encodes the situation as clearly as possible, as if it is taking a picture with a very still camera to avoid producing a fuzzy image. (Just keep in mind that, while memories are *encoded* in a way that is similar to taking a picture, memory *retrieval* is not like looking at a picture and works a bit differently, as will be discussed in the Treatment Implications section.) Finally, the hippocampus assigns to the memory a sequence of events, or order of operations of the memory. In other words, the hippocampus keeps track of not only what happens in a memory, but in what order (Eichenbaum, 2013).

However, during a traumatic event, when cortisol has flooded the hippocampus, the hippocampus may encode memories differently. Here are some ways in which trauma memory consolidation may differ from other (nontraumatic) memory consolidation. Not all of these encoding differences will apply to everyone nor all of the time, they simply describe what might happen during a traumatic event. One issue with trauma memory encoding is that the hippocampus may fail to take a panoramic picture of the situation, focusing instead on small details or fragments. In other words, the memory is not contextualized during encoding (van Ast et al., 2013). For example, in an active shooter situation, instead of encoding the entire scene, the hippocampus might zoom in and "take a picture" of the intruder's weapon. It may also encode other fragments of the situation, such as the color of someone's shoes, a door, a person's face, etc. This lack of contextualization may be the hippocampus's way of encoding what it believes to be the most important parts of a memory.

Additionally, during the encoding of trauma memories, the hippocampus may not take clear still pictures of all of the fragments. There may be some memory fragments that are blurred, while others are clear (Pozzulo et al., 2020). Finally, during a traumatic event the hippocampus may fail to keep track of the order of events of the situation, making it difficult to piece together exactly what happened, when, and in what order (Hayes et al., 2011).

Trauma and the Hippocampus: How It Presents

In trauma- or stressor-related disorders such as PTSD, the presentation of an underactive, atrophied hippocampus is similar to that seen in depression and anxiety. Individuals with PTSD often report memory deficits and have difficulty with stress management. However, they may also struggle with additional PTSD symptoms as a result of how trauma memories might have been encoded and consolidated by the hippocampus.

If a client's hippocampus encoded some details or pieces of a traumatic situation with very little context, and if some of those fragments are depicted as blurry images, the person may experience generalized fear. Using the example of an active shooter situation, depending on how the hippocampus encoded and consolidated that memory, the person might not become fearful only of masked men of a particular race holding a firearm in the context of a shopping mall around Christmas time, but instead become fearful of any number of those individual elements. For instance, the individual may develop a fear of Christmas music, or Christmas decorations, or all men, or all people of a certain race, or shopping malls, or smallish black objects that might share some elements in common with a firearm. When memories are stripped of context and are reduced to fragments, all of which are encoded as traumatic, the result can be individuals who fear each of those fragments and *anything sharing some commonality* with those fragments. If, however, the hippocampus were able to fully activate during the event, the hippocampus would be more likely to encode the situation in context and clearly. This reduces the chances of the person encoding just fragments and assigning danger to each fragment. Instead, the exact same situation would have to present itself again for the person to feel "triggered," and generalization of fear would not occur. Generalization of fear is a common issue in PTSD (and some anxiety disorders), and it presents as an aversion to many things, such as a smell, sound, certain types of scenes or people or animals, or even temperature, linked in some way to a traumatic event.

Additionally, when the hippocampus does not encode the sequence of events of a trauma, it can present as a client appearing confused about parts of the traumatic event and often leads individuals to giving inconsistent accounts of the trauma. Sexual assault reports are a classic example of this phenomenon. Survivors of sexual assault are often accused of being dishonest because they have difficulty remembering exactly what happened, in what order, and their stories sometimes change over time. For instance, when asked by a police officer or investigator what time they arrived somewhere, when they left, who they saw in what order, etc., they often struggle and answer, "I'm not sure" or "I can't remember." During subsequent questioning, pieces of memory may return or may change as a result of the person attempting to put the fragments together in a way that makes sense. This can give the impression of dishonesty, but in reality, the messier the story, the more likely it is to be true.

Treatment Implications

The treatment recommendations for trauma mirror those outlined in the depression and anxiety Treatment Implications with one addition, which is relevant to anxiety treatment as well: In addition to medication (SSRIs and SNRIs), CBT, and BDNF-boosting habits such as exercise, exposure therapy is often helpful for treating PTSD symptoms and strengthening the hippocampus.

Exposure therapy, including but not limited to memory reconsolidation therapies such as EMDR, have been shown to increase hippocampal activation and volume (Bossini et al., 2012; Boukezzi et al., 2017). During exposure therapy, a client is confronted with a thought, sound, picture, emotion, etc. that is associated with a feared situation. The idea is to activate the neural network containing that feared "thing" in order to change one's relationship to it. More specifically, exposure therapy asks clients to confront feared situations, people, etc. in order to desensitize or habituate to it, making it feel less scary. This in turn reduces avoidance of the feared situation. When a client faces (is exposed to) a frightening memory and pairs this with a new experience, such as feeling safe in the moment, the memory becomes less scary. This less-scary, updated version of the memory is then *reconsolidated* and re-stored in the hippocampus.

Later, when memory retrieval occurs again, what is remembered is not the original memory itself, but the *updated* memory that was last reconsolidated (Lee et al., 2017). To put it another way, when we recall something, we remember it as we last re-encoded it, *not* as it actually happened. This becomes an iterative process in exposure therapy. The idea is to repeatedly retrieve and reconsolidate memories iteratively, making them less and less dangerous-feeling. Each time retrieval occurs, the most recent, less frightening version of that memory is what is remembered, and over time this leads to memories feeling more tolerable. This process is possible thanks to intimate collaboration between the hippocampus and the prefrontal cortex (see Chapters 8 and 9 for more information about the prefrontal cortex). Over time, exposure therapy can increase hippocampal activation and volume, reversing some of the damage caused by chronic stress and cortisol and allowing the client to better manage stress and improve memory.

HIPPOCAMPUS

ADDICTION

Addiction and the Hippocampus: What Happens?

It is perhaps not surprising that the hippocampus plays a large role in the development and maintenance of addiction, as memory and learning are required for addiction to develop (Goodman & Packard, 2016). For instance, recalling memories of past drug or alcohol use can contribute to drug-seeking behaviors, because the person desires to feel as good as they did in the past when they were using (Kutlu & Gould, 2016). Acute, short-term use of some drugs, such as cocaine or amphetamines, may not reduce hippocampal functioning and may actually enhance it (Garavan, 2008; Segal et al., 2010; Zeeuws & Soetens, 2007). However, longer term drug and alcohol misuse and withdrawal have been associated with learning deficits (Gulick & Gould, 2008; Kelley et al., 2005), decreased connectivity between the hippocampus and other brain regions (Gu et al., 2010), lowered hippocampal activation (North et al., 2013; Wang et al., 2012; Wilkinson et al., 2013), and reduced hippocampal volume (Hamelink et al., 2005).

It has been hypothesized that the hippocampus plays a role in the development of addiction through conditioning, a type of learning wherein individuals pair drug/alcohol use with reward and then remember this pairing in the future. This in turn leads to drug-seeking behaviors and increases the chance that addiction will develop. In addition to the hippocampus playing a role in addiction development, however, it may also contribute to relapse. Another theory, the self-medication hypothesis, posits that drug and alcohol withdrawal are so aversive that they prompt the individual to relapse simply to avoid the terrible experience of withdrawal (Khantzian, 1985). It is believed that the hippocampus may also play a role in this phenomenon, as it is the hippocampus that helps encode and store aversive withdrawal memories and associations (Kutlu & Gould, 2016).

Addiction and the Hippocampus: How It Presents

Hippocampal deficits associated with long-term drug or alcohol use may present similarly to those experiencing PTSD, depression, or anxiety. They may report or exhibit memory impairments, such as difficulty encoding new memories or retrieving old memories. These individuals may also report gaps of many years where they have no memories, especially if they were using during that time. Also, hippocampal damage may present as emotion dysregulation, as this area of the brain may not be able to downregulate cortisol during times of stress, making daily stressors feel overwhelming. Moreover, those trying to recover from substance abuse or dependence may find it difficult to avoid relapse and may experience cravings. This is because the hippocampus stores the person's past experiences with substances, including the rewarding ones, and possibly the painful ones associated with withdrawal.

Treatment Implications

The treatment recommendations detailed in the previous sections of this chapter apply here, but there are added considerations when treating addiction. One is that, while some types of cognitive therapy and CBT have been shown to improve hippocampal functioning, these therapies may be less effective when treating addiction, at least in the early stages of treatment. This may be due to prefrontal cortex deficits (including underactivation and damage to this area), in addition to reduced hippocampal activation and connectivity, both of which can make it difficult for a client to focus on and remember cognitive tasks.

Addiction treatment that aims to rebuild the hippocampus may focus on behavioral techniques, such as behavioral activation (including employment, engaging in hobbies, etc.), exercise, dietary changes, and social support, as these can help the person re-engage with the world and also increase BDNF. Additionally, it is imperative for addiction treatment to focus on drug and alcohol cessation (or, in some cases, harm reduction), as this is necessary to halt hippocampal damage. Intensive or inpatient treatment may be required for cessation and may include approaches such as motivational interviewing (Miller & Rollnick, 2012), which helps clients become more dedicated to change, and Seeking Safety (Najavits, 2001), which simultaneously addresses both trauma and substance use.

HIPPOCAMPUS

OTHER MENTAL HEALTH CONDITIONS

Three additional conditions commonly associated with hippocampal deficits include epilepsy, schizophrenia, and Alzheimer's disease. In epilepsy, the hippocampus is commonly the origin of seizures (Chang & Lowenstein, 2003), possibly because it tends to be an easily excitable brain region that can engage in neurogenesis (Kuruba et al., 2009). Because seizures have been shown to damage the hippocampus (Sloviter, 2005), it is critical that epilepsy be treated as effectively as possible, though epilepsy itself is not a mental health condition. Some treatment options include medication, dietary changes, and/or surgery (Shorvon, 2010).

Schizophrenia has also been linked to hippocampal deficits, which might explain the long-term memory impairment often reported by those with schizophrenia (Ragland et al., 2017). In individuals with schizophrenia, the hippocampus may be smaller (Allen et al., 2016) and weakly connected to other key brain regions (Harrison, 2004), such as the prefrontal cortex (Goto & Grace, 2008). Interestingly, recent research suggests that those with treatment-resistant schizophrenia may benefit from exercise, which may promote schizophrenia symptom reduction (Woodward et al., 2018).

Moreover, hippocampal deficits, such as memory impairment, have been linked to Alzheimer's disease. Alzheimer's disease is associated with smaller hippocampus volumes (Halliday, 2017; Scheff et al., 2006) and reduced connectivity to other brain regions (Allen et al., 2007). While it is not currently possible to reverse the course of Alzheimer's disease, some medications that might slow its progression are available (Hashimoto et al., 2005; Weller & Budson, 2018).

CHAPTER 5

The Insula

THE INSULA'S LOCATION

The insula, initially referred to as the "Island of Reil" by Johann Christian Reil in 1809 (Fusar-Poli et al., 2009), lies at the base of the Sylvian fissure, hidden beneath the frontal and temporal lobes (Cauda et al., 2011). To better conceptualize the location of the insula, place your index fingers on your temples and then move them toward the back of your head by about an inch. This is the approximate location of the insula, deep inside the brain (see Figure 5.1).

Until recently, the insula had been an overlooked brain structure in affective and clinical neuroscience research (Craig, 2010), as its functions and structure were unclear. Though the number and locations of distinct regions of the insula have been debated, three main regions have been identified: anterior agranular area intermediate (or "transitional" or "central") dysgranular zone (Cauda et al., 2011; Kutlu et al., 2013), and posterior granular area. Additionally, the insula can be further divided into seven subdivisions not described here (Shura et al., 2014). The three main regions of the insula appear in Figure 5.2.

THE INSULA'S FUNCTIONS
In a Nutshell

The insula is involved in several functions, a few of which are detailed below. However, if you lack the time to read about the insula in depth, here is a brief summary of this little-known structure that plays a critical role in mental health.

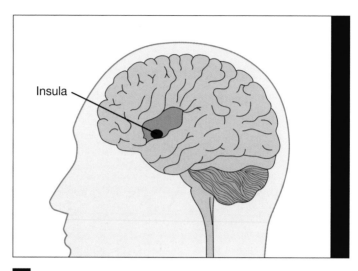

FIGURE 5.1: INSULA

In a nutshell, the insula can be conceptualized as the "mind-body connection center" of the brain. It is a brain structure where external sensory information, internal physical sensations (called interoception), and some aspects of cognitive control are integrated (Simmons et al., 2013; Uddin & Menon, 2009; Cauda et al., 2011). This integration gives rise to the experience of emotion (Uddin & Menon, 2009), self-awareness (Craig, 2010; Herbert & Pollatos, 2012), and cognition (Herbert & Pollatos, 2012). Thus, the insula can also be thought of as the birthplace of emotion.

When sensory information enters the body, the signals move up the spinal cord to the thalamus, sometimes referred to as the relay station of the brain. All sensory information except for smell, which bypasses this area and travels directly to the amygdala ("threat center"), passes through the thalamus. From the thalamus, sensory information is projected to multiple locations, including the posterior section (back part) of the insula. The posterior insula creates a physical representation of the bodily sensations (Namkung et al., 2017), noting where these sensations are felt and to what extent. This information is then communicated to the anterior insula (front, higher section), which translates this sensory information into con-

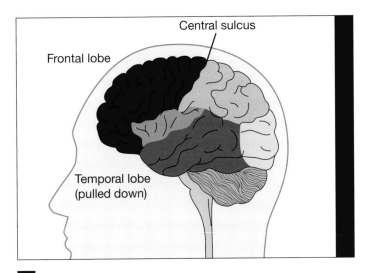

Central sulcus

Frontal lobe

Temporal lobe
(pulled down)

FIGURE 5.2: INSULA SUBREGIONS

INSULA

scious, subjective feeling states and emotion (Craig et al., 2011; Herbert &
Pollatos, 2012; Menon & Uddin, 2010; Naqvi & Bechara, 2009). Additionally, the anterior insula is involved in integrating emotion, which is produced in this subregion, with motivation and cognitive tasks (Craig et al.,
2011; Simmons et al., 2013). This is primarily accomplished through the
anterior insula's bidirectional connections to multiple cortical structures,
such as the anterior cingulate cortex ("self-regulation center"; see Chapter
7 for more information on this brain region).

As described above, the insula is involved in translating sensory experiences into emotion and integrating emotion and subjective feeling states
with cognition. These main functions of the insula suggest a couple of key
points relevant to mental health and psychotherapy. First, insula research
indicates that emotion is involved in cognition. While emotion and cognition are sometimes presented as separate, opposing phenomena, the insula's role in emotional and cognitive integration suggests that emotion is
part of (at least some forms of) cognition. This is consonant with LeDoux
and Brown's (2017) higher-order theory of emotional consciousness, which
asserts that emotion itself can be conceptualized as a type of cognition.

A second important lesson gleaned from insula research is that physical sensations are a critical component of emotion. Without physical sensation, there is no emotion. This can be a profound piece of psychoeducation for clients, who may not realize that a large portion of anxiety distress is *physical*. It is often the case that what makes anxiety unbearable is not a distressing thought, but the physical sensations associated with it. Consistent with this, it has been posited that the development of some mental health conditions, such as anxiety and depression, might be linked to the insula's inability to accurately translate physical sensations into subjective feeling states, emotion, and self-awareness (Herbert & Pollatos, 2012; Simmons et al., 2009).

The following sections describe the insula's functions in specific domains.

INTEROCEPTION

Interoception is the ability to detect, feel into, and process internal bodily states and sensations (Craig, 2002; Barrett & Simmons, 2015; Wager & Barrett, 2017). Simmons et al. (2009) define interoception as "the perception of one's internal physiological, sensory, and emotional status" (p. 373). Interoception allows individuals to experience hunger, temperature, pain, and other common sensations, such as rapid heart rate, muscle tension, or an itch. Additionally, insula activation has been linked to other types of interoceptive functions, such as limb ownership (Karnath & Baier, 2010) and nausea. For example, a 1955 study (Penfield & Faulk, 1955) found that direct stimulation of the insula produced sudden feelings of nausea in patients undergoing neurosurgery. This research, and subsequent studies, have led researchers to postulate that the insula is involved in translating feelings of sickness/nausea into disgust (Wicker et al., 2013).

Interoception is arguably the most researched function of the insula and is hypothesized to occur when incoming external and internal sensory information is processed in the posterior and then anterior subdivisions of the insula. Interoception is then translated into self-awareness and emotion (Craig, 2009; Zaki et al., 2012) and influences cognition (Wager & Barrett,

2017), motivated behavior (Contreras et al., 2007), and decision-making (Naqvi & Bechara, 2009).

~~~~~~

EMOTION AND CORE AFFECT

As stated in the previous section, interoception (which is produced in the insula) is a precursor to emotion. At a more basic level, interoception precedes something called core affect, which Bar-Anan et al. (2009) define as a "neurophysiological state that underlies simply feeling good or bad, drowsy or energized" (p. 1259). Similarly, Wager and Barrett (2017) describe core affect as "broadly tuned motivational states (e.g., excitement) with associated subjective feelings" (p. 102368) and found these nonspecific emotional states to be associated with the activation of a specific section within the anterior insula.

The insula is also involved in the experience of distinct emotions (Zaki et al., 2012) in addition to core affect. For instance, disgust is associated with insula activation (Wright et al., 2004), as is empathy (Singer et al., 2009). Notably, the insula produces the same response when an individual vicariously experiences, or simply observes (by looking at their facial expressions, for instance), feelings of disgust in others (Wicker et al., 2003). This suggests that, to an extent, the insula allows us to actually feel what others feel simply by observing them and that the insula may contain mirror neurons, which help produce empathy (Rizzolatti et al., 2009). Mirror neurons allow us to feel what others experience, presumably by activating similar areas of the brain when observing others that are activated when we ourselves have the same experience (for a review of mirror neurons, see Rizzolatti et al., 2001).

While not basic emotions, trust and uncertainty have also been linked to insula activation. Specifically, when engaged in an economic trust game, research participants' anterior insula activated when they did not trust anonymous partners (Kang et al., 2011). Interestingly, these participants were found to trust their partners less when they held ice packs than when they held warm packs. This implies there may be a neural basis for the common association between trust and warmth, both physically and emotionally. Finally, insula activation occurs when individuals experience uncertainty (Singer et al., 2009). Uncertainty intensifies both positive and negative emotions and thus can magnify subjective feeling states arising (at least in part) from physical sensations (Bar-Anan et al., 2009). Thus, the insula is not only a creator of core affect but an amplifier of emotion.

COGNITION

The insula is not typically considered a cognitive region of the brain, as is the prefrontal cortex (Gu et al., 2013). However, the insula plays an important role in cognition, as it introduces feeling states into cognitive processes (Chang et al., 2013; Namkung et al., 2017; Uddin et al., 2017), thereby influencing cognition, motivation, and ultimately behavior (de Divitiis et al., 2018). In particular, the anterior insula promotes the integration of cognition and feeling states (including both core affect and emotion). This integration is possible in large part due to the anterior insula's connections with the anterior cingulate cortex (de Divitiis et al., 2018).

Together, the anterior insula and anterior cingulate cortex subserve cognitive functions, such as intentional action (Gasquoine, 2014), decision-making in uncertain situations (Craig, 2009; Naqvi & Bechara, 2009), error-based learning (Singer et al., 2009), and cognitive control more generally (Menon & Uddin, 2010). This partnership between the anterior insula and anterior cingulate cortex, in which bidirectional influence occurs, helps us notice and pay attention to salient experiences (Menon & Uddin, 2010) so that we can take specific actions to either prolong (pleasant) or avoid (aversive) stimuli (de Divitiis et al., 2018). In this way, the insula is involved in motivation and behavior.

PAIN AND SOCIAL PAIN

The insula, especially the posterior insula, plays fundamental roles in the experience of physical pain (Isnard et al., 2011; Segerdahl et al., 2015), including pain perception, pain intensity, and pain expectancy (with the help of the anterior cingulate cortex; Fazeli & Buchel, 2018). As mentioned in the previous section, the insula also subserves motivation and intentional (i.e., goal-directed) behavior, and one way this is accomplished can be through pain, since pain is very aversive and most definitely motivating.

Approximately two decades ago, a fascinating journal article was authored by UCLA neuroscientist Dr. Naomi Eisenberger and her colleagues. In this 2003 paper, the researchers showed that social pain, defined as the aversive feeling associated with social exclusion (MacDonald & Leary, 2005), activated similar areas of the brain that tend to activate during the experience of physical pain, including (but not limited to) the insula and anterior cingulate cortex (Eisenberger et al., 2003). This finding, which has been replicated across multiple studies, further elucidates the relationship between physical and feeling states, including emotion.

THE INSULA: MENTAL HEALTH CONDITIONS
AND TREATMENT IMPLICATIONS

The insula plays a significant role in mental illness, making it a critical mental health brain region. The insula has been associated with anxiety disorders, mood disorders, autism, schizophrenia, eating disorders, chronic pain, addiction, and several other conditions (Gasquoine, 2014). However, most mental health clinicians have never heard of this brain structure and are thus unaware of how it contributes to distressing symptoms and how its functioning might be improved with psychotherapy.

INSULA

TRAUMA

Trauma and the Insula: What Happens?

In a traumatized brain, the insula can be hypoactive (Koch et al., 2016; Simmons et al., 2009) or hyperactive (Bruce et al., 2013; Rosso et al., 2014; Yan, 2013). While it seems contradictory to assert that the insula can be both under- and overactivated in trauma, there are a couple of explanations for this. First, there is some evidence that hypoactivation in individuals with PTSD occurs specifically in the posterior insula (Koch et al., 2016), whereas hyperactivation tends to occur in the anterior region of the insula (Garfinkel & Liberzon, 2009; Hopper et al., 2007). Thus, inconsistencies in the literature may be attributable to the particular areas within the insula that different studies investigated.

A second explanation for the discrepant findings is that the insula's activation may depend in part on whether an individual suffers from the dissociative subtype of PTSD. During symptom provocation (where individuals' symptoms were triggered), Nicholson et al. (2016) found hypoactivation of the insula in dissociative PTSD and hyperactivation in nondissociative PTSD. This distinction fits well with research showing that the insula becomes inactive when individuals dissociate or otherwise engage in mind wandering (i.e., when the default mode network is activated; Craig, 2009). Thus, it is possible that insula underactivation *and* hyperactivation may occur in the same individual, depending on whether dissociation is present.

Trauma and the Insula: How It Presents

Insula functioning in trauma is complex. This is because a traumatized client's insula will sometimes hyperactivate and other times switch off, becoming underactivated. When the insula is underactive in the context of trauma, it is often experienced as dissociation, numbing, or difficulty experiencing one's own sense of self. The dissociative experience can be intense and extreme, as in the case of a flashback, or it can present more mildly, such as when the client simply "goes blank" for a moment or experiences brief mind wandering. When this occurs, the client loses what Dr. Peter Levine calls "felt sense" (Levine, 1997), or a connection to the body, the present moment, and, ultimately, the self. When the insula shuts off, the client may experience a sort of nothingness, which may be identified by the therapist as physical or emotional numbing, derealization, or depersonalization. Because this nothingness can be an unsettling experience for clients, some clients may engage in cutting or other forms of self-harm in an attempt to reorient to the present moment and shift back into the body.

When the insula hyperactivates in trauma, the client's experience is quite different. A hyperactive insula may overreact to slight changes in sensations and feeling states, creating a sense of heightened vigilance to both external stimuli (such as noises) and internal experiences (interoception).

When a client's insula is hyperactive, the therapist may notice the client catastrophizing mild physical discomfort ("My stomach hurts, my appendix is bursting!"), or otherwise misinterpreting sensory information as dangerous ("I just felt turbulence on the plane, which means it is crashing!").

Additionally, anterior insula activity has been shown to positively correlate with the re-experiencing symptoms of PTSD, and hyperactivation has been linked to the experience of flashbacks (Hopper et al., 2007; Whalley et al., 2013). For instance, Hopper et al. (2007) found that re-experiencing symptom severity was positively associated with anterior insula activation but negatively correlated with avoidance severity (consistent with the previous paragraph). Moreover, several researchers, including Whalley et al. (2013), have found flashbacks to be associated with high insula activation.

Treatment Implications

As described in the previous sections, in traumatized clients the insula can show hypoactivation or hyperactivation, depending on a client's symptom profile. Whether the goal is to increase insula activation or better regulate already-high insula functioning (for instance, when it is too activated or overreactive), psychotherapy offers promising techniques for clients wanting to reduce distressing symptoms.

When treating clients with a hypoactive insula, as evidenced by numbing (both physical and emotional), dissociation, alexithymia, or a lack of sense of self, the main objective is to *get the client back into their own body and into the present moment*, which will activate the insula. Any technique or approach that meets this criterion is likely to increase insula activity, though research has yet to confirm this. Some options may include grounding exercises (Najavits, 2002), Somatic Experiencing (Levine, 1997), diaphragmatic breathing (Brown et al., 2013), and body-based techniques, such as progressive muscle relaxation and autogenic training (Schlamann et al., 2010), though specific research focusing on these techniques is needed. Also, meditations have been shown to increase insula activation (Brewer et al., 2011). Specifically, body scan meditations, such as the ones taught in Kabat-Zinn's (2003) mindfulness-based stress reduction have been found to reduce emotional numbing in traumatized clients

(Frewen & Lanius, 2015), and meditations more broadly have been found to reduce alexithymia and increase insula thickness (Santarnecchi et al., 2014). All of these techniques help clients become more attuned to their own internal states, both emotional and physical.

To help clients with hypoactive insulae reestablish a sense of self, Lanius et al. (2015) recommend trauma treatment interventions that address self-referential deficits. Therapy interventions, such as cognitive processing therapy, dialectical behavioral therapy, EMDR, and prolonged exposure, and cognitive behavioral therapy (broadly) may thus be beneficial (Lanius et al., 2015). While the impact of these therapies on the insula, specifically, remains a mystery, there is strong reason to believe these therapies may help clients restore a sense of self by activating the anterior insula.

In other traumatized clients, the objective may be to help them better manage strong negative internal experiences (for instance, when the insula is hyperactive or hyperreactive). In other words, the goal is to help clients *manage and relate differently* to their internal experiences. Strong reactions to negative experiences can be mitigated using bottom-up stress reduction techniques or top-down cognitive exercises (Borsook et al., 2016). Top-down cognitive exercises include cognitive therapy, CBT, and other types of primarily cognitive interventions (such as cognitive processing therapy). Bottom-up methods and stress-reduction exercises that can be utilized include exercise, yoga, or other movement-based or mindfulness techniques, such as diaphragmatic breathing. Because the insula is involved in stress management (Christianson et al., 2008), improving stress management can likely help regulate the insula, making negative feelings and sensations less distressing. However, more research is necessary to better understand the impact of bottom-up techniques on the insula.

ANXIETY

Anxiety and the Insula: What Happens?

The insula has been consistently found to be both hyperactive (Duval et al., 2018; Garfinkel & Liberzon, 2009; Shah et al., 2009; Simmons et al.,

2009; Stein et al., 2007) and hyperreactive (Klumpp et al., 2012; Klumpp, Post, et al., 2013; Puhl et al., 2018; Rosso et al., 2014) in individuals suffering from a variety of anxiety disorders. Conversely, a decrease in insula activation has been associated with reduced anxiety symptoms (Carlson & Mujica-Parodi, 2010; Duval et al., 2018). As described in the next section, insular hyperactivation and hyperreactivity in anxiety have been found to correlate with deficits in uncertainty tolerance and the accurate interpretation of internal physical states.

Anxiety and the Insula: How It Presents

Anxious individuals tend to experience difficulty in at least two areas, each of which is connected to insular activity: tolerance of uncertainty and appraisal of internal experiences. Intolerance of uncertainty is common in anxious individuals and is associated with insula hyperactivation in anxiety disorders, including panic disorder, obsessive–compulsive disorder, and generalized anxiety disorder (Simmons et al., 2008). For instance, in one study the anterior insula was found to be hyperactive in anxious individuals when they anticipated an unpredictable threat (Alvarez et al., 2015). These authors, and other researchers, have posited that anxious individuals' intolerance of uncertainty might reflect a diminished sense of control, contributing to insula hyperactivity (Alvarez et al., 2015; Ramautar et al., 2006).

Thus, anxious individuals may be prone to feeling out of control, and the more out of control they feel, the higher their intolerance for uncertainty. This intolerance for uncertainty may clarify why anxious individuals experience strong emotional reactions to worrisome thoughts about potential (negative, scary, or horrifying) events; their uncertainty and unpredictability feel insufferable (Carlson & Mujica-Parodi, 2010; Simmons et al., 2011). Also, this may explain why it is difficult for anxious individuals to feel at ease when they cognitively reconstruct their fears, because no matter how slight the chances of a catastrophe, such as a plane crash, feeling out of control on the plane may result in their having no tolerance for the slightest possibility of disaster.

Second, individuals with anxiety often have difficulty with the appraisal of internal experiences, overinterpreting or catastrophizing them (as described in the previous section on trauma). Thus, clients may perseverate on physical sensations or misinterpret them as threatening or dangerous (Reiss et al., 1986), which can exacerbate anxiety and even lead to panic attacks ("My heart is beating so fast I'm having a heart attack and dying!"; Engel et al., 2016). Additionally, nausea, which is commonly experienced in anxiety, is likely due partly to high insula activation (Napadow et al., 2013; Wicker et al., 2003).

Treatment Implications

In anxiety disorders the insula tends to be hyperactive and hyperreactive, as discussed in previous sections. This hyperactivation resembles the insula activation seen in many traumatized clients who often also suffer from symptoms such as worry, nervousness, hypervigilance, etc. Thus, the treatment recommendations for managing hyperactive insulae outlined in the trauma Treatment Implications section apply to this section as well. For example, techniques that teach clients how to relate differently to and better manage negative physical and emotional experiences are likely to be helpful to anxious clients. Some of these approaches might include stress-reduction exercises (mindfulness, breathing, yoga, etc.) as well as cognitive techniques (such as CBT).

For instance, Johnson et al. (2014) found that mindfulness training attenuated insula activation in Marine Corps soldiers experiencing an aversive interoceptive stimulus. In other words, mindfulness practice reduced the soldiers' distress related to the aversive experience. The authors concluded that mindfulness can help modulate the insula's response to negative or painful experiences and promotes resilience. Lutz et al. (2013) concluded something similar in their study, in which expert meditators reported less unpleasantness of pain than novice meditators despite experiencing equivalent pain intensity.

Moreover, Carlson and Mujica-Parodi (2010) found that successful cognitive reappraisal (a type of cognitive restructuring) was associated with decreased anterior insula reactivity when individuals were anticipating a negative or painful experience/stimulus. Concurrent increased activation in other brain areas, including some subregions of the cingulate cortex (see Chapter 7 for more information about the anterior cingulate cortex), suggests that as the insula becomes attenuated, brain regions involved in emotion regulation activate and may downregulate insula activity. These findings also imply that as the insula becomes attenuated, an individual's ability to manage anticipatory anxiety may improve.

Finally, a small number of studies have examined the effects of specific approaches on the insula in individuals suffering from anxiety disorders. For example, Klumpp, Fitzgerald, et al. (2013) found that individuals with social anxiety disorder who completed CBT showed reduced insula reactivity when presented with anxiety-provoking information. Similarly, Lipka et al. (2014) found that anxious subjects who engaged in CBT showed lowered insula activation over time, presumably as they became more skilled in cognitive behavioral techniques such as cognitive restructuring.

~~~~~~

DEPRESSION

Depression and the Insula: What Happens?

Similar to the trauma research, studies examining insula activation in depression have drawn inconsistent conclusions. Some studies have found hyperactivation of the insula in depression (Hamilton et al., 2011; Palaniyappan & Liddle, 2012), whereas others have shown hypoactivation in this area (Brooks et al., 2009; Fitzgerald et al., 2008; Simmons et al., 2016). Sliz and Hayley (2012) attribute these contradictory findings to population sample inconsistencies. For instance, some studies recruited depressed clients who had received treatment or taken medication, while others recruited clients who had not. Also, most studies did not distinguish between one-time depressive episode sufferers and chronically depressed subjects and did not mention any comorbid disorders.

Another explanation for the discrepant findings is that the insula's functioning in depression may depend on factors such as whether the individual was engaged in interoception efforts, emotion regulation, or other functions at the time of the study, as opposed to examining the insula while the subject was at rest (doing nothing at the time the brain was imaged).

INSULA

A thorough look at the current state of the research on depression and the insula indicates that in depression, the insula may be hypoactive or hyperactive, depending on the task the individual is engaged in.

Specifically, depressed individuals have been found to show hyperactivation of the insula when processing negative information (Hamilton et al., 2011), implying that they experience negative stimuli in a strong, and perhaps exaggerated, manner (Palaniyappan & Liddle, 2012). Consistent with this, Mayberg et al. (1999) found increased anterior insula activation and decreased activation in the cingulate (which is involved in emotion regulation) in depressed subjects, leading to an inability to successfully downregulate negative emotion. Finally, research studies have found increased insula activity in depressed subjects compared to healthy controls when subjects were instructed to restructure a negative feeling to make it more positive (Johnstone et al., 2007) or to suppress feelings of sadness (Beauregard et al., 2006).

Conversely, hypoactivation of the insula in depression has been associated with anhedonia (Dunn et al., 2002) and interoception (Avery et al., 2014). Underactivation of the insula has been found when depressed individuals attempt interoception in the absence of negative or aversive stimuli (Avery et al., 2014; Simmons et al., 2016; Yao et al., 2009).

Depression and the Insula: How It Presents

Depressed clients may be particularly sensitive to negative information, emotions, or physical sensations, as evidenced by insula hyperactivity during the processing of negative stimuli (Hamilton et al., 2011; Mayberg et al., 1999). Negative stimuli are likely to be particularly salient to depressed clients, who may seem to focus on and ruminate about negative experiences. This is likely in part due to an insula that overreacts to negativity but seems to ignore or underreact to neutral or positive physical and emotional experiences (Avery et al., 2014; Simmons et al., 2016). In other words, depressed clients may find it difficult to feel into and describe internal physical states or to feel positive emotions instead perseverating on negative feelings and experiences.

Treatment Implications

When treating depression, the goal is to be able to address both insula hyper- and hypoactivation, as both have been found in depression. In particular, clinicians need to help clients attenuate insula hyperactivation when processing negative information, sensation, or feelings, and to increase insula activation when experiencing neutral or positive stimuli. Thus, it is important for clinicians to help depressed clients connect with the body and strengthen emotional awareness. However, when it comes to negative experiences, it is more helpful to teach these clients how to manage, downregulate, and de-emphasize these physical and emotional experiences, as the insula often presents this information in a magnified, exaggerated manner.

To help depressed clients reenter the body but also modulate insula hyperactivation, the approaches described in the trauma Treatment Implications section can be effective. While clients suffering from depression do not suffer from dissociation and thus may not experience the extreme insula hypoactivation seen in trauma, they nonetheless often struggle with disconnection from the body and a weakened sense of self. Approaches that may help depressed clients increase their insula activation include grounding and/or interoceptive exercises, such as heart rate monitoring (Critchley et al., 2004), body scan meditations, deep breathing, and body-based exercises, though more research is needed to examine the impact of some of these specific techniques on the insula. With increased insula activity, it becomes easier for clients to connect with the body to experience neutral and positive feelings, not just the negative ones.

To regulate insula activation in response to negative information, top-down approaches such as cognitive behavioral therapy or cognitive therapy may be effective, as cognitive training has been shown to attenuate insula reactivity (Borsook et al., 2016). Of similar relevance, other research has shown that cognitive behavioral therapy can lower insula connectivity to "hot" emotional brain structures, such as the amygdala, leading to lowered reactivity to negative information (Chattopadhyay et al., 2017). Finally, stress-reduction techniques, such as exercise, have

INSULA

been associated with less insula reactivity (Christianson et al., 2008; Villemure et al., 2013).

~~~~~~

ADDICTION

Addiction and the Insula: What Happens?

Insula activation has been found to play a large role in substance use relapse, as it activates when an individual anticipates using a drug (or alcohol) or remembers what it feels like to use ("interoceptive memory"; Naqvi & Bechara, 2010; Naqvi et al., 2014). Also, the experience of cravings (Naqvi & Bechara, 2009), along with motivation to use alcohol or drugs (Naqvi et al., 2014), has been linked to insula activation. In these ways, insula activation in individuals suffering from addiction may contribute to relapse (Kutlu et al., 2013).

Interestingly, some insula research has found that damage to the insula, which prevents it from fully activating, eliminates cravings and substance use. For example, Naqvi et al. (2007) found that sudden insula damage in smokers resulted in immediate smoking cessation. These individuals denied experiencing cravings for cigarettes and reportedly had no desire to smoke again. Similarly, Contreras et al. (2007) deactivated the insula in rats who had experienced amphetamines, and this resulted in the rats becoming completely disinterested in amphetamines. Thus, under conditions where insula activation is not possible, cravings and motivation for drug use may be eliminated.

Addiction and the Insula: How It Presents

According to Kutlu et al. (2013), the insula first activates during the conscious pleasure induced by drug use. Once addicted, clients who experience insula activation may experience interoceptive memory about how pleasurable (physically and emotionally) it feels to engage in drug use, leading to a strong desire to use the drug to experience those reinforcing sensations and feelings again (Naqvi & Bechara, 2010). Thus, not only drug use but also *remembering what it feels like to use the drug* activates the insula. When the insula activates during interoceptive memory, it sends signals to other regions of the brain, leading to the release of dopamine even though the client has not actually used. This, often called "anticipatory dopamine," gives the client a bit of pleasure similar to the pleasure they experience during drug use (but less intense). This anticipatory dopamine can produce strong cravings for the drug and is likely to lead the client to relapse.

Treatment Implications

In the context of addiction, insula activation has been linked to substance-related cravings, motivation, anticipation, and interoceptive memory (in which the individual remembers the reinforcing physical effects of a substance). More research is necessary to determine how insula functioning can be therapeutically manipulated to treat addiction, but some potentially helpful approaches can be inferred. As discussed in the previous section, anticipatory dopamine released as a result of interoceptive memory can produce strong substance cravings, leading to relapse. Thus, one main goal of addiction treatment for many clients is to learn how to reduce cravings, thereby reducing the motivation to use and subsequent relapse. Three ways clients can better manage cravings are to notice the physical sensations associated with cravings, practice techniques that downregulate emotional responses to triggers (thereby making clients less reactive to these triggers), and help clients distract from images, thoughts, and sensory memories related to past experiences with substances (which may prevent the release of anticipatory dopamine).

Approaches for managing hyperactive insulae described in the trauma and anxiety Treatment Implications sections, such as cognitive behavioral therapy, mindfulness techniques, and other stress-reduction exercises, are applicable here. However, when working with addiction the goal is slightly different; instead of regulating the insula through relating or reacting differently to threatening stimuli, clients need to regulate the insula through the management of the physical and emotional correlates of craving triggers. While in anxiety and trauma the objective is to manage one's reactions to negative information/experiences, in addiction it is to manage one's reactions to *both negative and positive* feelings, such as interoceptive memories of past use. This may be a substantially more

INSULA

difficult goal, as clients tend to be more motivated to nullify negative experiences than positive ones.

To help clients manage craving triggers, a few approaches are recommended, though their specific impacts on the insula are currently unknown. First, it can be helpful for clients to identify where they experience cravings in their body, as a way of becoming more aware of the physical sensations associated with cravings. For instance, clients may notice feelings of hunger, pain in certain areas, rapid heart rate, etc. These and other physical sensations may indicate that a client is experiencing the early signs of a craving. Self-awareness of early craving signals is critical if clients are to eventually learn how to manage cravings. Unfortunately, clients often realize they are experiencing a craving when it has become too intense to manage, which is why learning to detect these physical signals early is critical.

If clients have difficulty feeling into internal physical states, which can happen if a client is depressed or traumatized (and thus have an underactive insula most of the time), it may be beneficial for them to incorporate treatment techniques that help them reenter and connect with the body, such as body-awareness techniques, diaphragmatic breathing exercises, and other approaches discussed in the trauma and depression Treatment Implications sections. Becoming more connected to internal sensations may help clients notice craving triggers in the body more easily (Garavan, 2010).

To manage craving triggers, clients need to learn how to recognize and modulate sensations (usually negative) related to cravings (such as pain, rapid heart rate, etc.) as well as interoceptive memories (usually positive) of past substance use. When clients experience the negative feelings associated with cravings along with positive memories about how reinforcing it felt to use, cravings substantially increase and can become unmanageable. To address these two issues, clinicians may consider utilizing the techniques described in the trauma and anxiety Treatment Implications sections for managing overactive insulae. Moreover, clinicians treating addiction may focus on helping clients work directly with negative sensations, teaching ways of reducing rapid heart rate and other indices of the stress response, for example, thereby decreasing the distressing feelings that prompt clients to relapse. These techniques can complement evidence-based cognitive approaches to relapse prevention, such as motivational interviewing (Navqi et al., 2014).

Finally, many clients may find it helpful to turn their focus away from thoughts, memories, or images related to substance use, because interoceptive memory (and anticipatory dopamine, prompted through increased insula activation) can intensify cravings dramatically. To accomplish this, clinicians can teach clients meditations (for a review, see Tapper, 2018) or alternative behaviors that help clients disengage from thoughts and images related to using, such as having them focus on something else (other thoughts, images, or behaviors). While not yet examined empirically, it has also been proposed that repetitive transcranial magnetic stimulation (rTMS) may be a promising approach for attenuating insula function in addiction (Yao et al., 2016).

OTHER MENTAL HEALTH CONDITIONS

The insula appears to be involved in additional mental health conditions, two of which include schizophrenia and autism. For instance, Wylie and Tregellas (2010) noted that subjects suffering from schizophrenia struggle with processing representations of the self, perhaps partially due to insula dysfunction that makes it difficult to maintain a clear sense of self. Moreover, Modinos et al. (2011) found that in schizophrenic subjects, higher insula activation was associated with psychosis. Additionally, the insula may be involved in autism. For example, studies have found hypoactivation in the anterior insula in autism (Ebisch et al., 2011; Uddin & Menon, 2009), which may be related to impairments in the emotional awareness (of both oneself and of others). While the treatment implications of insula functioning in autism and schizophrenia are unclear at this time, it is recommended that clinicians treating these conditions keep up to date with the burgeoning research in these areas.

CHAPTER 6

The Nucleus Accumbens

THE NUCLEUS ACCUMBENS'S LOCATION

The nucleus accumbens is a limbic (or, "emotional") brain structure (Goto & Grace, 2008) that is part of a larger region called the striatum, known for its involvement in movement, motivation, and reinforcement (Yager et al., 2015). The striatum is a part of a larger brain region called the basal ganglia (Dafny & Rosenfeld, 2017). The nucleus accumbens is situated a little bit above the amygdala and below the thalamus and more in front of (or, anterior to) both structures (see Figure 6.1). As such, it is well-positioned to integrate information from and send feedback to cortical and other limbic structures, such as the medial prefrontal cortex, hippocampus, and amygdala (Groenewegen et al., 1999; O'Donnell et al., 1997). The nucleus accumbens is also a key structure in the mesolimbic, or reward, pathway (see Figure 6.2; Ikemoto, 2010).

THE NUCLEUS ACCUMBENS'S FUNCTIONS
In a Nutshell

The nucleus accumbens plays a role in reward expectation (Scott et al., 2007), pain (Seminowicz et al., 2019), learning (Day & Carelli, 2007), sleep (Oishi et al., 2017), motivation (Cardinal et al., 2002), the placebo effect (Scott et al., 2007), and music (Gold et al., 2019), and through its connections it can influence emotions, motor movements, and memory (Kerfoot & Williams, 2018; Yager et al., 2015). As noted in the previous section, the nucleus accumbens is an integrative hub that connects many brain areas to one another, and as such it is well-positioned to be involved

NUCLEUS ACCUMBENS

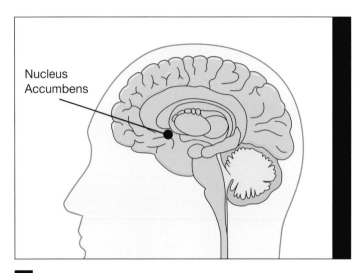

Nucleus
Accumbens

FIGURE 6.1: NUCLEUS ACCUMBENS

NUCLEUS
ACCUMBENS

in several functions, either directly or indirectly (Goto & Grace, 2008). Three main functions of the nucleus accumbens that will be detailed in this discussion are goal-directed behavior, reinforcement and aversion, and love and attachment.

GOAL-DIRECTED BEHAVIOR

It is perhaps not surprising, on account of it being a central part of the reward circuit, that the nucleus accumbens influences goal-directed behavior. When the nucleus accumbens is regulated and working well, it integrates information from limbic (emotional) areas of the brain and cortical (cognitive) areas of the brain to help individuals execute behaviors that are important for achieving a goal (Scofield et al., 2016). Brain lesions in this area, as well as drug use, can disrupt nucleus accumbens function, leading to a decrease in goal-directed behavior (Day & Carelli, 2007). The nucleus accumbens produces the experience of reinforcement with the help of dopamine, which is a neurotransmitter that makes situations, people, drugs, or behaviors feel pleasant. When a person's behavior aligns with

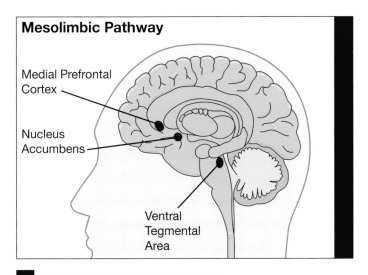

FIGURE 6.2: REWARD PATHWAY

a goal, dopamine is released, which reinforces the behavior because the dopamine is experienced as pleasant or exciting.

The nucleus accumbens, being tightly connected to cortical areas of the brain such as the prefrontal cortex, can help individuals make decisions and plan behaviors that will achieve their goals (Grubert et al., 2011; Volman et al., 2013). For example, if an individual wants to earn a raise because they anticipate it will make them feel happy, they may strategize about how to best achieve that goal. The nucleus accumbens will facilitate this process by merging information from the limbic areas of the brain about the emotions and desire for the goal with information from the cortical areas of the brain about the logical steps that would make the goal possible. The nucleus accumbens thus combines rational thinking and problem solving with emotions and motivation in order to help individuals plan and execute goal-directed behavior.

NUCLEUS
ACCUMBENS

REINFORCEMENT AND AVERSION

The nucleus accumbens is a reward brain structure and is part of the meso-limbic (reward) pathway, along with the ventral tegmental area (VTA) and medial prefrontal cortex (Volman et al., 2013). As described in the last section, the reinforcing, pleasant experience associated with nucleus accumbens activation is attributable to the presence of dopamine, which is released from the VTA and activates nucleus accumbens neurons. Thus, the nucleus accumbens has historically been considered the main reinforcement center of the brain and is believed to be involved in positive emotion and reward expectation (Wager et al., 2008; Volman et al., 2013). The nucleus accumbens has been associated with reinforcement; the amygdala has been associated with punishment or aversion.

However, the distinction between the nucleus accumbens and amygdala may not be so straightforward. Some research has shown, for instance, that the nucleus accumbens may be involved in reinforcement *and* aversion (along with the amygdala; Mccutcheon et al., 2012; Salamone, 1994), wherein dopamine substantially decreases in this region in response to aversive stimuli (Volman et al., 2013). Some researchers find this to be expected given the nucleus accumbens's role in goal-directed behavior; for goal-directed behavior to be successful, an individual needs to be able to predict not only pleasant outcomes of behaviors, but unpleasant ones as well. Thus, effective goal-directed behavior requires both the ability to approach rewards and the ability to withdraw from punishments. To do this, one must be able to evaluate the aversiveness of an action. It is posited that the nucleus accumbens's role in reinforcement and aversion is critical to learning and conditioning (Volman et al., 2013).

LOVE AND ATTACHMENT

The nucleus accumbens also plays a role in love and attachment, two experiences that are related to reinforcement and reward. For example, the nucleus accumbens activates when an individual looks at a picture of a close friend (Acevedo et al., 2012), during the experience of yearning for another

NUCLEUS
ACCUMBENS

person (O'Connor et al., 2008), and in romantic love (Seshadri, 2016). The activation of the nucleus accumbens in intense, passionate, romantic love has been likened to addiction (Fisher et al., 2016), wherein romantic love has been conceptualized as a sort of behavioral addiction (Burkett & Young, 2012). Relatedly, heart break and romantic rejection can also activate the nucleus accumbens (Fisher et al., 2010), and researchers believe this reflects a yearning, or craving, for the rejecting partner. Intense romantic love, whether requited, unrequited, or rejected, appears to activate the nucleus accumbens and may indicate obsessive, intrusive thinking about the love interest and a strong desire to be united with the person. Thus, nucleus accumbens activation is not only associated with the reinforcement that accompanies requited love but also with anticipated contact with a loved one and even with the yearning for a permanently unavailable lover.

THE NUCLEUS ACCUMBENS: MENTAL HEALTH CONDITIONS AND TREATMENT IMPLICATIONS

Nucleus accumbens alterations have been identified in several psychiatric disorders, reflecting its connection to several limbic and cortical brain regions. Individuals diagnosed with these disorders tend to experience anhedonia (a result of low dopamine in the nucleus accumbens), reduced motivation, and difficulties with positive emotions. The following sections detail the nucleus accumbens's specific role in addiction, schizophrenia, and depression.

ADDICTION

Addiction and the Nucleus Accumbens: What Happens?

There are many types of addiction, which tend to be categorized as behavioral or chemical. Because different types of addiction impact the brain in various ways, it is difficult to generalize what addiction looks like in the brain, especially in limbic structures. This section will emphasize chemical addictions and how the nucleus accumbens responds to this type of addiction, but keep in mind that behavioral addictions also alter the brain and in some ways resemble chemical addictions.

NUCLEUS ACCUMBENS

The nucleus accumbens has long been identified as a main area of the brain involved in reward and addiction (Goto & Grace, 2008; Salgato & Kaplitt, 2015). This brain region activates in response to reinforcing (and aversive) stimuli, including everyday experiences such as eating, laughing, sex, spending time with social supports, and even petting the dog. These activities lowly or moderately activate the nucleus accumbens, providing individuals with reinforcement and pleasure that motivate them to continue engaging in these behaviors. However, when individuals excessively consume alcohol (Boileau et al., 2003) or use drugs such as cocaine (Hyman, 1996), opiates (Koob et al., 1992), nicotine (Dani & Heinemann, 1996), methamphetamine (Rocha & Kalivas, 2010), or heroin (Tanda et al., 1997), the nucleus accumbens reacts more strongly and becomes flooded with dopamine (Di Chiara & Imperato, 1988). This increased nucleus accumbens activation creates a magnified reinforcing experience that is much more intense than, say, petting the dog. This in turn prompts the individual to repeatedly seek out the chemical in the future, facilitating the development of addiction.

Additionally, as an individual continues to use drugs or alcohol, two other shifts begin to occur in the nucleus accumbens. First, the nucleus accumbens begins to activate, releasing dopamine, when the chemical is *anticipated*, not just when the chemical enters the person's body (Salgato & Kaplitt, 2015). This is referred to as anticipatory dopamine, and it occurs when the person experiences strong reinforcement simply by thinking about the chemical, not just while using it. The release of anticipatory dopamine in the nucleus accumbens also leads to addiction, as it produces strong cravings.

Second, as individuals develop addiction, they often notice that as their interest in drugs or alcohol increases, their interest in other naturally reinforcing stimuli decreases. For example, they may begin to engage in drug seeking behaviors, feeling consumed by the pursuit of a particular drug, and at the same time lose interest in their job, family, or hobbies. This is because nucleus accumbens activation for those previously reinforcing behaviors decreases over time as the brain focuses solely on the drugs/alcohol. In other words, addiction is more than just desiring the thing a person is addicted to; it's also losing interest in and reinforcement from the things the person used to value and enjoy. While petting the dog used to be enjoyable, if a person becomes addicted to methamphetamines, the dog may not feel so reinforcing anymore, leading the person to disengage from the dog. This is why individuals with addiction give up the things, including the people, they love the most. Over time, the nucleus accumbens fails to activate in response to those stimuli, activating only when the person uses drugs or alcohol (Melis et al., 2005; Saal et al., 2003; Scofield et al., 2016).

Addiction and the Nucleus Accumbens: How It Presents

Clients experiencing nucleus accumbens dysfunction as a result of addiction may report feeling preoccupied by thoughts of alcohol or the drug that they are addicted to and less interested in things they used to care about. Because these clients may have neglected the natural reinforcers in their lives, such as spouses, children, friends, other family, hobbies, and/ or work, it is common for them to lose the people and activities they previously valued. Thus, they may report feeling lonely and disconnected, and their lives may be in disarray. This can make psychotherapy difficult, because these clients may not have the social supports, resources, or other stabilizing influences in their lives that can help facilitate recovery.

Moreover, addicted clients will often struggle with intrusive and overwhelming thoughts about using drugs or alcohol, including memories of past usage and what those experiences were. These strong thoughts or fantasies about using may be attributable to the nucleus accumbens activation and dopamine release that occurs in addiction when the individual simply thinks about the drug or alcohol (anticipatory dopamine). Addiction-related thoughts may in turn produce strong cravings, which clients may struggle to manage. When mismanaged or too strong, these cravings make the client susceptible to relapse.

Treatment Implications

A main goal of addiction treatment is to help clients reduce, and in most cases abstain from, substance use. A little-known effect of long-term abstinence from drug or alcohol use is dopamine/nucleus accumbens regulation

(Volkow et al., 2001; Volkow et al., 2004). Also, nucleus accumbens volume atrophy that is sometimes observed in drug addiction can be reversed (Korponay et al., 2017). When the nucleus accumbens is allowed to repair itself, and it recovers from the effects of substance abuse or dependence, the client is then able to re-engage with their life, enjoy the people and activities they value, and improve their functioning overall. The good news about dopamine in the nucleus accumbens, according to research, is that it has the ability reregulate after abstinence. Specifically, when clients stop using drugs or alcohol, their nucleus accumbens relearns how to activate in response to naturally rewarding stimuli, activities, and people, in part due to dopamine transporters (Laine et al., 1999; Sekine et al., 2001). Thus, while clients may have lost the ability to connect with support systems or enjoy the activities that used to be important to them, interest in these things can be reignited when the nucleus accumbens is repaired and dopamine is reregulated, and this happens naturally with abstinence. Also, when there is prolonged abstinence, anticipatory dopamine decreases over time, which attenuates cravings, promoting recovery. Thus, focusing on abstinence is the best way to improve nucleus accumbens functioning.

Pharmacotherapies may help clients maintain sobriety, which in turn can facilitate nucleus accumbens repair. These medications may target dopamine, glutamate, or other neurotransmitters and, in many clients, can help reduce cravings, relapse, and the reinforcing effects of addictive substances. For example, pharmacotherapies that act on glutamate may reduce relapse (Scofield et al., 2016). Additionally, the opioid agonist naltrexone may reduce or prevent the release of dopamine in the nucleus accumbens, which can make drugs or alcohol less reinforcing (Jayaram-Lindstrom et al., 2017).

Finally, deep brain stimulation (DBS), a neurosurgical procedure wherein electrodes are implanted into specific brain regions for the purpose of activating those areas, may show promise for those experiencing addiction. Several studies have suggested that DBS may help individuals recover from addiction by stimulating the nucleus accumbens in the absence of drugs or alcohol (Luigjes et al., 2012; Pierce & Vassoler, 2013;

NUCLEUS ACCUMBENS

Voges et al., 2013; Wang et al., 2018). However, this extremely invasive treatment is unlikely to be recommended for most individuals with substance use disorders or other addictions.

~~~~~~

DEPRESSION

Depression and the Nucleus Accumbens: What Happens?

Neuroimaging research studies have consistently found nucleus accumbens hypoactivation in depressed individuals (Drevets et al., 1992; Heller et al., 2009; Macpherson & Hikida, 2019; Mayberg et al., 2000; Russo & Nestler, 2013; Satterthwaite et al., 2015), likely reflecting anhedonia, a reduced ability to experience reward or reinforcement, and difficulty accessing positive emotions (Linden et al., 2012). In addition, reduced nucleus accumbens volume in this population has been observed in several studies (Baumann et al., 1999; Husain et al., 1991; Krishnan et al., 1992), though a few studies found no nucleus accumbens volume changes in depression (Bremmer et al., 2000; Hannestad et al., 2006). It is unclear if volume changes are associated with nucleus accumbens hypoactivation. Finally, reduced connectivity between the ventral striatum and cortical regions has been found (Oathes et al., 2015), which is consistent with generalized findings linking depression with overall reduced connectivity in the brain (Schultz et al., 2019).

Depression and the Nucleus Accumbens: How It Presents

Depressed clients experiencing low nucleus accumbens activation may report feeling numb, unhappy, apathetic, and/or unable to enjoy activities, hobbies, or people they used to value. Anhedonia, which is the inability to experience pleasure or reinforcement, is a common depression symptom and can make it difficult for people to engage in behavioral activation. This in turn often leads to low motivation, withdrawal, and isolation, as depressed individuals may notice that "nothing feels good" and "everything feels like a chore." This anhedonia is believed to be a result of lowered dopamine and hypoactivation of the reward circuit of the brain, including the nucleus accumbens. Because everyday life can feel laborious and unrewarding when clients are depressed it is common for these clients to become even more depressed as a result of behavioral inactivation, which is why behavioral activation is often recommended as a part of cognitive behavioral therapy.

Treatment Implications

Some therapeutic approaches may help activate the nucleus accumbens/ventral striatum and strengthen its connection with cortical areas, but research as much more to explore with regard to this topic. For example, CBT may help increase ventral striatum activity. In one study, individuals with major depressive disorder who practiced CBT skills aimed at increasing positive emotion showed increased ventral striatum activation, suggesting the ventral striatum to be involved in positive affect and emotion regulation (Greening et al., 2014). While more research would need to be conducted to conclude that CBT results in sustained nucleus accumbens/ventral striatum activation and reduced depression symptoms, the study by Greening et al. suggests this may be the case. Additionally, one study concluded that depressed individuals with reward-processing deficits responded better to CBT treatment than depressed individuals who did not show those same deficits (Burkhouse et al., 2016). The authors concluded that the results suggest CBT may target reward circuit functioning and increase activation in those areas (including the nucleus accumbens). Other researchers made a similar assertion regarding reward circuit functioning and depression, stating that "neural responsiveness to reward [may be] both a mechanism and predictor of depression symptom change. . ." (Burkhouse et al., 2018). It is possible that CBT may alter reward circuit responsiveness in depressed individuals.

Additionally, neurofeedback has been shown to increase nucleus accumbens/ventral striatum activation in depressed individuals (Johnston et al., 2010; Linden & Lancaster, 2011; Linden et al., 2012; Mehler et al., 2018), and this activation is associated with a reduction in depression symptoms. Thus, neurofeedback is becoming widely accepted as a promising therapeutic tool in depression treatment. Research has found that neurofeedback can reduce depression symptoms by about 40% (Mehler et al., 2018), and the nucleus accumbens/ventral striatum is one brain region, along with other regions such as the insula and ventrolateral prefrontal cortex, targeted by neurofeedback (Buhle et al., 2014).

Similarly, DBS (described above in the Treatment Implications section for addiction) is another, though much more invasive way, to activate the nucleus accumbens/ventral striatum. Several studies have shown DBS to activate this brain region and reduce depression symptoms (Bewernick et al., 2010; Malone et al., 2009; Shlaepfer et al., 2008), even in those with severe and recalcitrant depression (Nauczyciel et al., 2013). More specifically, one study found that depression symptoms after DBS diminished by 50% (Macpherson & Hikida, 2019). These findings indicate DBS that targets the nucleus accumbens/ventral striatum is an effective depression treatment for some depressed individuals.

Finally, antidepressant medication, specifically SSRIs, may alter nucleus accumbens/ventral striatum connectivity. While very few studies have shown SSRIs to activate this region in response to reinforcing stimuli (Stoy et al., 2012), SSRIs may be helpful in strengthening the connection between the nucleus accumbens/ventral striatum and other key areas of the brain, leading to better neural integration and reduced depression symptoms (Chen et al., 2008; Wang et al., 2017). In some patients, however, SSRIs may blunt emotional responses, both positive and negative. Diminished neural processing of rewarding stimuli was found in one study, wherein healthy participants showed reduced ventral striatum activation in response to pleasant stimuli, such as chocolate (McCame et al., 2010). This study only included individuals not diagnosed with depression (or other psychiatric disorders), thus the findings may not be generalizable to depressed clients, but the authors proposed that this underactivation of the ventral striatum in response to rewarding stimuli may account for the emotional numbing reported by some depressed individuals who are prescribed SSRIs.

NUCLEUS
ACCUMBENS

ANXIETY

Anxiety and the Nucleus Accumbens: What Happens?

While nucleus accumbens activity likely varies across anxiety disorders, some patterns have been observed, and this brain region has recently started to gain attention for its possible role in anxiety. However, much of the research on this region's link to anxiety has focused on the ventral striatum, which includes the nucleus accumbens (see The Nucleus Accumbens's Location section of this chapter; Yager et al., 2015). The nucleus accumbens is the largest subregion of the ventral striatum, thus ventral striatum findings usually include the nucleus accumbens and other subregions (Salgado & Kaplitt, 2015). In particular, the nucleus accumbens specifically, and the ventral striatum more broadly, tend to be less activated in anxious individuals (Engelmann et al., 2015; Macpherson & Hikida, 2019), including those who meet criteria for GAD (Lee et al., 2015; Wu et al., 1991) and those with SAD who anticipate a stressful performance demand (Boehme et al., 2014). Conversely, high nucleus accumbens activation is associated with lowered anxiety (Ericson et al., 2011). Also, nucleus accumbens connectivity with the dorsolateral prefrontal cortex has been found to be weak in anxious and depressed individuals (Du et al., 2018).

However, increased activation of the ventral striatum has also been associated with anxiety, especially during anticipation of an aversive event (Pohlack et al., 2012), such as a punishment (Levita et al., 2012). One study found that individuals with SAD showed increased ventral striatum activation in response to their partners during a trust game, and this activation occurred even when the partner was untrustworthy and elicited anxiety (Sripada et al., 2013). Similarly, another study found increased activation in the ventral striatum in socially anxious individuals who anticipated engaging in a confrontational arithmetic task (Kilts et al., 2006). Together, these findings suggest the striatum (including the nucleus accumbens) is involved in the processing of both reward and aversion. This is consistent with other nucleus accumbens findings that indicate that the reward circuit activates in response to both reinforcing and aversive stimuli (Mccutcheon et al., 2012). Moreover, nucleus accumbens volume has been found to be larger in anxious than nonanxious individuals (Günther et al., 2018; Kühn et al., 2011), though nucleus accumbens volume does not necessarily predict nucleus accumbens activity.

The contradictory findings regarding anxiety and nucleus accumbens/ventral striatum activity are not simple to resolve, and more research will be required to better understand when and why anxiety is associated with nucleus accumbens hyperactivation versus hypoactivation. However, the results of one study may begin to clarify the discrepant findings. Levita et al. (2012) conducted an fMRI study with anxious individuals, observing nucleus accumbens activity in response to anxiety-related avoidance. They found increased nucleus accumbens activation in anxious individuals during active avoidance of anxiety-producing stimuli, but decreased nucleus accumbens activation during passive avoidance of the same stimuli. Thus, nucleus accumbens activation may not reflect the *experience* of one's anxiety as much as one's *strategy* for avoiding anxiety-related situations.

ANXIETY AND THE NUCLEUS ACCUMBENS: HOW IT PRESENTS

Nucleus accumbens hypoactivation may present as anhedonia or emotional numbing in anxious clients. Nucleus accumbens underactivation has been linked to the numbing symptoms of PTSD (Mehta et al., 2020), and anxious clients may show similar symptoms, wherein they report either feeling anxious or "turned off" from their emotions. Because of this, clients may no longer pursue previously enjoyed activities or hobbies, and they may seem preoccupied by their anxious feelings and thoughts. This may make it difficult for clients to comply with treatment recommendations that include engagement with other people or enjoyable activities. Moreover, the nucleus accumbens hyperactivation sometimes observed in anxious individuals may present as active avoidance of anxiety-inducing situations, people, or stimuli, and may reflect a strong experience of aversion.

NUCLEUS ACCUMBENS

Treatment Implications

Research on nucleus accumbens/ventral striatum activity and connectivity in anxiety treatment is sparse at this time, likely because interest in these brain regions with regard to anxiety has only recently received attention. However, a few therapeutic approaches show promise for healthy nucleus accumbens alterations. For instance, repetitive transcranial magnetic stimulation (rTMS) has been shown to strengthen dorsolateral prefrontal cortex–nucleus accumbens connectivity, which in turn is associated with lowered anxiety (Du et al., 2018).

Additionally, deep brain stimulation (DBS) has repeatedly been found to reduce anxiety symptoms (Bewernick et al., 2010; Macpherson & Hikida, 2019; Sturm et al., 2003). When DBS is combined with cognitive behavioral therapy for the treatment of OCD, patients may experience additional anxiolytic effects (Mantione et al., 2014). However, as stated in previous sections of this chapter, given the invasiveness of DBS and the resources and risks involved, this is not a therapeutic approach that will likely be accessible by most individuals. Thankfully, preliminary research indicates that CBT/exposure therapy alone may regulate ventral striatum activity, at least in those with panic disorder (Wittmann et al., 2018).

OTHER MENTAL HEALTH CONDITIONS

The nucleus accumbens/ventral striatum likely contributes to the development and maintenance of several psychiatric disorders, though research on this region's connection to mental health conditions other than addiction is still fairly limited. Some research suggests that the nucleus accumbens is involved in psychopathy (usually diagnosed as antisocial personality disorder), wherein the nucleus accumbens tends to be hyperactive both during and in anticipation of a rewarding event or stimulus (Buckholtz et al., 2010). This may explain why individuals with high levels of psychopathy reportedly enjoy engaging in antisocial behaviors without regard for the rights of others. Also, the nucleus accumbens appears to be hypoactivated in some individuals with ADHD, presumably due to reduced dopamine synaptic markers in this region (Volkow et al., 2009). In ADHD, hypoactivation of the nucleus accumbens may be related to symptoms of inattention. The nucleus accumbens may be involved in other conditions as well, including OCD, bipolar disorder, neurocognitive disorder secondary to Parkinson's disease, and Alzheimer's disease (Idris & Abdullah, 2017). Future research may elucidate the nucleus accumbens's role in these and other conditions.

CHAPTER 7

The Anterior Cingulate Cortex

THE ANTERIOR CINGULATE CORTEX'S LOCATION

The anterior cingulate cortex is part of a much larger structure, the cingulate cortex, which is comprised of four subsections (see Figure 7.1; Vogt et al., 1995). Considered both a limbic and cortical structure, the anterior cingulate cortex is located at the front of the cingulate cortex (toward your forehead), and slightly in front of (i.e., anterior to) and around the corpus callosum (Jumah & Dossani, 2019), which consists of the fibers that connect the left and right hemispheres. To give you a better idea, the anterior cingulate cortex is located approximately three inches behind your "third eye," which is the center on your forehead between your eyebrows.

Within the anterior cingulate cortex are two distinct substructures, the dorsal anterior cingulate cortex (dACC) and ventral anterior cingulate cortex (vACC; Bush et al., 2000). The word "dorsal" refers to an animal's back, and in brain research it means the part of a structure closest to the top of the head. In the brain, ventral refers to the lower-most part of a brain structure (see Figure 7.2 to view the dACC and vACC). The dACC has been associated with cognitive functions, whereas the vACC (sometimes called the rostral ACC) has been found to be involved in emotional functions and error detection (Bush et al., 2000; for a more elaborate explanation, see the next section).

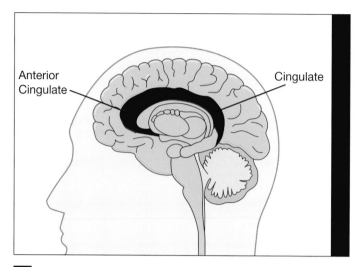

FIGURE 7.1: **ANTERIOR CINGULATE CORTEX**

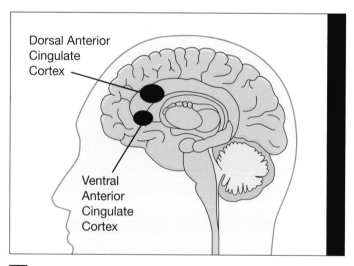

FIGURE 7.2: **DACC AND VACC**

THE ANTERIOR CINGULATE CORTEX'S FUNCTIONS
In a Nutshell

The anterior cingulate cortex functions as a sort of judge; it considers several pieces of information from various brain structures and integrates them to help make decisions about how to feel, what to think, and how to behave. Thus, the anterior cingulate cortex has strong connections to areas of the brain involved in learning and memory (hippocampus), self-referential thinking (prefrontal cortex), sensation (sensorimotor cortex), reward (basal ganglia), interoception (insula), and others (Margulies et al., 2007). The anterior cingulate cortex is both a limbic and cortical structure and is often considered the bridge between the cognitive and emotional regions of the brain. Best of all, activation of this brain region is within conscious control, thus with practice, the anterior cingulate cortex can be strengthened using a variety of techniques!

COGNITIVE FUNCTIONS

The anterior cingulate cortex, the dACC in particular, is best known for its involvement in cognitive functions such as response/conflict monitoring, real-time monitoring more broadly, error detection, and decision-making (Heilbronner & Hayden, 2016; To et al., 2017). It also helps assess the effort needed to accomplish a goal and determines whether the effort is worth the likely outcome (Chong et al., 2017). The dACC is involved in real-time monitoring of situations (and effort) by assessing one's internal experiences and external environment. This continuous monitoring allows ongoing calibration of one's decision-making based on internal and external cues and promotes cognitive flexibility.

Additionally, the dACC activates during conflict monitoring (Iannaccone et al., 2015; Yeung, 2014), which is when an individual thinks or feels two conflicting things at once, or when a person is faced with multiple pieces of contradictory information that need to be reconciled. For instance, cognitive dissonance presents a conflict, such as a smoker who knows research shows smoking to be detrimental to health. To reconcile these conflicting parts—the smoking behavior and the knowledge of harm

ANTERIOR CINGULATE CORTEX

done by smoking—the dACC will likely activate to attempt to solve the conflict. Related to conflict monitoring, this same brain region has been shown to help detect errors (O'Connell et al., 2007; Ridderinkhof et al., 2004; Wessel et al., 2011), such as when you make a typing error or make a grammatical error that you are aware of.

EMOTIONAL FUNCTIONS

The anterior cingulate cortex, specifically the vACC, has been shown to be involved in multiple emotional functions. This brain region has strong connections to emotional, limbic areas of the brain, including the amygdala and insula, and is believed to play a role in emotion processing and regulation and in the generation of emotional responses appropriate to different situations. Because of this, the vACC is sometimes considered to be the emotional subsection of the anterior cingulate cortex (Bush et al., 2000). For example, vACC activation would occur when you have a strong emotional reaction to a situation but attempt to control your response to it or try to talk yourself out of feeling the emotion. Therefore, the anterior cingulate cortex may also be called the "self-regulation" center of the brain (Tang & Tang, 2013).

Moreover, the vACC helps the brain determine the emotional significance, if any, of one's context and helps the dACC with decision-making by contributing emotional reactions to the situation at hand (Sander & Scherer, 2010). While a common misconception is that sound rational decision-making should not include emotion, anterior cingulate cortex functioning indicates the opposite, that emotions are critical to the process of decision-making. Finally, the vACC has also been shown to help modulate heart rate and bodily arousal states (Critchley et al., 2003), which may also contribute to decision-making and emotion regulation.

EMPATHY

The anterior cingulate cortex has also been shown to activate during the experience of empathy (Larson et al., 2010; Klimecki-Lenz & Singer,

ANTERIOR CINGULATE CORTEX

2013; Apps et al., 2016), often along with the anterior insula (Melloni et al., 2014). It is possible that the anterior cingulate cortex and anterior insula together allow individuals to "feel" what others experience: the insula allows the individual to experience the sensations of empathy (i.e., racing heart), and the anterior cingulate cortex (especially the dACC) helps provide an interpretation of the sensations (i.e., "That is stressful!"). Conversely, when research subjects report experiencing low empathy, their anterior cingulate cortex is significantly less activated (Bloom, 2017). Thankfully, empathy is a skill that can be built with dedication and training. Empathy-building practices, such as loving kindness meditation (Lippelt et al., 2014) and other compassion practices (Lown, 2016), have been linked to higher anterior cingulate cortex activation, suggesting that it is possible to strengthen this brain region and, in the process, create new emotional experiences for ourselves.

THE ANTERIOR CINGULATE CORTEX: MENTAL HEALTH CONDITIONS AND TREATMENT IMPLICATIONS

The anterior cingulate cortex is an extensively studied, large brain region involved in several psychiatric conditions, including depression, PTSD, OCD, addictions, schizophrenia, anxiety, and others (Yücel et al., 2003). The following sections detail the roles of the anterior cingulate cortex in three different mental health conditions and how psychotherapy may help alter the functioning of the anterior cingulate cortex in the direction of health.

ANTERIOR CINGULATE CORTEX

TRAUMA
Trauma and the Anterior Cingulate Cortex: What Happens?

A consistent finding in PTSD research is that the anterior cingulate cortex tends to be underactivated in those who meet criteria for this disorder (Hopper et al., 2007; Rosso et al., 2014; Zweerings et al., 2018). This is perhaps not surprising, as PTSD is characterized, in part, by deficits in self-regulation (Koenen, 2006), including emotion regulation (Weiss et al., 2012). The anterior cingulate cortex has been found to be involved in self-regulation, broadly, and emotion regulation, more specifically (Kohn et al., 2014).

PTSD is believed to have a specific "neural profile," in which the insula and amygdala are hyperreactive and the anterior cingulate cortex is under-activated (along with some areas of the prefrontal cortex, such as the ven-tromedial prefrontal cortex; Etkin & Wager, 2007). While activation of the amygdala and insula are observed not only in PTSD but in several anx-iety disorders as well, underactivation of the anterior cingulate cortex is posited to be a defining feature of PTSD, as it is not consistently found in anxiety disorders or in individuals who have experienced trauma who do *not* meet criteria for PTSD (Patel et al., 2012). The underactivation of the anterior cingulate cortex in PTSD suggests that those with PTSD not only experience exaggerated fear and startle responses but likely also struggle with emotion regulation more broadly, even in the absence of fear-inducing stimuli. Interestingly, an increase in anterior cingulate cortex activation in individuals with PTSD has been correlated with PTSD symptom reduction (Dickie et al., 2011).

Additionally, several studies have found altered connectivity between the anterior cingulate cortex and other brain regions, which may fur-ther explain why individuals with PTSD experience difficulties with self-regulation. In particular, research has shown increased connectivity between the anterior cingulate cortex and the amygdala in PTSD (Brown et al., 2014; Sripada et al., 2012). This may allow the amygdala, the threat detection center of the brain, to easily override and suppress functioning of the anterior cingulate cortex in PTSD, leading to "amygdalar hijack-ings," wherein the individual feels triggered and cannot think clearly or regulate their emotional reactions. Moreover, the connection between the anterior cingulate cortex and some areas of the prefrontal cortex, includ-ing those involved in self-referential thinking (medial prefrontal cortex), is often weaker in those with PTSD compared to healthy controls (Clausen et al., 2017). This reduced functional connectivity may explain why it is difficult for those with PTSD, and other psychiatric disorders, to regulate and reduce negative self-talk and ruminations.

ANTERIOR
CINGULATE
CORTEX

Trauma and the Anterior Cingulate Cortex: How It Presents

Anterior cingulate cortex-related changes in those experiencing PTSD likely contribute to several key symptoms from multiple DSM-5 PTSD symptom clusters. Specifically, anterior cingulate cortex underactivation and functional connectivity alterations may be linked to the re-experiencing symptoms of PTSD. For example, research has found re-experiencing symptoms to be negatively correlated with anterior cingulate cortex activation (Hopper et al., 2007; Nicholson et al., 2017). In other words, the lower the anterior cingulate cortex activation, the more severe the re-experiencing symptoms. It can be presumed that this is because the anterior cingulate cortex, the self-regulation center of the brain, is too weak to modulate or downregulate distressing reactions to trauma reminders produced by the amygdala. Many clients with PTSD, whose anterior cingulate cortex is likely underactivated, often report that they experience overwhelmingly distressing trauma reminders. Once triggered, they may find it challenging to self-soothe by engaging in calming, positive self-talk, which requires anterior cingulate cortex activation.

Anterior cingulate cortex alterations may also play a role in arousal and reactivity symptoms. Risky and impulsive behavior has been associated with reduced anterior cingulate cortex activation in those with PTSD (Strom et al., 2012; Weiss et al., 2012), as the inhibition of these behaviors requires self-regulation and anterior cingulate cortex dominance over other brain regions, such as the amygdala. Also, lowered anterior cingulate cortex activation has been linked to concentration difficulties, another arousal and reactivity symptom of PTSD (Koso & Hansen, 2006), in addition to hypervigilance (Rosso et al., 2014). Given these findings, it is understandable that those experiencing PTSD will often seem anxious, on guard, and distracted. While these individuals often report feeling fearful and hypervigilant, they may simultaneously engage in high-risk behaviors due to difficulty with inhibiting (often self-destructive) impulses.

Treatment Implications

The anterior cingulate cortex is an area of the brain that is within conscious awareness and control and that can be altered by many different therapeutic approaches. This makes the anterior cingulate cortex a central focus of PTSD treatment research. Psychotherapy, broadly, has been associated with increased activation of the anterior cingulate cortex in PTSD clients (Thomaes et al., 2014). In particular, exposure and cognitive behavioral therapies show the most promise for shifting anterior cingulate cortex activation and connectivity in the direction of health and are considered the preferred treatment approaches for PTSD.

A combination of exposure therapy and cognitive behavioral therapy is the general, frontline approach for treating PTSD (Roy et al., 2014), and both approaches have been found to increase anterior cingulate cortex activation and strengthen functional connectivity between the anterior cingulate cortex and the prefrontal cortex. Helpman et al. (2016) examined the connectivity between the anterior cingulate cortex and ventromedial prefrontal cortex before and after completion of prolonged exposure therapy, an evidence-based exposure therapy for PTSD, and found enhanced connectivity after therapy completion. This suggests that exposure therapy strengthened the relationship between the self-regulation area of the brain (anterior cingulate cortex) and the self-referential area of the brain (ventromedial prefrontal cortex), possibly helping individuals regulate their reaction to trauma reminders by remaining self-aware and staying present in the here and now.

Moreover, multiple neuroimaging studies have found EMDR, an exposure-based therapy, to be associated with increased anterior cingulate cortex activation and PTSD symptom improvement (Rousseau et al., 2019; Boccia et al., 2015). EMDR is an evidence-based therapy for PTSD that emphasizes repeated, imaginal exposure to salient trauma memories. It has been suggested that the increased anterior cingulate cortex activation observed after EMDR completion reflects desensitization to previously feared stimuli, as successful desensitization is correlated with anterior cingulate cortex activation (Boccia et al., 2015).

Compared to CBT, EMDR has been associated with faster symptom reduction (Solomon & Rando, 2012). One explanation for this finding is that EMDR may directly strengthen the anterior cingulate cortex through desensitization and habituation, whereas CBT may primarily strengthen the prefrontal cortex, only indirectly improving anterior cingulate cortex activation (Boccia et a., 2015). Nonetheless, the link between increased anterior cingulate cortex activation and cognitive approaches in general, including CBT, is well-established in the PTSD literature (Corrigan, 2004; Felmingham et al., 2007; Yang et al., 2018). For example, individuals with PTSD showed increased anterior cingulate cortex activation in response to anticipated trauma reminders after completing cognitive therapy (Aupperle et al., 2013). This was associated with a positive response to treatment. Such findings indicate that those suffering from PTSD may benefit from a top-down approach to post trauma symptoms, wherein cortical areas such as the anterior cingulate cortex are strengthened, enabling top-down regulation of the amygdala.

A proposed mechanism of cognitive and exposure-based therapies is that they tend to encourage mindful self-awareness, including awareness of and attention to thoughts and emotions, which can promote healing (Corrigan, 2004). This real-time monitoring of oneself is associated with anterior cingulate cortex activation and is emphasized (to varying degrees) in cognitive therapies, psychodynamic psychotherapy, EMDR, dialectical behavioral therapy, and various mindfulness approaches (King et al., 2016). However, more research is needed on these specific therapeutic interventions to determine their potential effects on the anterior cingulate cortex.

ADDICTION

Addiction and the Anterior Cingulate Cortex: What Happens?

Anterior cingulate cortex underactivation has also been found in a variety of addictions, including (but not limited to) opiates (Forman et al., 2004), nicotine (Kutlu et al., 2013), cocaine (Goldstein et al., 2009), heroine (Ma et al., 2010), and even Internet addiction (Dong et al., 2011). It's been posited that anterior cingulate cortex underactivation observed in addiction may play a role in impulsive drug use (Forman et al., 2004), relapse (Naqvi & Bechara, 2010), impaired self-control (Tang et al., 2015), and difficulties with cognitive processing in general (Goldstein et al., 2009). In fact, anterior cingulate cortex hypoactivation during cognitive tasks is a key finding in addiction neuroimaging research (Goldstein et al., 2010). One noteworthy example of this comes from research indicating that when evaluating behaviors that may elicit a reward or punishment, individuals with Internet addiction show less anterior cingulate cortex activation when considering an action likely to result in punishment (Dong et al., 2011). The authors of this study concluded anterior cingulate cortex underactivation in addiction to be associated with decreased risk and loss sensitivity.

Altered anterior cingulate cortex connectivity has also been observed in addicted individuals. Multiple studies have found increased connectivity between the anterior cingulate cortex and the nucleus accumbens, a main reward and reinforcement center of the brain, in addicted subjects compared to healthy controls (Ma et al., 2010). This, along with underactivation of the anterior cingulate cortex, may contribute to the reinforcing properties of drug use becoming more salient than the possible consequences of using. Additionally, increased connectivity between the anterior cingulate cortex and thalamus has been linked to increased risk-taking in nicotine addicts and implies decision-making difficulties in addiction (Wei et al., 2016).

Addiction and the Anterior Cingulate Cortex: How It Presents

Those experiencing active addiction will often exhibit impulsivity and lack of self-control, engaging in risky behavior that can be self-destructive and seem irrational. This is especially the case when the individual is under stress, as distress tolerance can be low in those experiencing addiction (Bornovalova et al., 2012; Tang et al., 2015). While it may be the case that risky and self-destructive behavior is limited to drug or alcohol use or to other addiction behaviors, these behaviors may be broader and can include self-harm (de Cates et al., 2017) or sensation-seeking activities (Ersche et al., 2010). In a clinical context, addicted individuals who experience low anterior cingulate cortex activation and altered anterior cingulate cortex connectivity may appear restless, distracted, and prone to noncompliance or intermittent compliance with psychotherapy. They may also report engagement in several different sensation-seeking activities in addition to

ANTERIOR CINGULATE CORTEX

addictive behaviors, and these behaviors may increase as replacements to the addiction(s) once abstinence is achieved.

Treatment Implications

Therapeutic approaches that help improve cognitive control and emotion regulation show promise for activating the anterior cingulate cortex and promoting recovery in those suffering from addiction (Konova et al., 2013). Many of these approaches, which tend to be cognitive behavioral in nature, are similar to the ones described in the section discussing the treatment of PTSD. While CBT likely shifts the activation and connectivity of several brain regions and circuits (Potenza et al., 2011), the anterior cingulate cortex is likely targeted in techniques that emphasize the development of coping skills for craving management, impulsivity, and distress tolerance (Bornovalova et al., 2012; Garrison & Potenza, 2014; Wexler et al., 2001) and in exercises that promote body awareness (along with the insula; Janes et al., 2010). Additionally, research suggests that in individuals suffering from addiction, cognitive control (and anterior cingulate cortex activation) can be improved with CBT, mindfulness techniques, neurofeedback, and motivation-enhancing interventions (Tang et al., 2015; Zilverstand et al., 2016).

Moreover, pharmacological treatment may also improve anterior cingulate cortex functioning in addicted individuals. Naltrexone, commonly used to reduce relapse in those experiencing substance use disorders, has been shown to increase connectivity between the anterior cingulate cortex and ventromedial prefrontal cortex, possibly improving self-regulation and inhibition and reducing impulsivity (Elton et al., 2019). Also, modafinil, a medication originally developed to treat narcolepsy and obstructive sleep apnea, has been shown to improve cognitive control and attention and to increase anterior cingulate cortex activation (Ghahremani et al., 2011). Finally, oral methylphenidate, otherwise known as Ritalin, has been associated with increased anterior cingulate cortex responsiveness and decreased impulsivity during cognitive tasks in cocaine addicted individuals (Goldstein & Volkow, 2011a. It is likely that cognitive behavioral approaches, combined with some pharmacological interventions, may

ANTERIOR
CINGULATE
CORTEX

help improve anterior cingulate cortex functioning in addiction in general (Goldstein & Volkow, 2011b).

~~~~~~

DEPRESSION

Depression and the Anterior Cingulate Cortex: What Happens?

Depression has been associated with changes in anterior cingulate cortex functioning and connectivity. While the depression research showing reduced anterior cingulate cortex connectivity is well-established and straightforward, anterior cingulate cortex activation changes in depression are more complex. Depression has been repeatedly associated with lowered activation of the anterior cingulate cortex overall (Halari et al., 2009; Holsen et al., 2012; Pizzagalli et al., 2001), but this general finding does not capture the entirety of the relationship between depression and anterior cingulate cortex activation.

As discussed earlier in this chapter, the anterior cingulate cortex contains multiple subregions, including the dACC and vACC (sometimes referred to as rACC), which are involved in slightly different functions. The dACC's role is primarily in the regulation of cognition, whereas the vACC is more involved in emotion processing and error detection (meaning, this area activates when you've made a mistake, to alert you to it). In depression, the dACC tends to be underactivated, while the vACC— especially the portion involved in error detection—tends to be hyperactivated (Disner et al., 2011; Levkovitz et al., 2011; Roiser et al., 2012).

Underactivation of the dACC in depression suggests these individuals may experience reduced cognitive control (Liotti & Mayberg, 2001). For instance, dACC activation has been found to be lower during attempts at suppressing of task-irrelevant information in depressed individuals, indicating a lack of cognitive and attentional control (Roiser et al., 2012). Put more simply, depressed individuals may have a hard time disengaging from thoughts even when they want to, and this is likely linked to the dACC's inability to activate as well as it does in nondepressed individuals (Ladouceur et al., 2012). This finding is further supported by research showing decreased dACC activation in depressed individuals during completion of a Stroop task (Pizzagalli et al., 2001). Stroop tasks require the participant to state the font *color* of a particular word while ignoring what the word *says*. To do this successfully, the individual must be able to engage in thought suppression, which is difficult in depression. Additionally, underactivation of the dACC has been associated with a stronger stress response in the body and with autonomic nervous system dysregulation (Holsen et al., 2012).

Conversely, the vACC has been found to be hyperactive in depression. Given that the vACC is involved in error detection, hyperactivation of this area suggests that depressed individuals may struggle with self-blame and self-criticism, as vACC activation can relentlessly insist that the person has done something wrong (Levkovitz et al., 2011). vACC activation in depression has also been associated with biased self-referential thoughts and rumination (Disner et al., 2011). It is possible that in depression, the vACC produces negative self-talk and ruminations that the dACC then has difficulty disengaging from or downregulating (Disner et al., 2011; Roiser et al., 2012).

Moreover, anterior cingulate cortex connectivity with other brain regions tends to be weak in depression (Anand et al., 2007; Philippi et al., 2015). For example, the reduced connectivity between the dACC and some areas of the limbic system, such as the thalamus, insula, and amygdala (Veer et al., 2010), has been associated with increased negative thoughts and attitudes as well as an inability to control those thoughts (Disner et al., 2011). It has been posited that overall decreased connectivity between the anterior cingulate cortex and other regions may contribute to the initial development of depression (Philippi et al., 2015).

ANTERIOR CINGULATE CORTEX

Depression and the Anterior Cingulate Cortex: How It Presents

When working with depression, altered anterior cingulate cortex functioning may become apparent in two ways. First, it is common for depressed clients to report a high frequency of distressing, self-deprecating, pessimistic thoughts. While nondepressed individuals also experience these thoughts, they are usually much less prevalent and intrusive. When depressed, some individuals can recognize that the thoughts they are having may not be accurate, but the thoughts continue to materialize anyway and can be persistent and convincing to the person even when they are irrational.

Second, depressed clients find it difficult to focus away, or disengage from, their distressing thoughts. Thus in therapy sessions, depressed individuals may be repetitive and seem like "broken records" when sharing their thoughts and perspectives. They may also have difficulty seeing themselves, situations, or others from different perspectives. Various cognitive behavioral techniques, such as cognitive reframing, aim to help clients shift their thinking from distressing thoughts to more helpful ones. However, it can take time for clients to successfully practice cognitive restructuring because it requires retraining the brain. More specifically, clients must learn how to activate the dACC (allowing them to shift away from negative thoughts) while also reducing their vACC activation (which can produce negative thoughts). This takes time and effort.

Treatment Implications

Several treatment approaches have been shown to positively alter anterior cingulate cortex functioning in depression. Perhaps most notable are cognitive therapy techniques, which alter anterior cingulate cortex activations and connectivity in the direction of health. For example, neuroimaging research has established a positive association between cognitive restructuring/reappraisal and dACC activity (Giuliani et al., 2011), especially when confronted with distressing emotional information (Vanderhasselt et al., 2013; Hermann et al., 2014). Cognitive reappraisal is a cognitive restructuring strategy wherein an individual attempts to think differently about some emotional content to make it feel less distressing. Research suggests that cognitive reappraisal training (and perhaps cognitive restructuring techniques more broadly) may help strengthen the dACC, thereby helping the individual change their thinking away from distressing thoughts to more helpful, adaptive thoughts. It is also possible that the amygdala may be downregulated by the dACC during cognitive reappraisal (Kanske et al., 2012).

Also, CBT has been associated with decreased vACC activation in response to negative stimuli (Yoshimura et al., 2014) in depressed individ-

ANTERIOR CINGULATE CORTEX

uals, suggesting that CBT may help reduce the frequency and/or intensity of negative self-talk. Finally, CBT has been linked to improved connectivity between the anterior cingulate cortex and other limbic regions in depressed individuals (Pantazatos et al., 2020), which may also explain why those who complete CBT and other psychotherapies often exhibit an improved ability to regulate distressing thoughts and emotions (Etkin & Schatzberg, 2011).

Psychiatric medications, broadly, and SSRIs, more specifically, may also alter anterior cingulate cortex functioning. Some SSRIs have been associated with increased connectivity between the anterior cingulate cortex and limbic structures of the brain (Anand et al., 2005; Anand et al., 2007) as well as decreased vACC activation in depressed individuals (Fu et al., 2004; Mayberg et al., 2005). Overall increases in anterior cingulate cortex activation have also been observed in depressed individuals who responded well to escitalopram (Godlewska et al., 2016) and paroxetine (Goldapple et al., 2004), suggesting possible improved cognitive control.

In addition to psychotherapy and medication management of depression symptoms, there is a growing trend to treat depression using neurofeedback, which has also been linked to anterior cingulate cortex alterations. Neurofeedback may help decrease vACC activation (Hamilton et al., 2011) and is associated with improved anterior cingulate cortex connectivity with the prefrontal cortex (Cannon et al., 2009). Neurofeedback may also increase overall anterior cingulate cortex activation (Zilverstrand et al., 2017).

ANTERIOR CINGULATE CORTEX

OTHER MENTAL HEALTH CONDITIONS

The anterior cingulate cortex is a large brain region believed to be involved in many psychiatric disorders (Devinsky et al., 1995), including ADHD (Ende et al., 2016), bipolar depression, schizophrenia (Sanders et al., 2002; Benes, 1993), autism (Yücel et al., 2003), borderline personality disorder (BPD; Ende et al., 2016), OCD (Rauch et al., 1994; Melcher et al., 2008), and anxiety disorders (Shang et al., 2014). The anterior cingulate cortex's role in these disorders is often complex, unlike the amygdala's role in most psychiatric conditions, which is usually that it is hyperactive or hyper-reactive. This complexity is likely attributable to the size of the anterior cingulate cortex, which is large compared to other brain structures and contains several subregions. Each subregion of the anterior cingulate cortex is believed to be involved in different functions, making it difficult to make generalizations about anterior cingulate cortex functioning in some psychiatric disorders. However, what the aforementioned disorders have in common, to an extent, is that they are characterized by cognitive and/or emotion regulation difficulties. Not surprisingly, the techniques that tend to help treat depression, addiction, and PTSD are often ones that show promise for treating the other disorders noted here. It is possible that anterior cingulate cortex alteration may be one mechanism of change that these therapeutic techniques have in common.

ANTERIOR
CINGULATE
CORTEX

CHAPTER 8

The Ventromedial Prefrontal Cortex

THE VENTROMEDIAL PREFRONTAL CORTEX'S LOCATION

The ventromedial prefrontal cortex is situated within the prefrontal cortex, which comprises a large part of the frontal lobe. Specifically, the ventromedial prefrontal cortex is located in the ventral (meaning, "under" or "lower part") and medial (meaning, "center" or "near center") section of the frontal lobe (see Figure 8.1.). It is an extremely well-connected region of the brain, receiving inputs from the amygdala, thalamus, hippocampus, temporal lobe, areas involved in the reward system, and others (Carlson, 2013). It projects to the amygdala, hippocampus, hypothalamus, nucleus accumbens, posterior cingulate cortex, and other regions (Bhanji et al., 2019). Because of its extensive connections, ventromedial prefrontal cortex is able to receive and synthesize information from, and influence, several other areas of the brain (Euston et al., 2012).

THE VENTROMEDIAL PREFRONTAL CORTEX'S FUNCTIONS
In a Nutshell

The ventromedial prefrontal cortex's extensive connectivity allows it to be involved in, and influence, a variety of functions in several domains (Carlson, 2013), including social cognition, self-awareness, self-perception, emotion regulation, memory, envisioning future events, decision-making, and self-regulation more broadly (Chester et al., 2017; Davidson et al., 2000; Gage & Baars, 2018; Mitchell et al., 2005; Roy et al., 2012). Over-

VENTROMEDIAL PREFRONTAL CORTEX

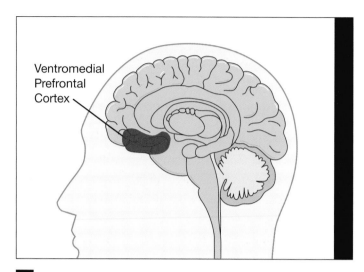

FIGURE 8.1: **VENTROMEDIAL PREFRONTAL CORTEX**

all, the ventromedial prefrontal cortex can be thought of as a hub that integrates several experiences related to the self. It's the site where self-referential thinking takes place, and it is involved in memories and simulations of potential future events related to the self.

EMOTION REGULATION

The ventromedial prefrontal cortex's strong outputs to the amygdala (see Chapter 3 for more information on the amygdala) position it well to facilitate emotion regulation, because it can downregulate amygdala activation. The dual inhibition model of emotion regulation posits that the ventromedial prefrontal cortex, anterior cingulate cortex (this chapter provides more information on the anterior cingulate cortex), and orbitofrontal cortex work together to inhibit amygdala activation during times of stress, resulting in improved emotion regulation (Andrewes & Jenkins, 2019). For example, research has shown that when healthy research subjects are instructed to control their emotional reactions to strongly emotional stimuli, ventromedial prefrontal cortex activation increases while amygdala activation decreases (Johnstone et al., 2007). Relatedly, studies have indicated that fear extinction is likely facilitated through ventromedial prefrontal cortex activation, which leads to a reduction of fear-related amygdala activation (Milad et al., 2007; Phelps et al., 2004).

MEMORY AND SIMULATED EVENTS

The ventromedial prefrontal cortex has repeatedly been found to play a role in memory reconsolidation. Specifically, the process of memory consolidation has been associated with increased ventromedial prefrontal cortex activation, especially in the later phases of consolidation (Nieuwenhuis & Takashima, 2011). For example, Bonnici and Maguire (2018) demonstrated that remote memories, more than two years old, were represented in the ventromedial prefrontal cortex in addition to the hippocampus, whereas recent (two-week-old) memories were mainly represented in the hippocampus. Thus, the ventromedial prefrontal cortex appears to be involved in long-term autobiographical memory storage.

Additionally, the ventromedial prefrontal cortex has been shown to be involved in the construction of simulated future events (Benoit et al., 2014). Autobiographical, episodic memories and imaginal, simulated future events have a neural correlate in common: ventromedial prefrontal cortex activation (Addis et al., 2007). In fact, these two phenomena appear to interact; simulated events (which have never happened) are easier to imagine and are associated with greater ventromedial prefrontal cortex activation if they have elements in common with real past events (D'Argembeau et al., 2010). This is perhaps because the ventromedial prefrontal cortex is one area of the brain where remote (long-term) autobiographical memories are stored. Put another way, our past experiences, which are represented in the ventromedial prefrontal cortex (and the hippocampus as well), help us envision future events, which are also represented in the ventromedial prefrontal cortex. Interestingly, individuals with ventromedial prefrontal cortex damage find it difficult to remember details of autobiographical memories *and* to construct theoretical future events (Campbell et al., 2018).

VENTROMEDIAL PREFRONTAL CORTEX

SELF-PERCEPTION

The ventromedial prefrontal cortex has been shown to play a key role in self-perception, including self-knowledge, self-awareness, self-monitoring, self-esteem, and other types of self-referential cognition (D'Argembeau, 2013; Wagner et al., 2012; Will et al., 2017). It has been shown to be especially sensitive to self-relevant information (Macrae et al., 2004) and to activate when an individual recalls memories involving themselves or when one imagines themselves in the future (Mitchell et al., 2011). For example, the ventromedial prefrontal cortex has been shown to activate when individuals are asked to imagine achieving an important goal in the future (D'Argembeau et al., 2010), and this ventromedial prefrontal cortex activation appears to be positively correlated with an individual's ability to delay gratification and avoid shortsighted decision-making (Ersner-Hershfield et al., 2009; Wagner et al., 2012). Conversely, damage to the ventromedial prefrontal cortex has been associated with deficits in self-monitoring and socially inappropriate behavior (Beer et al., 2006).

THE VENTROMEDIAL PREFRONTAL CORTEX: MENTAL HEALTH CONDITIONS AND TREATMENT IMPLICATIONS

The ventromedial prefrontal cortex plays an integral role in several functions and domains, including memory, emotion regulation, and self-perception. As such, it is likely involved in several mental health conditions. Research has demonstrated ventromedial prefrontal cortex dysfunction in depressive disorders, autism spectrum disorder, OCD, PTSD, schizophrenia, and various anxiety disorders (Hiser & Koenigs, 2018). The following sections detail the ventromedial prefrontal cortex's role in trauma, anxiety, and depression and provide research-based clinical recommendations.

TRAUMA

Trauma and the Ventromedial Prefrontal Cortex: What Happens?

In individuals with PTSD, the ventromedial prefrontal cortex is underactive both at rest (Koch et al., 2016) and during fear extinction efforts, such as when an individual attempts to avoid feeling upset when faced with trauma reminders (Hayes et al., 2012; Rougemont-Bucking et al., 2011). The ventromedial prefrontal cortex's hypoactivation during fear extinction has been associated with increased amygdala activation (Herzog et al., 2019; Miller et al., 2017) and a sensitive startle response (Fitzgerald et al., 2018), possibly indicating the ventromedial prefrontal cortex's inability to downregulate fear responses to promote successful fear extinction (Rauch et al., 2006; VanElzakker et al., 2018). Similarly, research has shown that individuals with PTSD show reduced ventromedial prefrontal cortex activation, in comparison to individuals without a PTSD diagnosis, when thinking about traumatic events (Pitman et al., 2012). This, too, may indicate emotion dysregulation, wherein the ventromedial prefrontal cortex is not recruited to modulate the amygdala activation associated with traumatic memories. Not surprisingly, multiple studies have found ventromedial prefrontal cortex hypoactivation to be negatively correlated with PTSD symptom severity (Dickie et al., 2008; Pitman et al., 2012): the less the ventromedial prefrontal cortex activation, the more severe the PTSD symptoms.

Ventromedial prefrontal cortex connectivity may also be altered in PTSD. Specifically, low ventromedial prefrontal cortex connectivity has been repeatedly demonstrated in neuroscientific research. Reduced ventromedial prefrontal cortex connectivity with other brain regions may suggest the ventromedial prefrontal cortex's influence on those structures to be weak. For example, weak projections from the ventromedial prefrontal cortex to the amygdala may help explain why the ventromedial prefrontal cortex has difficulty downregulating the amygdala (Nicholson et al., 2017), thus preventing successful emotion regulation and fear extinction. Notably, the ventromedial prefrontal cortex is weakly connected to both the amygdala and the hippocampus (Akiki et al., 2017; Koch et al., 2016), suggesting a more generalized top-down processing deficit in PTSD. Conversely, bottom-up connections, such as those originating in the amygdala and projecting upward to the ventromedial prefrontal cortex, tend to be stronger in those with PTSD, suggesting bottom-up processing is dominant (Nicholson et al., 2017).

VENTROMEDIAL
PREFRONTAL
CORTEX

Trauma and the Ventromedial Prefrontal Cortex: How It Presents

Ventromedial prefrontal cortex underactivation and underconnectivity, in the context of trauma, may present as emotion dysregulation. Clients who experience difficulty accessing and activating their ventromedial prefrontal cortex may become easily "hijacked" by amygdala activation, leading to emotional overwhelm, dissociation, or even flashbacks. When confronted with trauma triggers, they may feel out of control and flooded, which can lead to intense efforts to avoid trauma reminders. Also, while some clients may be able to recognize that their fears and triggers are not rational, this awareness will rarely change their emotional experience. Clients may describe this as their "heart and head not agreeing," when in fact it reflects a disconnect between lower limbic areas of the brain (such as the amygdala) and higher cortical areas (such as the ventromedial prefrontal cortex) and reflects an inability to use logic and rationality to modulate fear responses.

Additionally, ventromedial prefrontal cortex dysfunction may temporarily compromise a client's ability to engage in self-reflection, self-monitoring, and self-referential thinking more broadly. This is usually most apparent when the client is experiencing a trauma reminder. Trauma triggers may lead the person to behave uncharacteristically, such as impulsively reacting with fear, terror, or rage in ways they later regret. Clients may recall such behaviors in therapy sessions and may also engage in destructive, therapy-interfering behaviors during the session that they regret when the ventromedial prefrontal cortex later becomes accessible again. Thus, some clients with PTSD experience themselves as both Jekyll and Hyde and experience distress and lowered self-esteem due to these often unexpected shifts in emotion and behavior.

Treatment Implications

Research on exposure-based therapies demonstrates post-treatment activation of the ventromedial prefrontal cortex in PTSD subjects, but there is a dearth of research on the effectiveness of other interventions. Fear extinction is posited to be a primary mechanism of action of most exposure therapies and likely requires ventromedial prefrontal cortex activation, as noted in the previous sections of this chapter. Individuals with PTSD often experience difficulty with fear extinction, and this difficulty can contribute to arousal and re-experiencing symptoms. The ventromedial prefrontal cortex underactivation that underlies both extinction difficulties and these PTSD symptom clusters is not unalterable.

Exposure-based therapies in particular have been shown to increase ventromedial prefrontal cortex activation in those with PTSD, both at rest and in response to distressing or trauma-related stimuli (Fonzo, et al., 2017; Reddy, Greenberg, & Philip, 2017; Roy et al., 2014). Virtual reality exposure therapy (Roy et al., 2014), prolonged exposure (Fonzo et al., 2017), and EMDR (Calancie et al., 2018) have been associated with increased ventromedial prefrontal cortex activation and reduced PTSD symptoms. More broadly, exposure therapies such as EMDR have been associated with more cortical activation and less limbic activation in the brain (Pagani et al., 2012). Moreover, the desirable effects of exposure therapy may be enhanced by incorporating noninvasive brain stimulation (Reddy, O'Brien, et al., 2017).

ANXIETY

Anxiety and the Ventromedial Prefrontal Cortex: What Happens?

While it is likely that anxiety disorders have different neural profiles, it has consistently been found that anxiety, including social anxiety (Evans et al., 2009), panic disorder (Killgore et al., 2014), generalized anxiety (Greenberg et al., 2013), and specific phobias (Killgore et al., 2014), is associated with chronic ventromedial prefrontal cortex underactivation (Myers-Schulz & Koenigs, 2012). Much like with trauma, ventromedial prefrontal cortex hypoactivation in anxious individuals is apparent both at rest and during fear inhibition and extinction attempts. This suggests an inability for anxious individuals to recruit this area to regulate emotion, modulate the amygdala, and feel calmer (Greenberg et al., 2013; Kim et al., 2011).

Additionally, research has shown ventromedial prefrontal cortex underreactivity when anxious individuals are presented with safety cues.

VENTROMEDIAL PREFRONTAL CORTEX

Healthy controls, however, show increased ventromedial prefrontal cortex activation, possibly indicating that they are able to use self-referential cognition to make themselves feel safer and more at ease (Via et al., 2018). In theory, the presence of safety cues helps individuals self-soothe and feel less fear and anxiety, presumably through amygdala downregulation. However, this appears to be difficult for anxious individuals, as they may be unable to sufficiently activate the ventromedial prefrontal cortex to suppress amygdala activation. Not surprisingly, ventromedial prefrontal cortex activation is also negatively correlated with worry severity in GAD. The more intense the worrying in those with generalized anxiety disorder, the less the activation in ventromedial prefrontal cortex observed (Via et al., 2018). This, too, suggests the ventromedial prefrontal cortex is unable to regulate distressing emotions and thoughts commonly experienced in anxiety disorders.

Moreover, ventromedial prefrontal cortex *hyperactivation* has consistently been found in anxious individuals, but only when anticipating threat (Hu, 2018; Morriss et al., 2015). Specifically, this occurs when anxious individuals think of something terrible happening to them. As discussed earlier in this chapter, the ventromedial prefrontal cortex activates in response to thoughts about future events or simulations. Thus, thoughts about terrible things that might happen to a person would likely activate the ventromedial prefrontal cortex. In anxiety, heightened ventromedial prefrontal cortex activation in response to threat suggests anxious individuals' mental simulations about awful things happening may be particularly salient, vivid, and distressing. This, too, may explain why individuals with anxiety have trouble tolerating uncertainty about possible negative outcomes; the possibility of the bad thing happening, no matter how remote, may feel unbearable (Morriss et al., 2015). In nonanxious individuals, however, threat anticipation elicits less ventromedial prefrontal cortex activation (Myers-Schulz & Koenigs, 2012). This may allow tolerance for possible negative outcomes or events because they are more difficult to envision and emotionally simulate.

Anxiety and the Ventromedial Prefrontal Cortex: How It Presents

Much like with trauma, ventromedial prefrontal cortex underactivation in anxiety often presents as emotion dysregulation. Anxious clients may say that they realize their worries are excessive or, in the case of OCD, individuals may note that they understand their compulsions do not make logical sense, but their emotions and thoughts feel out of control. Anxious individuals experience difficulty activating the ventromedial prefrontal cortex to downregulate the amygdala, whose hyperactivation is likely contributing to the formation of catastrophic thoughts and worries by creating a diffuse stress response throughout the brain and body that sets the stage for distressing thoughts and emotions to develop. Thus, both under and overactivation of the ventromedial prefrontal cortex are associated with anxiety, just in different ways, and perhaps at different times. While overactivation has been linked to vivid and emotionally intense imagining of terrible future events, underactivation is associated with emotion dysregulation and a failure to downregulate the amygdala.

Additionally, anxious clients may describe potential future events vividly, which might make them overestimate the likelihood of them occurring. This is referred to as "emotional reasoning" and is a cognitive distortion often discussed in cognitive behavioral therapies. Anxious individuals often describe simulations of potential terrible events in more sensory detail than one might expect and appear very distressed as they discuss them. In fact, these simulations may produce almost as much distress as in vivo exposure to feared situations. For these clients, assurance that the negative potential events are statistically rare is unlikely to calm them; when a simulation feels intense and real, clients tend to engage in emotional reasoning and conclude it *will* become real.

Treatment Implications

Different anxiety treatments may address both the ventromedial prefrontal cortex underactivation associated with fear extinction deficits and the hyperactivation associated with vivid, distressing simulations of negative future events. For example, exposure therapy may facilitate fear extinction in individuals with anxiety (Ball et al., 2017), and individuals who

VENTROMEDIAL PREFRONTAL CORTEX

have a snake phobia and completed exposure therapy showed decreased anxiety symptoms and increased ventromedial prefrontal cortex activation, and these effects were enhanced when participants were simultaneously given D-cycloserine, an antibiotic (Nave et al., 2012). D-cycloserine has been shown to augment exposure therapy, according to recent research (Hofmann et al., 2019; Klass et al., 2017). Additionally, exposure therapy may activate the ventromedial prefrontal cortex in individuals with acrophobia, and these effects may be enhanced by also applying high-frequency transcranial magnetic stimulation over the ventromedial prefrontal cortex (Herrmann et al., 2017).

Meditations and meditation-based interventions that instruct the participant to attend to their internal experiences—whether emotional, physical, etc.—have been shown to increase ventromedial prefrontal cortex activation and connectivity and to decrease amygdala activation (Kral et al., 2018). In particular, increased ventromedial prefrontal cortex activation and reduced amygdala activation have been found in mindfulness-based stress reduction (Kral et al., 2018) and mindfulness meditation (Zeidan et al., 2014), both of which train participants to become aware of, and to focus on, their internal experiences. Thus, mindful attention to oneself may improve self-regulation and emotion regulation capabilities via these brain changes. Similarly, a finding by Creswell et al. (2007) demonstrated an association between affect-labeling, wherein participants identified and labeled their emotions, ventromedial prefrontal cortex activation, and amygdala de-activation, providing further support for the benefit of attending to one's experience as a way to improve emotion regulation.

However, fear extinction and ventromedial prefrontal cortex activation may not be the only goal in anxiety treatment. As discussed in the previous sections, ventromedial prefrontal cortex hyperactivation often occurs when anxious individuals envision, or simulate, distressing potential future events in their mind. This exacerbates anxiety because it makes feared situations, people, events, etc. feel real and more likely to happen than they might actually be. When intense worry and/or vivid distressing future scenarios are present, the goal may be to *decrease* ventromedial prefrontal cortex activation in those moments, not to increase it. One cognitive strategy that has been shown to decrease ventromedial prefrontal cortex activation during distressing self-referential thoughts is called "decentering" (Lebois et al., 2015). Decentering is a concept taught in Mindfulness-Based Cognitive Therapy that closely resembles a concept in Acceptance and Commitment Therapy referred to as "cognitive defusion." Both concepts emphasize the externalization of distressing thoughts and feelings, wherein the client creates space, or distance, between themselves and the thought or feeling. Decentering may also be thought of as a way an individual can disengage a bit from their distressing experience while still observing and acknowledging it. This is in contrast to what anxious clients usually do when they simulate future events, which is to immerse themselves in the experience without recognizing it. Decentering has been shown to reduce ventromedial prefrontal cortex activation, and it is associated with lowered anxiety (Lebois et al., 2015).

DEPRESSION
Depression and the Ventromedial Prefrontal Cortex:
What Happens?

There are two consistent findings in the research about ventromedial prefrontal cortex functioning in depression. First, a well-established finding is that the ventromedial prefrontal cortex tends to be hyperactive in depressed individuals (An et al., 2017; Grimm et al., 2009; Kühn & Gallinat, 2013), both at rest (Greicius et al., 2007) and during self-critical thinking (Di Simplicio et al., 2012). Ventromedial prefrontal cortex hyperactivation in depression is believed to reflect the experience of negative affect (Zald et al., 2002), rumination, and negative self-referential thoughts and feelings more broadly (An et al., 2017). When ventromedial prefrontal cortex hyperactivation, indicating negative affect and negative self-referential cognition, is considered in tandem with the low dorsolateral prefrontal cortex activation found in depression (which suggests possible deficits in cognitive regulation; see Chapter 9), it is perhaps not surprising that depressed individuals find it difficult to control negative thoughts and feelings about themselves (Drevets, 1998; Koenigs & Grafman, 2009). Not

VENTROMEDIAL PREFRONTAL CORTEX

surprisingly, improvements in depression symptoms have been associated with a decrease in ventromedial prefrontal cortex activation (Brody et al., 2001; Scopinho et al., 2010).

Second, the ventromedial prefrontal cortex's resting and functional connectivity with several other brain regions is often weak (Guo et al., 2016) in depressed individuals. For example, the ventromedial prefrontal cortex has been shown to be weakly connected to the striatum (Felger et al., 2016; Furman et al., 2011), which plays a large role in movement. While this weak connectivity may not seem important, it is associated with increased stress and inflammation in the body (Felger et al., 2016). Moreover, research has shown the ventromedial prefrontal cortex to be weakly connected to the cerebellum (Cao et al., 2012), another area of the brain involved in movement, and to the amygdala (Connolly et al., 2017; Jalbrzikowski et al., 2017). A weak connection between the ventromedial prefrontal cortex and the amygdala is also related to inflammation in the body; ventromedial prefrontal cortex/amygdala functional connectivity is negatively correlated with inflammation (Mehta et al., 2018). The biomarkers of inflammation that are commonly observed in depression, such as cytokines (Farooq et al., 2017), may be associated with emotion dysregulation; the ventromedial prefrontal cortex may be unable to downregulate the amygdala due to weakened connectivity between the two regions. Cytokines may also contribute to the lethargy and fatigue some individuals with depression experience. Additionally, the ventromedial prefrontal cortex's weak connection to areas of the brain involved in movement may explain why some individuals with depression experience psychomotor changes.

However, the ventromedial prefrontal cortex has also been shown to be hyperconnected to the default mode network (DMN; Kaiser et al., 2015). The DMN is a large neural network that, when activated, can produce mind wandering and daydreaming (Kucyi & Davis, 2014; Poerio et al., 2017). Thus, it is sometimes referred to as the "mind wandering network." DMN's strong connection to the ventromedial prefrontal cortex suggests that the ventromedial prefrontal cortex may activate when the DMN activates, so the two essentially activate together. When this happens, depressed individuals' minds wander (due to DMN activation), and as their minds wander, the mind then produces ruminations and negative thoughts about themselves (due to ventromedial prefrontal cortex activation). This coactivation may make it especially difficult for depressed individuals to control their negative self-referential thoughts, as these thoughts are occurring while the mind is wandering, which may make the thoughts difficult to recognize.

Depression and the Ventromedial Prefrontal Cortex: How It Presents

Ventromedial prefrontal cortex hyperactivation in depression may be apparent in clients' reports of feeling depressed, sad, or otherwise down. These individuals may have difficulty accessing positive emotions and may not be able to see the "bright side" of a situation. During cognitive behavioral work with these clients, it may also become apparent that they experience frequent or ongoing ruminations, wherein their mind produces negative thoughts about themselves that they cannot easily control. Sometimes these negative thoughts are obvious to the client, but at other times they seem to play in the back of the client's mind, outside of awareness until the therapist begins to notice themes in the client's therapy. This lack of awareness may be attributable to the hyperconnectivity between the DMN and ventromedial prefrontal cortex described above, as ruminative thoughts often occur during mind wandering. While it is sometimes the case that the client will question the validity, or truthfulness, of their ruminative thoughts, they often tend to believe the thoughts, which can lead to more intense negative affect.

Ventromedial prefrontal cortex hypoconnectivity in depression may be more difficult to infer but may contribute to some depressed individuals' experience of psychomotor retardation, lethargy, and/or fatigue. Thus, some depressed clients may present in session as low-energy, and in severe forms of depression, clients may find it difficult to get out of bed or consistently engage in activities of daily living. At times, clients' lethargy may make them appear disengaged during therapy sessions, which can feel draining for the therapist, who may attempt to engage and energize the

VENTROMEDIAL PREFRONTAL CORTEX

client. Moreover, depressed clients may complain of somatic symptoms, such as a general feeling of malaise or a nondescript "sickness," and these experiences may be associated with the presence of inflammation.

Treatment Implications

The gold standard treatment approach for depression is a combination of psychotherapy and medication, both of which have been shown to alter ventromedial prefrontal cortex functioning in the direction of health. For instance, SSRIs such as venlafaxine and citalopram have been found to reduce ventromedial prefrontal cortex activation (Kennedy et al., 2007; Di Simplicio et al., 2012), and this deactivation was associated with diminished attention to self-referent thoughts and negative emotions (Di Simplicio et al., 2012). Moreover, research has indicated that some SSRIs, such as escitalopram (An et al., 2017) and sertraline (Anand et al., 2007), may increase functional connectivity between the ventromedial prefrontal cortex (including subregions of the ventromedial prefrontal cortex, such as the subgenual anterior cingulate cortex [sgACC]) and the amygdala. These effects were apparent after only eight weeks of taking escitalopram or sertraline. Thus, one way in which SSRIs may help reduce depression symptoms is by acting on the ventromedial prefrontal cortex.

Psychotherapies may also alter ventromedial prefrontal cortex functioning in individuals experiencing depression symptoms. For example, one study found reduced ventromedial prefrontal cortex activation after 14 sessions of CBT (Rubin-Falcone et al., 2018), whereas another showed lowered ventromedial prefrontal cortex activation after 12 sessions of CBT (Kennedy et al., 2007). A third study was able to show similar improvements in the sgACC, a subregion of the ventromedial prefrontal cortex, after only five sessions of CBT (Straub et al., 2015). A review article by Franklin et al. (2016), summarizing 10 studies on the neuroscience of CBT in depression, concluded that CBT is consistently associated with reduced activation in the anterior cingulate cortex and ventromedial prefrontal cortex.

As described in the anxiety Treatment Implications section earlier in this chapter, decentering (a cognitive approach) may also decrease ventromedial prefrontal cortex activation (Lebois et al., 2015). In the context of depression, the reduced ventromedial prefrontal cortex activation associated with decentering training may help depressed individuals focus away from, or externalize, negative self-referential thoughts, rumination, and distressing emotions so that they are felt less intensely. More research needs to be conducted on the neuroscience of decentering and cognitive defusion, a similar cognitive concept, to fully understand the neural correlates of these strategies. However, it is possible that Mindfulness-Based Cognitive Therapy, an effective, evidence-based therapy for major depressive disorder that incorporates decentering, owes some of its success to ventromedial prefrontal cortex regulation via decentering training. Further research may clarify this.

Finally, other therapeutic approaches such as electroconvulsive therapy (ECT) and transcranial magnetic stimulation (TMS) may also alter ventromedial prefrontal cortex functioning. One study indicated ECT may reduce ventromedial prefrontal cortex activation (Nobler et al., 2001). TMS may also be a promising approach for depressed individuals, as it has been linked to reduced ventromedial prefrontal cortex activation (Kito et al., 2012), and it has also been associated with decreased resting-state connectivity between the sgACC and the DMN (Long et al., 2020).

OTHER MENTAL HEALTH CONDITIONS

Abnormal ventromedial prefrontal cortex functioning has also been found in other psychiatric conditions. In most of these conditions, the ventromedial prefrontal cortex is underactive. For example, underactivation of ventromedial prefrontal cortex in autism is well-established (Kohls et al., 2013; Lombardo et al., 2010) and may indicate difficulties with self-referential thinking. Similarly, ventromedial prefrontal cortex underactivation presents in individuals with schizophrenia (Holt et al., 2012; Kuhn & Gallinat, 2013), and this, too, suggests possible impairments in self-reflection and self-referential thinking more broadly. Those high in psychopathy (usually diagnosed as antisocial personality disorder) also demonstrate lowered ventromedial prefrontal cortex activation compared to healthy controls (Decety et al., 2014; Harenski et al., 2010), especially when processing moral violations (Harenski et al., 2010). This may signal deficits in self-evaluation. An exception to the ventromedial prefrontal cortex underactivation observed in several disorders occurs in OCD, which is associated with hyperactivation of the ventromedial prefrontal cortex (Milad at al., 2013). The hyperactivity of the ventromedial prefrontal cortex in OCD may precipitate the obsessions and ruminations commonly experienced in OCD.

VENTROMEDIAL PREFRONTAL CORTEX

CHAPTER 9

The Dorsolateral Prefrontal Cortex

THE DORSOLATERAL PREFRONTAL CORTEX'S LOCATION

The dorsolateral prefrontal cortex is a cortical region of the brain located on the dorsal (meaning "back" or "top") and lateral (meaning far from the center) part of the frontal lobe (see Figure 9.1.) in both the left and right hemispheres (Rajkowska & Goldman-Rakic, 1995). Thus, sometimes a distinction is made between functions of the left dorsolateral prefrontal cortex and the right dorsolateral prefrontal cortex. The dorsolateral prefrontal cortex is adjacent to the ventromedial prefrontal cortex (see Chapter 8 for more information) and very close to and a little bit above the anterior cingulate cortex (See Chapter 7 for more information).

THE DORSOLATERAL PREFRONTAL CORTEX'S FUNCTIONS
In a Nutshell

The dorsolateral prefrontal cortex is involved in a variety of executive functions and higher order processes, such as reasoning, decision-making, emotion regulation, reality testing, and working memory (Carter, 1999; Krawczyk, 2002; Curtis and D'Esposito, 2003). In addition, this brain region plays a role in selective attention, drive, and motivation (Ballard et al., 2011; Miller, 1999). Thus, individuals who have suffered damage to the dorsolateral prefrontal cortex often experience attentional difficulties, decreased motivation, impairments in planning and inhibition, and other executive functioning deficits (Clark & Manes, 2004; Robinson et al.,

DORSOLATERAL PREFRONTAL CORTEX

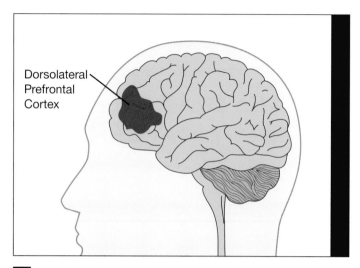

Dorsolateral
Prefrontal
Cortex

FIGURE 9.1: DORSOLATERAL PREFRONTAL CORTEX

2014). The following sections detail the dorsolateral prefrontal cortex's specific roles in cognitive control, decision-making, and social cognition and behavior.

COGNITIVE CONTROL

Several studies have associated dorsolateral prefrontal cortex activation, especially left dorsolateral prefrontal cortex activation (Li, Wang, et al., 2017), with improved cognitive control (Brosnan & Wiegand, 2017; Egner & Hirsch, 2005; MacDonald et al., 2000), which is a person's ability to align their thoughts, emotions, and behavior with their goals (Cieslik et al., 2013; Stuss & Knight, 2013). Similar to the anterior cingulate cortex (especially the dACC), the dorsolateral prefrontal cortex is believed to be involved in self-regulation (Hare et al., 2009), which requires cognitive control (Metcalf & Mischel, 1999). For example, the dorsolateral prefrontal cortex has been shown to activate, along with the dACC, when an individual attempts to monitor and resolve internal conflicts through self-regulation efforts (Smith et al., 2019).

DORSOLATERAL PREFRONTAL CORTEX

Additionally, the dorsolateral prefrontal cortex appears to play a role in delaying gratification, which also requires cognitive control, usually over emotions (Drobetz et al., 2014; Nejati et al., 2018). Individuals with dorsolateral prefrontal cortex atrophy tend to have difficulty delaying gratification and may be more impulsive (Drobetz et al., 2014), indicating the dorsolateral prefrontal cortex may play a role in these functions. Delay of gratification and, more broadly, cognitive control are important skills to develop because they are associated with high academic performance (Wang et al., 2017), low BMI (Schlam et al., 2013), high net worth (Benjamin et al., 2020), and strong social skills (Duckworth et al., 2013).

DECISION-MAKING

Along with the anterior cingulate cortex and orbitofrontal cortex, the dorsolateral prefrontal cortex is believed to strongly influence decision making through working memory and reasoning (Rosenbloom et al., 2012) and the integration of multiple information sources (Krawczyk, 2002). The dorsolateral prefrontal cortex has been found to play a role in multiple types of decision making. For instance, the dorsolateral prefrontal cortex activates during decision making related to moral dilemmas, such as when individuals are asked to decide how to allocate a limited number of resources to others (Greene et al., 2001). The dorsolateral prefrontal cortex also activates when individuals try to make fair, equitable decisions that minimize personal gain (Knoch & Fehr, 2007).

Moreover, research has shown that the dorsolateral prefrontal cortex activates when working through emotionless dilemmas (Greene, 2007; Prehn et al., 2008). For example, the dorsolateral prefrontal cortex is involved in legal decision-making. One study found dorsolateral prefrontal cortex activation when individuals ascribed responsibility to fictional characters for an adverse outcome (Buckholtz et al., 2008). Interestingly, when those individuals were asked to decide these characters' level of punishment, no dorsolateral prefrontal cortex activation was found, but activation was apparent in the amygdala, the posterior cingulate cortex, and the medial prefrontal cortex (Buckholtz et al., 2008). Thus, the

DORSOLATERAL PREFRONTAL CORTEX

dorsolateral prefrontal cortex likely plays roles in both emotional and emotionless decision-making.

SOCIAL COGNITION AND BEHAVIOR

Dorsolateral prefrontal cortex activation, especially in the right dorsolateral prefrontal cortex, has been associated with prosocial behaviors (Fehr & Kraibich, 2014), such as reciprocation, behaving unselfishly (van den Bos et al., 2011), or paying back money an individual believes they owe to avoid feeling guilty (Chang et al., 2011). Research has shown that suppression of the right dorsolateral prefrontal cortex, conversely, leads to more selfish behavior, such as accepting blatantly unfair offers or advantages (Knoch et al., 2006; Knoch et al., 2008). Activation in this area has also been associated with navigating complex social situations (Miller & Cummings, 2017) and complying with social norms (Buckholtz et al., 2008). In addition, the dorsolateral prefrontal cortex plays a role in social cognition (Miller & Cummings, 2017). For instance, the dorsolateral prefrontal cortex is involved in perspective taking (van Lange et al., 2014), which is the ability to infer another person's thoughts or feelings, and helps individuals understand other people's intentions (Hunt & Behrens, 2011).

THE DORSOLATERAL PREFRONTAL CORTEX: MENTAL HEALTH CONDITIONS AND TREATMENT IMPLICATIONS

Given the dorsolateral prefrontal cortex's role in decision making, social cognition and behavior, cognitive control, and several other executive functions, it is not surprising that deficits in this region have been associated with a variety of symptoms of mental illness, distress, and functional impairment. In fact, many psychiatric disorders are characterized by persistent difficulties in one or more of these areas. The following sections describe the dorsolateral prefrontal cortex's specific role in trauma sequelae, depression, and addiction, and clinical implications are discussed.

DORSOLATERAL PREFRONTAL CORTEX

~~~~~~

TRAUMA

Trauma and the Dorsolateral Prefrontal Cortex: What Happens?

Depending on the task at hand, dorsolateral prefrontal cortex activation in individuals experiencing PTSD can be low or high, and both underactivation and overactivation of this region can contribute to PTSD symptoms. In general, activation of the dorsolateral prefrontal cortex is associated with the ability to inhibit unwanted thoughts, feelings, or behaviors (Shackman et al., 2009; Vrtička et al., 2012). Dorsolateral prefrontal cortex activation has also been linked to the experience of vigilance and feelings of uncertainty (Shackman et al., 2009). Thus, when an individual encounters a situation that elicits feelings of uncertainty, the dorsolateral prefrontal cortex tends to activate, presumably in an attempt to control one's anxiety about this uncertainty (Shackman et al., 2009). In individuals with PTSD, dorsolateral prefrontal cortex hyperactivation may indicate attempts at self-regulation, as described in previous sections. However, compared to healthy controls, the dorsolateral prefrontal cortex in those with PTSD tends to be hypoactive under some circumstances and hyperactive in others.

Increased activation in the dorsolateral prefrontal cortex in those with PTSD (compared to healthy controls) has been observed when these individuals are confronted with distressing information. For example, in one study, women with PTSD who had experienced interpersonal violence (IPV) showed increased dorsolateral prefrontal cortex activation compared to healthy controls when shown videos that depicted negative (but not violent) interactions between men and women (Moser et al., 2015). This activation may reflect the women's efforts to avoid becoming dysregulated or "triggered" by these videos, and it suggests an attempt at top-down attenuation of the amygdala that may not be needed for healthy controls with no history of IPV (Moser et al., 2015). Similarly, when told to anticipate the presentation of negative emotional information in a research setting, women with PTSD showed increased dorsolateral prefrontal cortex activation in comparison to a control group (Aupperle et al., 2012). This is consistent with other findings that indicate dorsolateral prefrontal cor-

DORSOLATERAL
PREFRONTAL
CORTEX

tex activation in response to distressing (but not trauma-related) stimuli in those with PTSD (see Selemon et al., 2019 for a review).

Decreased activation of the dorsolateral prefrontal cortex has also been observed in individuals with PTSD, particularly when engaged in working memory or other cognitive tasks and/or when experiencing stress. For instance, reduced BOLD response has been found in the dorsolateral prefrontal cortex in PTSD subjects when they attempt to recall and focus on memories (Tian et al., 2014). Also, underactivation of the dorsolateral prefrontal cortex in PTSD has been found when individuals engage in working memory tasks (Bruce et al., 2012; Geuze et al., 2008; Hou et al., 2007; Rabinak et al., 2014). This underactivation has been found in multiple areas of the brain that comprise the executive network (including but not limited to the dorsolateral prefrontal cortex) and suggests broad frontal lobe dysfunction in PTSD that may be apparent during working memory (Moores et al., 2008) and other cognitive tasks (Koenen et al., 2001).

Working memory impairment and dorsolateral prefrontal cortex underactivation is also apparent during acute and chronic stress, even in those without PTSD. For example, healthy individuals experiencing acute stress after watching a violent movie showed dorsolateral prefrontal cortex underactivation and poor performance on a working memory task (Gärtner et al., 2014). Even highly trained soldiers have shown similar tendencies; Special Forces soldiers exhibited working memory impairments when under severe, acute stress, and these impairments were more evident in those with a history of traumatic stress (Morgan et al., 2006). Thus, it is possible that acute stress is associated with low dorsolateral prefrontal cortex activation in general and may be more pronounced in those with a trauma history. This is especially evident when the acute stressor is perceived as uncontrollable (Amat et al., 2006).

Moreover, several studies have found more general dorsolateral prefrontal cortex hypoactivation in PTSD (Milad & Quirk, 2012; Philip et al., 2018; VanElzakker et al., 2014), which may explain why those with PTSD report difficulty suppressing fear responses and downregulating amygdala activation when confronted with trauma reminders (Chen et al., 2018; Kan et al., 2020). This in turn may compromise one's ability to engage in real-

DORSOLATERAL
PREFRONTAL
CORTEX

ity testing, a function that requires dorsolateral prefrontal cortex involvement (Simons et al., 2008), leading to an inability to distinguish between memories and real-time events (Arnsten et al., 2015). This is perhaps why flashbacks are so aversive: with lowered dorsolateral prefrontal cortex activation, memories are experienced as occurring in the present, not the past.

Finally, reduced dorsolateral prefrontal cortex volume (Herringa et al., 2012; Kühn & Gallinat, 2013) and connectivity have been reported in PTSD. For instance, individuals with a history of trauma tend to show reduced dorsolateral prefrontal cortex gray matter, and the link between dorsolateral prefrontal cortex gray matter loss and trauma is accentuated when an individual has suffered multiple traumas (Ansell et al., 2012). Also, those with PTSD show reduced dorsolateral prefrontal cortex connectivity with other key brain regions (Holmes et al., 2018; Olson et al., 2018), including the orbitofrontal cortex and dACC (Selemon et al., 2019) and the amygdala (Liston et al., 2006). The weak connection between the dorsolateral prefrontal cortex and the amygdala may further explain why it is difficult for those with PTSD to downregulate amygdala activation (Kim et al., 2013; Quirk & Mueller, 2008).

Trauma and the Dorsolateral Prefrontal Cortex: How It Presents

Dorsolateral prefrontal cortex alterations may contribute to the arousal and reactivity symptoms, and the re-experiencing symptoms, of PTSD. While arousal and reactivity symptoms tend to be associated with subcortical activation, such as amygdala activation, they may also be related to the dorsolateral prefrontal cortex's inability to downregulate amygdala activation when trauma reminders are present (Kim et al., 2013). Thus, dorsolateral prefrontal cortex underactivation and underconnectivity have been linked to arousal symptoms, such as lack of concentration (Robinson et al., 2014), as well as reactivity symptoms, such as hypervigilance (Shackman et al., 2009) and anger outbursts (Bertsch et al., 2019). Given the dorsolateral prefrontal cortex's role in attention, problem solving, self-regulation, and cognitive control, these findings are perhaps to be expected.

Dorsolateral prefrontal cortex functioning may also be associated with some of the re-experiencing symptoms of PTSD (Olson et al., 2018). Stud-

DORSOLATERAL PREFRONTAL CORTEX

ies have suggested that low dorsolateral prefrontal cortex activation and/ or connectivity may play a role in flashbacks (Arnsten et al., 2015), intrusive thoughts that are difficult to control (Lindauer et al., 2008; Vrtička et al., 2012), and emotion dysregulation (Buhle et al., 2014; Golkar et al., 2012). As described in the previous section, dorsolateral prefrontal cortex underactivation may compromise reality testing, leading to distressing flashbacks when trauma triggers are presented. Also, because dorsolateral prefrontal cortex activation is required for cognitive control, low activation in this region may make it difficult for individuals with PTSD to suppress trauma-related thoughts and accompanying emotions.

Treatment Implications

Healthy dorsolateral prefrontal cortex alterations may be facilitated through psychotherapy, medication, and transcranial magnetic stimulation. Commonly utilized evidence-based therapies such as CBT, cognitive processing therapy (CPT), EMDR, prolonged exposure (PE), and other cognitive or exposure-based therapies may activate the dorsolateral prefrontal cortex and improve connectivity with other brain structures as well as increase dorsolateral prefrontal cortex volume.

One study found a positive association between PE and improved dorsolateral prefrontal cortex connectivity, which was also linked to improved attenuation of negative emotions during stressful situations (Stojek et al., 2018). In other words, as dorsolateral prefrontal cortex connectivity strengthened, so did the individuals' ability to downregulate negative emotions. A similar finding was reported by King et al. (2016), who found that mindfulness-based exposure-based therapy was linked to improved dorsolateral prefrontal cortex connectivity and reduced PTSD symptoms, including hyperarousal and avoidance symptoms. Moreover, Helpman et al. (2016) noted that after desensitizing to traumatic material (as a part of PE), individuals with PTSD showed increased connectivity between the dorsolateral prefrontal cortex, ventromedial prefrontal cortex, amygdala, and hippocampus, which are all areas of the brain involved in memory reconsolidation and fear conditioning. Improved dorsolateral prefrontal cortex connectivity has also been shown after the completion of CPT and

CBT (Shou et al., 2017). It has been posited that increased dorsolateral prefrontal cortex connectivity and activation after psychotherapy, including exposure therapy (Roy et al., 2010), may indicate improved control over distressing, unwanted thoughts, emotions, and memories (Lindauer et al., 2008).

Psychotherapy has also been associated with increased dorsolateral prefrontal cortex activation and volume. Exposure-based therapies such as EMDR may increase dorsolateral prefrontal cortex volume. For example, Boukezzi et al. (2017) found that as PTSD symptoms decreased (as individuals completed EMDR), gray matter density increased in areas of the prefrontal cortex, such as the dorsolateral prefrontal cortex. Additionally, CBT has been linked to increased activation in the dorsolateral prefrontal cortex and other cortical regions in individuals with PTSD during an emotional conflict task (Yang, Oathes, et al., 2018). This suggests these individuals demonstrated greater cognitive control and emotion regulation after completing CBT. It has been proposed that psychotherapies can help individuals learn how to extinguish fear responses, reduce arousal and reactivity symptoms, and reduce intrusive thoughts and memories through top-down modulation of the amygdala, brainstem, hippocampus, and other regions via the prefrontal cortex (including the dorsolateral prefrontal cortex; Arnsten et al., 2015).

Psychiatric medications may also alter dorsolateral prefrontal cortex functioning and may be helpful when psychotherapy alone is insufficient (Arnsten et al., 2015). The SSRI paroxetine, for instance, has been found to increase dorsolateral prefrontal cortex activation, which is associated with improved cognitive reappraisal (MacNamara et al., 2016). Also, prazosin, an antihypertensive medication, is now commonly prescribed to individuals experiencing PTSD symptoms. Prazosin has been shown to reduce nightmares and other arousal and reactivity symptoms of PTSD (Germain et al., 2012; Taylor et al., 2008) and is associated with dorsolateral prefrontal cortex activation (and prefrontal activation more broadly; Taylor et al., 2006), presumably via the blocking of α-1 receptors in this region. When α-1 receptors are blocked, which occurs with prazosin, healthy prefrontal cortex activation is restored (Arnsten et al., 2015).

DORSOLATERAL
PREFRONTAL
CORTEX

Finally, transcranial magnetic stimulation (TMS) may also improve dorsolateral prefrontal cortex functioning in those experiencing PTSD. TMS uses an electromagnetic field to stimulate different brain regions (George & Post, 2011) and is increasingly being used to treat PTSD (Yan et al., 2017). TMS has been found to increase dorsolateral prefrontal cortex activation and is linked to improved dorsolateral prefrontal cortex connectivity in individuals with PTSD (Karsen et al., 2014; Nakama et al., 2014). Moreover, a meta-analysis concluded TMS to be helpful for reducing PTSD symptoms (Yan et al., 2017) and identified the dorsolateral prefrontal cortex as a primary brain region to target (Cirillo et al., 2019). Thus, TMS shows promise as an alternative treatment for PTSD (Kan et al., 2020).

ADDICTION

Addiction and the Dorsolateral Prefrontal Cortex: What Happens?

Similar to dorsolateral prefrontal cortex activity in PTSD, the dorsolateral prefrontal cortex in addicted individuals can be hyperactive or hypoactive, depending on the circumstance and task at hand. Research has shown the dorsolateral prefrontal cortex in addiction to be hyperactive during negative emotion processing compared to healthy controls (Asensio et al., 2010; Goldstein & Volkow, 2011). Additionally, dorsolateral prefrontal cortex activation has been found in response to drug- or smoking-related cues in those addicted to drugs or cigarettes (Yalachkov et al., 2009; Heinz et al., 2007; Grüsser et al., 2004). For example, dorsolateral prefrontal cortex activation occurred in smokers who watched a smoking-related video (Brody et al., 2002). Similar results were found for those addicted to video games: dorsolateral prefrontal cortex activation was observed in addicted individuals compared to healthy controls when confronted with video game-related stimuli (Ko et al., 2009). It has thus been proposed that the dorsolateral prefrontal cortex may be involved in attempts to control cravings when faced with addiction-related temptation, attention bias toward addiction-related stimuli, the formation of addiction-related memories, and motivation to obtain drugs or alcohol (Goldstein et al., 2011).

DORSOLATERAL PREFRONTAL CORTEX

However, underactivation and reduced volume of the dorsolateral prefrontal cortex has also been associated with addiction (Cooper et al., 2017). For instance, the dorsolateral prefrontal cortex is often hypoactive in addiction during some cognitive tasks requiring inhibitory control, such as the Stroop Task (Azizian et al., 2010; Hester et al., 2009; Salo et al., 2009). Moreover, dorsolateral prefrontal cortex gray matter volume is often lower in those suffering from substance use disorders, such as abuse of alcohol (Chanraud et al., 2007), heroin (Yuan et al., 2009), methamphetamines (Schwartz et al., 2010), nicotine (Kühn et al. 2010), and cocaine (Sim et al., 2007). Generally speaking, the longer and more severe the substance use, the more pronounced the reduction in dorsolateral prefrontal cortex volume (Goldstein & Volkow, 2011). Low dorsolateral prefrontal cortex volume may contribute to addicted individuals' denial of their being sick, their cognitive impairment, and their impulsivity (Golstein & Volkow, 2011).

Addiction and the Dorsolateral Prefrontal Cortex: How It Presents

The dorsolateral prefrontal cortex often strongly activates when an addicted individual is confronted with addiction-related cues, such as a video depicting smoking or using drugs. This suggests the person may be trying very hard to resist craving-related feelings and impulses. Thus, those suffering from addiction may report that resisting cravings is difficult and exhausting, and at times they may feel helpless to overcome the cravings. When working with these individuals, therapists often note that their clients feel as though they are trying very hard to combat their addiction and that they find the effort to be tiring.

Moreover, underactivation of the dorsolateral prefrontal cortex during some cognitive tasks indicates addicted individuals may experience difficulty regulating thoughts and moods and might find it hard to concentrate on some tasks. Dorsolateral prefrontal cortex atrophy may exacerbate these cognitive difficulties and contribute to these individuals' denial about their addiction and to their unwillingness to seek professional help. While overactivation of the dorsolateral prefrontal cortex can help the individual fight a craving, the frequent underactivation of this area when engaging in cognitive tasks, combined with dorsolateral prefrontal cortex atrophy, may contribute to impulsive urges that feel overpowering in the moment. Thus, therapists may notice that individuals recovering from addiction seem distracted and exhibit difficulty focusing on one topic for a long period of time. Recovering individuals may also report feeling well-regulated and in control of their impulses in one moment but completely out of control in the next (especially if under stress), which is when they are likely to relapse.

Treatment Implications

The research on addiction treatment and dorsolateral prefrontal cortex functioning is sparse; however, some recommendations can be gleaned from the literature. First, though not specific to addiction treatment, multiple types of treatments and techniques have been associated with improved dorsolateral prefrontal cortex activation and connectivity, including mindfulness-based stress reduction (Farb et al., 2007), Zen meditation (Kozasa et al., 2008), other mindfulness techniques (Chiesa, 2010; Hölzel et al., 2007), and CBT (Shou et al., 2017; Yang, Oathes, et al., 2018; see previous section for more details). SSRIs, such as fluoxetine (Mayberg et al., 2000) and paroxetine (Kennedy et al., 2001), have also been shown to increase dorsolateral prefrontal cortex activation. Moreover, CBT has been associated with increased dorsolateral prefrontal cortex volume (Seminowicz et al., 2013). It has been proposed that psychotherapeutic techniques, including mindfulness practices or cognitive exercises, may strengthen and repair the same areas of the brain that are involved in distressing emotions, cravings, and relapse, including the dorsolateral prefrontal cortex (Garland et al., 2014; Witkiewitz et al., 2013). Additionally, abstinence alone may repair the dorsolateral prefrontal cortex, and abstinence has been associated with increased volume in this area even when no other interventions are used (Chanraud et al., 2010; Wobrock et al., 2009). This is likely one reason that abstinence is usually a main objective of treatment.

While there is a dearth of research exploring the neural correlates of addiction treatment in particular, multiple studies have found that the dorsolateral prefrontal cortex may play a key role in addiction recovery. For instance, in one study, CBT completion was associated with at-rest increased dorsolateral prefrontal cortex activation, and this in turn was

DORSOLATERAL
PREFRONTAL
CORTEX

linked to improved emotion regulation and reduced alcohol craving (Suzuki et al., 2020). Also, increased dorsolateral prefrontal cortex activation has been found in smokers who completed mindfulness-based interventions, and this was associated with decreased cravings (Tang et al., 2013; Vinci et al., 2016). Moreover, TMS has been shown to be a promising approach to addiction treatment and has been shown to stimulate dorsolateral prefrontal cortex activity (Barr et al., 2011; Coles et al., 2018; Lupi et al., 2017). In TMS studies, increased dorsolateral prefrontal cortex activation tends to be negatively correlated with cravings and drug and alcohol consumption (Bellamoli et al., 2014; Li, Du, et al., 2017; Tik et al., 2017).

DEPRESSION

Depression and the Dorsolateral Prefrontal Cortex: What Happens?

The dorsolateral prefrontal cortex has been repeatedly identified as a key region involved in depressive disorders (Mayberg, 2009; Rajkowska & Stockmeier, 2013). Specifically, compared to healthy controls, in depression the dorsolateral prefrontal cortex is often underactive (Hamilton et al., 2012), which may lead to difficulty downregulating the amygdala (Wang et al., 2020). This may explain why cognitive and emotion regulation tend to be difficult in depression (Joormann & Stanton, 2016; Salehinejad et al., 2017). Relatedly, hypoactivation of the dorsolateral prefrontal cortex has been observed during working memory tasks and negative emotion processing (Grieve et al., 2013), suggesting difficulty regulating negative emotion and possible memory impairment (Fitzgerald et al., 2006; Korgaonkar et al., 2013). Also, dorsolateral prefrontal cortex underactivation has been associated with emotion-processing biases in depression: depressed individuals recognize distressing emotional stimuli more easily than pleasant emotional cues (Auerbach et al., 2015).

Research examining possible dorsolateral prefrontal cortex volume changes in depression has resulted in mixed findings, with some studies finding volume loss in depression (Grieve et al., 2013) and some finding no significant volume differences between depressed and nondepressed individuals (Bora, Fornito, et al., 2012). Approximately half of the published studies examining dorsolateral prefrontal cortex volume in depression have concluded there is atrophy in this area of depressed individuals' brains (Bora, Harrison, et al., 2012). Several studies have also found synaptic loss in the dorsolateral prefrontal cortex in depression (Duman et al., 2016; Holmes et al., 2019). Lower dorsolateral prefrontal cortex volume has been linked to depressive rumination (Wang et al., 2015), which may further explain the cognitive and emotional dysregulation characteristic of depression.

Dorsolateral prefrontal cortex connectivity with other brain regions may also be altered in depression (Holmes et al., 2019; Murrough et al., 2016; Scheinost et al., 2018). Specifically, dorsolateral prefrontal cortex connectivity with areas such as the nucleus accumbens and ventral tegmental area, brain regions involved in reward, has been found to be weaker in depressed individuals than in healthy controls (Bracht et al., 2014). This may contribute to the common experience of anhedonia in depression; the reward areas of the brain, which help promote motivation, reinforcement, and behavioral activation (Yang, de Jong, et al., 2018), are weakly connected to cognitive areas such as the dorsolateral prefrontal cortex and thus cannot interact much with, or influence, the dorsolateral prefrontal cortex.

Depression and the Dorsolateral Prefrontal Cortex: How It Presents

Dorsolateral prefrontal cortex alterations in depression may contribute to multiple depression symptoms and presentations. For example, depressed individuals may appear to have flat affect and report experiencing anhedonia, where they cannot easily access positive emotions. They may also have repetitive, self-focused negative thoughts and ruminations that they have a difficult time controlling, and this may be related to dorsolateral prefrontal cortex underactivation or atrophy, along with ventromedial prefrontal cortex hyperactivation (see Chapter 8 for more information on the ventromedial prefrontal cortex's role in depression). Additionally, depressed individuals may find it challenging to engage in cognitive restructuring or reframing, in which they attempt to replace negative thoughts with more positive ones. While this is an exercise often practiced in cognitive behav-

THE DORSOLATERAL PREFRONTAL CORTEX ■ 133

ioral therapy, it may be a task that is difficult for depressed individuals. Thus, it may take practice and patience for these clients to successfully learn how to restructure negative thoughts. Finally, those experiencing depression may find it difficult to simply "snap out of it" to feel better, as emotion dysregulation, in addition to cognitive dysregulation, is a common symptom of depression.

Treatment Implications

The treatment implications for depression are similar to those for PTSD and addiction (see above sections) and include SSRIs, TMS, and CBT-based interventions. As noted previously, SSRIs have been found to improve dorsolateral prefrontal cortex activation in general (Kennedy et al., 2001; Mayberg et al., 2000). This has also been found in depressed individuals in particular (Ma, 2015) and has been associated with a reduction in depression symptoms in these individuals (Cheng et al., 2017; Fales et al., 2009).

CBT has also been linked to improved depression symptoms and dorsolateral prefrontal cortex functioning. For example, CBT has been associated with improved dorsolateral prefrontal cortex–amygdala connectivity, possibly leading to better top-down control of the amygdala (Shou et al., 2017). Similarly, research has demonstrated increased overall dorsolateral prefrontal cortex connectivity in adolescents after completing group CBT (Sosic-Vasic et al., 2017). Improved connectivity may, in turn, facilitate better emotion regulation and cognitive regulation. Moreover, research has found increased dorsolateral prefrontal cortex activation in depressed individuals who completed CBT (Yang, Oathes, et al., 2018) and also in those who simply practiced cognitive reappraisal exercises (Dillon & Pizzagalli, 2013).

Finally, TMS and transcranial direct current stimulation (TDCS), a related technique, may increase dorsolateral prefrontal cortex activation and help reduce depression symptoms (Brunoni et al., 2013). Similar results have been found in trauma and addiction literature, as described in previous sections. Dorsolateral prefrontal cortex activation in depression after TMS/TDCS has been found in several studies (Nakamara et al., 2014; Salehinejad et al., 2017; Zrenner et al., 2020) and review articles (Downar

DORSOLATERAL PREFRONTAL CORTEX

& Daskalakis, 2013). Recovery from depression may be expedited by combining brain stimulation with other techniques, such as cognitive therapy or cognitive tasks (Segrave et al., 2014).

OTHER MENTAL HEALTH CONDITIONS

Dorsolateral prefrontal cortex dysfunction has been observed in several other mental health conditions, such as bipolar disorder (Radaelli et al., 2015), anxiety disorders (Balderston et al., 2017), schizophrenia (O'Connor & Hemby, 2007), and autism (Fujii et al., 2010). While the specific dorsolateral prefrontal cortex deficits vary by disorder, usually this brain region is found to be underactive. Also, it's common for this area to be weakly connected to other key brain regions, including limbic structures, making it difficult to successfully engage in emotional and cognitive regulation. Top-down, cognitive techniques such as cognitive restructuring or cognitive reappraisal, in addition to TMS and psychiatric medications, may be helpful for correcting some of the dorsolateral prefrontal cortex deficits described in this chapter.

DORSOLATERAL PREFRONTAL CORTEX

CHAPTER 10

Synthesis

This chapter synthesizes the main content chapters of the book (Chapters 2–9), providing synopses of each chapter and several summary tables to help readers process and consolidate the main points of the book. This chapter may also be used as a reference guide, to locate information that may be difficult to quickly glean from the more detailed content chapters. Specifically, this chapter is divided into five sections:

1. Summaries of Brain Regions
2. Tables of Brain Regions and Mental Health Conditions
3. Table of Brain Regions, Mental Health Conditions, and Therapeutic Approaches
4. Table of Therapeutic Approaches and Corresponding Brain Regions
5. Conclusion and Future Directions

SUMMARIES OF BRAIN REGIONS

THALAMUS

The thalamus is a small, subcortical structure located above the brain stem (see Figure 10.1). Its main function is to receive sensory inputs and reroute that information to several other brain regions for more in-depth processing. The thalamus is also involved in sleep and memory, as it produces slow wave sleep oscillations and sleep spindles, which help transfer information from working memory to long-term memory. In other words, the thalamus helps facilitate memory consolidation.

Altered thalamus activation has been found in individuals experiencing trauma, anxiety, and addiction symptoms. Research has shown the thalamus to be underactivated at rest and during re-experiencing of symptoms in individuals with PTSD. However, overactivation has been observed in individuals with PTSD who are experiencing dissociation and flashbacks. Increased thalamic activation has also been found in anxious individuals during fear anticipation and worry, and one specific region of the thalamus (the paraventricular nucleus) appears to be involved in fear acquisition. Finally, the thalamus may be indirectly involved in addiction, as it influences other brain structures known to be involved in the development and maintenance of addiction. It has been suggested that the thalamus may prompt activation of the nucleus accumbens, the addiction center of the brain, leading to drug-seeking behavior.

Clinical implications are difficult to identify, given the paucity of clinical research focusing on this brain region. However, EMDR has been shown to activate the thalamus when eye movements are utilized, and this may help clients reconsolidate memories and better filter sensory information related to the traumatic event. This, in turn, may facilitate desensitization to traumatic material. Additionally, both CBT and some SSRIs have been found to decrease thalamic activation (and connectivity with other key brain structures) in individuals with anxiety disorders, possibly leading to fear extinction and reduced worry. CBT may also alter thalamic activation to help addicted individuals learn how to anticipate and desire non-substance-related rewards and reduce cravings for substances.

AMYGDALA

The amygdala is a small, almond-shaped structure located deep in the temporal lobes (see Figure 10.1). It is widely known as the fear processing center of the brain, and has been called the "smoke detector," as its main function is to identify and respond to threat and danger. In addition, the amygdala plays a role in implicit memory formation (for aversive experiences in particular), in emotional information processing more broadly, and emotional empathy.

As a brain region deeply involved in emotional processing, the amygdala is implicated in several mental health conditions, including (but not limited to) anxiety disorders, trauma disorders, and depressive disorders. The amygdala's role in anxiety is complex, but several studies have found that the amygdala is hyperactive and hyperreactive in anxious individuals, and this appears to be the case at rest and during stressful experiences, such as public speaking or panic attacks. Additionally, the extended amygdala may play a role in worry and dread in those with anxiety. Similarly, individuals with depression have shown amygdalar hyperreactivity but not hyperactivation at rest. In PTSD, the amygdala has been shown to be hyperreactive but, unlike in anxiety, this hyperreactivity is not limited to aversive stimuli and can occur in response to neutral stimuli as well. Some research has also found the amygdalae of traumatized individuals to be hypoactivated in response to threatening information, and this is associated with the numbing symptoms of PTSD.

Exposure therapies, including prolonged exposure, exposure and response prevention, and EMDR, have been associated with reduced activation in individuals with anxiety disorders and/or PTSD. Research studies focusing on somatic and mindfulness-based practices, as well as those examining meditations and other cognitive approaches, have found similar results. Some psychiatric medications may reduce amygdala activation. Finally, a combination of psychiatric medication and cognitive techniques may strengthen amygdalar connectivity with other brain regions, leading to reduced depression symptoms.

HIPPOCAMPUS

The hippocampus is located in the temporal lobe very close to the amygdala (see Figure 10.1). As such, it has been found to collaborate with the amygdala and other nearby structures involved in emotional processing. While the hippocampus is best known as the long-term memory center of the brain, it is also involved in spatial navigation, goal-directed behavior, and stress regulation. However, long-term memory storage is considered the primary function of the hippocampus.

The hippocampus plays specific roles in anxiety, depression, trauma, and addiction. The hippocampus has been shown to be underactive and to exhibit atrophy in individuals with depression, anxiety, and/or PTSD, and this is likely a result of prolonged stress, which leads to cortisol damage to this brain region over time. Moreover, substance abuse been associated with reduced hippocampal activation, volume, and connectivity with other brain structures. Acute stress also affects the hippocampus, leading to underactivation that can alter how trauma memories are encoded and stored.

Hippocampal atrophy can be repaired, however, with the help of psychiatric medications, meditation, omega-3 fatty acids, and even exercise. Additionally, long-term abstinence from drugs and alcohol can halt the hippocampal damage resulting from substance misuse, and some types of behavioral activation may lead to hippocampal repair in those experiencing addiction. Also, CBT has been found to activate the hippocampus in individuals experiencing anxiety and depression, and EMDR and other memory reconsolidation techniques may increase hippocampal activation in those diagnosed with PTSD.

INSULA

The insula is a limbic structure located deep inside the brain, beneath the frontal and temporal lobes (see Figure 10.1). As a limbic structure, the insula is directly and indirectly involved in many functions, such as cognitive and emotional processing. In fact, the insula is the main brain region that facilitates the translation of sensory experiences into emotion, with the help of cognition. To do this, the insula first helps the individual to feel into their body, to become aware of internal experiences, including pain (this is called interoception). Next, the insula makes a determination about the physical sensations, deciding if the sensations are pleasant or aversive. Finally, the insula (with the help of other brain regions) creates an emotional experience by adding cognition to the physical sensations, as interpretations of those experiences.

Individuals experiencing symptoms of trauma, anxiety, depression, and/or addiction have shown altered insula functioning. For example, traumatized individuals have been found to exhibit insula hyperactivation or hypoactivation, depending on their symptom profiles (e.g., dissociation is associated with hypoactivation). Those with anxiety disorders consistently show hyperactive and hyperreactive insulae, whereas depressed individuals may experience over- or underactivation of this area (e.g., hypoactivation is associated with anhedonia). In addiction, insula activation has been linked to relapse and anticipation of substance use.

In traumatized individuals experiencing dissociation, grounding techniques, other sensory- or somatic-based techniques, and mindfulness practices have been associated with increased insula activation. For those depressed, anxious, or traumatized individuals needing to manage a hyperactive or hyperreactive insula, exercise, stress reduction techniques, mindfulness practices, and cognitive strategies may help regulate this brain region. Cognitive approaches may also reduce insula connectivity to other brain regions, thereby reducing negative reactivity to aversive information in those experiencing depression. In the context of addiction, insula modification may be achieved through helping clients become aware of the physical sensations and emotions associated with substance cravings, withdrawal, and memories of past usage.

NUCLEUS ACCUMBENS

The nucleus accumbens is located above the amygdala and below the thalamus and anterior to both of these structures (see Figure 10.1). Given its location, it is well-positioned to receive, integrate, and project information to several other limbic structures. As a central structure of the reward system, the nucleus accumbens is involved in many functions, such as reward expectation, motivation, goal-directed behavior, reinforcement and aversion, and love and attachment. All of these functions require the nucleus accumbens and other areas of the brain that comprise the reward circuit.

The activation of the nucleus accumbens has been found to be altered in addiction, depressive disorders, and anxiety disorders. In addiction, the nucleus accumbens hyperactivates in response to substance use (in chemical addictions) but becomes hypoactivated in response to "natural reinforcers," such as other people, animals, hobbies, etc. This pattern of activation is believed to reinforce and strengthen the individual's desire for the substance they are addicted to. In depression, the nucleus accumbens is often hypoactivated, resulting in anhedonia and accounting for the lack of dopamine in depressive disorders. In anxiety disorders, nucleus accumbens activity is a bit more complex: research has shown this region can be hyper-activated or hypoactivated, depending on multiple factors. Underactivation of this region in anxiety may indicate a lack of reward processing, whereas overactivation may suggest dread or anticipation of an aversive event (since nucleus accumbens activation activates during aversion as well as reinforcement).

Long-term abstinence from substance use often results in nucleus accumbens repair, even without additional interventions. Thus, absti-nence is a central treatment goal for substance use disorders, and various psychotherapies can help clients achieve and maintain abstinence. Deep brain stimulation may also facilitate addiction recovery and decrease some individuals' depression and anxiety symptoms by stimulating the nucleus accumbens. Similar findings have been observed with neurofeedback. Also, repetitive transcranial magnetic stimulation has been found to strengthen nucleus accumbens connectivity with cortical regions, leading to reduced anxiety symptoms, presumably due to strengthening of individuals' top-down control of anxiety. Moreover, CBT may specifically increase nucleus accumbens activation and generally increase reward circuit responsiveness in depressed individuals.

ANTERIOR CINGULATE CORTEX

The anterior cingulate cortex is considered a limbic and cortical structure due to its location above other limbic structures but beneath the prefron-tal cortex (see Figure 10.1). It is considered a bridge between emotional (limbic) and cognitive (cortical) brain regions. Considering it is a limbic and cortical structure, it is perhaps not surprising that the anterior cingulate cortex is involved in both emotional and cognitive functions, including empathy, emotion regulation, cognitive regulation, and conflict monitoring. Because of its roles in these functions, this area has been called the "self-regulation" center of the brain.

The anterior cingulate cortex is implicated in most psychiatric disorders, as most conditions include difficulty with thought and/or emotion regulation, which almost always involve this region in some way. However, the anterior cingulate cortex plays a strong role in three categories of conditions in particular: trauma/PTSD, addiction, and depression. In PTSD and depression, anterior cingulate activation is often lower than in healthy controls and connectivity is altered; specifically, the anterior cingulate cortex is strongly connected to the amygdala, and this tight wiring allows the amygdala to strongly influence, and even suppress, cingulate cortex activation. The anterior cingulate is also weakly connected to other cortical structures in those with PTSD, making collaboration with "rational" brain regions difficult. Similarly, anterior cingulate cortex underactivation has been found in addiction, especially when an individual considers consequences of addiction-related behaviors (substance misuse, for instance). This suggests that addiction may impair one's ability to consider or predict the consequences of their decisions. Conversely, it has been found that in some depressed individuals, one small part of the anterior cingulate cortex becomes overactivated, indicating hyperactivation of the "error detection center" within the anterior cingulate cortex. Researchers concluded that this activation may lead to self-blame and self-criticism, which depressed individuals commonly experience.

Broadly, psychotherapy has been shown to increase activation of the anterior cingulate cortex in those with PTSD. More specifically, both exposure therapies (such as prolonged exposure and EMDR) and CBT are associated with increased activation in this area in individuals with PTSD. CBT, neurofeedback, and mindfulness practices have also been linked to increased activation of the anterior cingulate cortex in those with substance use disorders, and this activation is associated with reduced cravings and impulsivity and increased distress tolerance in that population. Some medications, such as Naltrexone, may also alter anterior cingulate connectivity, leading to reduced relapse in addicted individuals. Finally, CBT, neurofeedback, and pharmacological approaches have been associated with improved anterior cingulate cortex functioning in depression, including improved functional connectivity and activation. These alterations are often accompanied by reduced depression symptoms.

VENTROMEDIAL PREFRONTAL CORTEX

The ventromedial prefrontal cortex is located near the top of the brain and includes the middle (or midline) portion of the prefrontal cortex, which can be found right behind the center of the forehead (see Figure 10.1). This area of the brain, though a cortical, cognitive region, is involved not only in cognitive functions but also emotional functions, such as emotion regulation. Overall, this area of the brain is dedicated to thoughts and emotions related to the self and thus tends to be involved in self-referential thinking, decision-making, envisioning future events, memories involving the self, and self-perception.

Altered functioning and connectivity of the ventromedial prefrontal cortex has been observed in individuals experiencing trauma, anxiety, and/or depression symptoms. In PTSD and most anxiety disorders, ventromedial prefrontal cortex underactivation has been found to occur both at rest and when individuals are faced with aversive stimuli (including, but not limited to, trauma reminders). This underactivation is often accompanied by amygdala hyperactivation. Under-connectivity between the ventromedial prefrontal cortex and other structures in PTSD and depression may imply reduced collaboration with, or influence over, other brain structures, and may compromise one's efforts to control negative thoughts about oneself. Additionally, hyperactivation of the ventromedial prefrontal cortex has been found in anxious individuals when they anticipate threatening stimuli (however, once the threat occurs, hypoactivation of this region is usually observed). This hyperactivation likely reflects the self-referential, future-based thinking that occurs during the anticipation of an event. Similarly, hyperactivation of the ventromedial prefrontal cortex is common in depression and likely explains why depressed individuals find it difficult to "turn off" negative thoughts about themselves.

Exposure therapies, such as prolonged exposure, EMDR, and virtual reality exposure therapy, have been associated with increased ventromedial prefrontal cortex activation in those with PTSD, both at rest and in response to distressing or trauma-related information. Similar results have been found in anxious individuals who have completed exposure therapy for fears and phobias. Additionally, anxious individuals appear to benefit from meditation-based interventions that instruct the participant to attend to internal physical and emotional experiences, as these also have been found to result in increased ventromedial prefrontal cortex activation. Conversely, cognitive strategies, such as decentering and cognitive defusion, have been linked to reduced ventromedial prefrontal cortex activation while anxious individuals imagine (or simulate) future distressing events. Finally, depression neuroimaging research reveals that both CBT and SSRI use may contribute to improved ventromedial prefrontal cortex activation and connectivity and are associated with reduced attention allocated to negative self-talk and distressing emotions. In severe, treatment-resistant depression, electroconvulsive therapy and transcranial magnetic stimulation may help diminish depression symptoms by reducing activity in the ventromedial prefrontal cortex.

DORSOLATERAL PREFRONTAL CORTEX

Like the ventromedial prefrontal cortex, the dorsolateral prefrontal cortex is located within the larger prefrontal cortex, but in the upper, lateral regions as opposed to the center of the prefrontal cortex (see Figure 10.1). Thus, the dorsolateral prefrontal cortex flanks the ventromedial cortex and is located slightly above that region. As a cortical structure, the dorsolateral prefrontal cortex is intimately involved in several cognitive functions, such as reasoning, reality testing, working memory, cognitive control, decision-making, and social cognition.

Research has shown the dorsolateral prefrontal cortex to be involved in PTSD, addiction, and depressive disorders. In PTSD, dorsolateral prefrontal cortex hypoactivation tends to occur when traumatized individuals engage in working memory of cognitive tasks, whereas hyperactivation is associated with the presentation of distressing stimuli, indicating strong attempts to down-regulate aversive emotions or "triggers." Similarly, in addiction, dorsolateral prefrontal cortex activation can be low or high. Hyperactivation of this brain region in addiction may suggest difficulties with processing negative emotions, whereas hypoactivation may indicate deficits in cognitive inhibitory control. Moreover, dorsolateral prefrontal cortex hypoactivation in depression has been linked to negative-emotion regulation difficulties and memory impairment as well as emotion-processing biases, wherein depressed individuals recognize distressing stimuli more easily than pleasant ones. Decreased dorsolateral prefrontal cortex volume has also been found in both addiction and depression.

In PTSD, dorsolateral prefrontal cortex activity and connectivity may be altered through CBT, exposure-based psychotherapy, medication, or transcranial magnetic stimulation (TMS). For instance, prolonged exposure, EMDR, and cognitive processing therapy have been shown to attenuate negative emotions, and this change has been associated with improved dorsolateral prefrontal cortex connectivity, increased activation in this region, and increased volume size. CBT and mindfulness techniques have also been shown to activate the dorsolateral prefrontal cortex in addicted and depressed individuals, who often experience less severe depression symptoms and/or fewer relapses and cravings after treatment. Additionally, TMS and SSRIs have been shown to activate the dorsolateral prefrontal cortex in PTSD and depression, and these approaches have been linked to reduced PTSD and depression symptoms.

Figure 10.1 depicts all eight main brain regions in one visual. Each of these regions can function both independently and interdependently with the other areas.

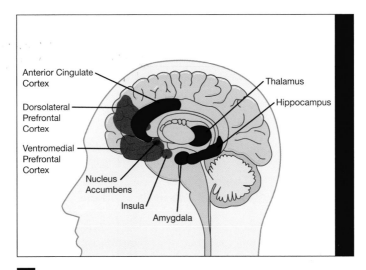

FIGURE 10.1: EIGHT MAIN BRAIN REGIONS

TABLES OF BRAIN REGIONS AND
MENTAL HEALTH CONDITIONS

The following two tables show the mental health conditions associated with each brain region, as described in the previous chapters. This is presented in two ways, using two separate tables. Table 10.1 lists each *brain region* and then identifies the mental health conditions more commonly and less commonly associated with alterations in those specific brain structures. Table 10.2 lists the *mental health conditions* discussed in this book and then connects those conditions to the specific brain regions shown to be impacted by those conditions. Note that the list of conditions and the brain regions' roles in these conditions are not exhaustive, but do reflect the current state of neuroscientific research. It is highly likely that the brain regions discussed here, and others not detailed in this book, are involved in many psychiatric disorders, but more research is required to understand the full extent of these brain regions' influence on mental health and illness.

Table 10.1: Brain Regions and Corresponding Mental Health Conditions

Brain Region	More Commonly Associated Conditions	Less Commonly Associated Conditions
Thalamus	PTSD Anxiety disorders Addiction-related disorders	Depressive disorders OCD

Amygdala	PTSD
	Anxiety disorders
	Depressive disorders
		Addiction-related
		   disorders
		Neurodevelopmental
		   disorders
		Bipolar disorder
		Psychosis
		Autism
		Personality disorders
		Antisocial personality
		   disorder
		OCD

Hippocampus	PTSD Anxiety disorders Depressive disorders Addiction-related disorders	Schizophrenia Alzheimer's disease
Insula	PTSD Anxiety disorders Depressive disorders Addiction-related disorders	Schizophrenia Autism

Nucleus Accumbens	Anxiety disorders
	Depressive disorders
	Addiction-related
	   disorders
		Antisocial personality
		   disorder
		ADHD
		Bipolar disorder
		Neurocognitive
		   disorder
		Alzheimer's disease
		OCD

Brain Region	More Commonly Associated Conditions	Less Commonly Associated Conditions

Anterior Cingulate Cortex	PTSD
	Depressive disorders
	Addiction-related
	   disorders
		ADHD
		Bipolar disorder
		Schizophrenia
		Autism
		Borderline personality
		   disorder
		Anxiety disorders
		OCD

Ventromedial Prefrontal Cortex	PTSD Anxiety disorders Depressive disorders	Autism Schizophrenia Antisocial personality disorder OCD
Dorsolateral Prefrontal Cortex	PTSD Depressive disorders Addiction-related disorders	Anxiety disorders Bipolar disorder Schizophrenia Autism

Table 10.2: Mental Health Conditions and Corresponding Brain Regions

Mental Health Condition	Brain Region(s) Involved
Addiction-related disorders	Thalamus Amygdala Hippocampus Insula Nucleus accumbens Anterior cingulate cortex Dorsolateral prefrontal cortex
ADHD	Nucleus accumbens Anterior cingulate cortex
Alzheimer's disease	Hippocampus Nucleus accumbens

TABLE 10.2: *continued*

Mental Health Condition	Brain Region(s) Involved
Antisocial personality disorder	Amygdala Nucleus accumbens Ventromedial prefrontal cortex
Anxiety disorders	Thalamus Amygdala Hippocampus Insula Nucleus accumbens Anterior cingulate cortex Ventromedial prefrontal cortex Dorsolateral prefrontal cortex
Autism	Amygdala Insula Anterior cingulate cortex Ventromedial prefrontal cortex Dorsolateral prefrontal cortex
Bipolar disorder	Amygdala Nucleus accumbens Anterior cingulate cortex Dorsolateral prefrontal cortex
Borderline personality disorder	Anterior cingulate cortex
Depressive disorders	Thalamus Amygdala Hippocampus Insula Nucleus accumbens Anterior cingulate cortex Ventromedial prefrontal cortex Dorsolateral prefrontal cortex
Neurocognitive disorders	Nucleus accumbens
Neurodevelopmental disorders	Amygdala

Mental Health Condition	Brain Region(s) Involved
OCD	Thalamus Amygdala Nucleus accumbens Anterior cingulate cortex Ventromedial prefrontal cortex
Personality disorders (broadly)	Amygdala
Psychosis	Amygdala
PTSD	Thalamus Amygdala Hippocampus Insula Anterior cingulate cortex Ventromedial prefrontal cortex Dorsolateral prefrontal cortex
Schizophrenia	Hippocampus Insula Anterior cingulate cortex Ventromedial prefrontal cortex Dorsolateral prefrontal cortex

TABLE OF BRAIN REGIONS, COMMONLY ASSOCIATED MENTAL HEALTH CONDITIONS, AND THERAPEUTIC APPROACHES

This section summarizes neuroscientific research findings regarding the eight main brain regions, the mental health conditions they are more or less commonly involved in, and the therapeutic approaches that have been shown to alter the functioning and/or structure of those brain regions in the direction of health (see Table 10.3.). Note that this chart does not specify the type of change each therapeutic approach elicits (reduced or increased activation, volume changes, etc.) nor the conditions the approaches are specifically linked to. Rather, therapeutic approaches that have been shown to alter these brain areas are simply listed. For more detail about the specific impacts of the therapeutic approaches and which conditions the findings are associated with, refer to the content chapters of this book (Chapters 2–9). This chart is intended to provide readers with a quick overview of the main brain regions detailed on the book, the conditions they are involved in, and the therapeutic strategies that have been shown to alter those specific brain areas.

Neuroscientific studies examining the effects of psychotherapy and pharmacological approaches vary widely in terms of the approaches that are examined and how they are described in publications. For example, some studies simply refer to utilizing CBT, whereas others specify a particular therapy that is cognitive behavioral in nature. Still other studies do not refer to specific therapies (such as cognitive processing therapy) nor broad categories of therapies (such as CBT), but instead investigate the effects of individual therapeutic techniques (such as cognitive restructuring). These individual techniques may be components of specific therapies but are not representative of the therapy as a whole. Cognitive restructuring is an example of this; cognitive restructuring is an individual technique, or skill, taught in various cognitive therapies, such as cognitive processing therapy. But practicing cognitive restructuring is not the same as completing cognitive processing therapy; it is just one part of cognitive processing therapy.

Given the wide range of semantics and therapeutic methods used in clinical neuroscience research, it can be difficult to draw generalizations about which techniques or therapies shift brain functioning in different mental health conditions. To allow this data to be as digestible as possible, the therapeutic approaches summarized in Table 10.3 have been organized into three levels. Level 1 includes broad categories of therapeutic interventions, such as CBT-based interventions, where CBT is conceptualized as a large umbrella category that may encompass several specific therapies. Level 2 approaches include specific therapies or intervention packages/protocols, such as EMDR, cognitive processing therapy, or other interventions. Many of these therapies can be thought of as specific examples of the broader categories included in Level 1 but are acknowledged separately when the neuroscientific research has specified findings directly related to

TABLE 10.3: Brain Regions, Commonly Associated Mental Health Conditions, and Therapeutic Approaches

Brain Region	Commonly Associated Mental Health Conditions	Therapeutic Approaches
Thalamus	PTSD Anxiety disorders Addiction-related disorders	Level 1: CBT-based interventions Exposure-based interventions SSRIs Level 2: EMDR Level 3: Deep breathing Progressive muscle relaxation
Amygdala	PTSD Anxiety disorders Depressive disorders	Level 1: Exposure-based interventions Cognitive therapies Mindfulness-based training Meditations SSRIs Anxiolytics Electroconvulsive therapy Level 2: Cognitive therapy for depression Exposure and response prevention Prolonged exposure EMDR Systematic desensitization Level 3: Tapping Progressive muscle relaxation Autogenic training Deep breathing Body scan Cognitive restructuring Neurofeedback Antibiotic (d-cycloserine) Acupuncture Neuromodulation

TABLE 10.3: *continued*

Brain Region	Commonly Associated Mental Health Conditions	Therapeutic Approaches
Hippocampus	PTSD Anxiety disorders Depressive disorders Addiction-related disorders	Level 1: CBT-based interventions SSRIs SNRIs Level 2: EMDR Level 3: Omega-3 supplements Physical exercise
Insula	PTSD Anxiety disorders Depressive disorders Addiction-related disorders	Level 1: CBT-based interventions Mindfulness-based training Meditations Grounding techniques Level 3: Physical exercise Cognitive restructuring

Nucleus accumbens	Anxiety disorders
	Depressive disorders
	Addiction-related
	   disorders
		Level 1:
		CBT-based interventions
		SSRIs
		
		Level 3:
		Naltrexone
		Neurofeedback
		Repetitive transcranial magnetic
		   stimulation
		Deep brain stimulation

TABLE 10.3: *continued*

Brain Region	Commonly Associated Mental Health Conditions	Therapeutic Approaches
Anterior cingulate cortex	PTSD Depressive disorders Addiction-related disorders	Level 1: CBT-based interventions Cognitive therapies Exposure-based interventions SSRIs Level 2: Prolonged exposure EMDR Level 3: Self-awareness/self-monitoring Cognitive restructuring Neurofeedback Naltrexone Modafinil Ritalin
Ventromedial prefrontal cortex	PTSD Anxiety disorders Depressive disorders	Level 1: CBT-based interventions Exposure-based interventions SSRIs Level 2: Virtual reality exposure therapy Prolonged exposure EMDR Mindfulness-based stress reduction Level 3: Mindfulness meditation Emotion identification Cognitive decentering/defusion Transcranial magnetic stimulation Electroconvulsive therapy d-cycloserine

TABLE 10.3: *continued*

Brain Region	Commonly Associated Mental Health Conditions	Therapeutic Approaches
Dorsolateral prefrontal cortex	PTSD Depressive disorders Addiction-related disorders	Level 1: CBT-based interventions Mindfulness-based training SSRIs Level 2: Prolonged exposure Cognitive processing therapy EMDR Mindfulness-based stress reduction Level 3: Cognitive reappraisal Zen meditation Transcranial magnetic stimulation Prazosin

those particular therapies. Level 3 includes individual techniques that have been examined in the neuroscience literature.

As a caveat, this chart, like the ones presented earlier in this chapter, aims to represent the current state of neuroscientific research but may not be exhaustive or comprehensive. For instance, it is likely that brain regions are altered by therapeutic techniques not listed here. Future studies will likely slowly "fill in the gaps" that currently exist between neuroscience research and clinical practice. Additionally, the Table 10.3 does not specify dosage effects, nor does it categorize therapeutic techniques according to the strength of the research supporting their use for specific brain changes. It is recommended that readers review the content chapters of this book to learn more about these therapeutic approaches and, when desired, refer to the original research studies cited throughout the book.

TABLE OF THERAPEUTIC APPROACHES
AND CORRESPONDING BRAIN REGIONS

Table 10.4 presents a summary of the therapeutic approaches mentioned in this book and the brain regions that research indicates they may therapeutically alter. The information contained in Table 10.4 is similar to that presented in Table 10.3 but is categorized by therapeutic approach, making it an easy reference for readers wanting to quickly locate information related to brain areas impacted by various therapies and techniques.

Table 10.4: Therapeutic Approaches and Corresponding Brain Regions

Therapeutic Approaches	Brain Region(s) Involved
Acupuncture	Amygdala
Anxiolytics	Amygdala
Autogenic training	Amygdala
Body scan	Amygdala Hippocampus
CBT-based interventions	Thalamus Insula Nucleus accumbens Anterior cingulate cortex Ventromedial prefrontal cortex Dorsolateral prefrontal cortex
Cognitive decentering/defusion	Ventromedial prefrontal cortex
Cognitive processing therapy	Dorsolateral prefrontal cortex
Cognitive restructuring	Amygdala Insula Anterior cingulate cortex Dorsolateral prefrontal cortex
Cognitive therapies	Amygdala Anterior cingulate cortex
Cognitive therapy for depression	Amygdala
d-cycloserine	Amygdala Ventromedial prefrontal cortex

TABLE 10.4: *continued*

Therapeutic Approaches	Brain Region(s) Involved
Deep brain stimulation	Nucleus accumbens
Deep breathing	Thalamus Amygdala
Electroconvulsive therapy	Amygdala Ventromedial prefrontal cortex
EMDR	Thalamus Amygdala Hippocampus Anterior cingulate cortex Ventromedial prefrontal cortex Dorsolateral prefrontal cortex
Exposure and response prevention	Amygdala
Exposure-based interventions	Thalamus Amygdala Anterior cingulate cortex Ventromedial prefrontal cortex
Grounding techniques	Insula
Meditations	Amygdala Insula Ventromedial prefrontal cortex Dorsolateral prefrontal cortex
Mindfulness-based training	Amygdala Insula Dorsolateral prefrontal cortex
Mindfulness-based stress reduction	Ventromedial prefrontal cortex Dorsolateral prefrontal cortex
Modafinil	Anterior cingulate cortex
Neurofeedback	Amygdala Nucleus accumbens Anterior cingulate cortex
Neuromodulation	Amygdala

Therapeutic Approaches	Brain Region(s) Involved
Naltrexone	Nucleus accumbens Anterior cingulate cortex
Omega-3 supplements	Hippocampus
Physical exercise	Hippocampus Insula
Prazosin	Dorsolateral prefrontal cortex
Progressive muscle relaxation	Thalamus Amygdala
Prolonged exposure	Amygdala Anterior cingulate cortex Ventromedial prefrontal cortex Dorsolateral prefrontal cortex
Ritalin	Anterior cingulate cortex
Self-awareness/self-monitoring/emotion identification	Anterior cingulate cortex Ventromedial prefrontal cortex
SNRIs	Hippocampus
SSRIs	Thalamus Amygdala Hippocampus Nucleus accumbens Anterior cingulate cortex Ventromedial prefrontal cortex Dorsolateral prefrontal cortex
Systematic desensitization	Amygdala
Tapping	Amygdala
Transcranial magnetic stimulation	Nucleus accumbens Ventromedial prefrontal cortex Dorsolateral prefrontal cortex
Virtual reality exposure therapy	Ventromedial prefrontal cortex

CONCLUSION AND FUTURE DIRECTIONS

The summaries and charts presented in this chapter are intended to help readers to quickly access information otherwise buried deep in the content chapters and to synthesize the large amount of data described in this book. As mentioned, the four mental health conditions most extensively studied by neuroscientists are PTSD, anxiety disorder, depressive disorders, and addiction-related disorders. The eight main brain regions involved in mental health and illness are the thalamus, amygdala, hippocampus, insula, nucleus accumbens, anterior cingulate cortex, ventromedial prefrontal cortex, and dorsolateral prefrontal cortex. The four main mental health conditions identified are those for which clinicians have the most information in terms of brain regions involved and promising therapeutic approaches (according to neuroscientific research). From the tables in this chapter, it is also clear that more research needs to be completed before clinicians have a comprehensive, detailed understanding of mental health and illness in the brain as well as of the therapies and interventions that most reliably change key brain regions in the direction of health.

However, I hope this book provides clinicians with a way to begin integrating neuroscience research into clinical practice. When a basic understanding of the brain regions involved in mental health and illness is gained, including the locations and functions of those structures and the therapy approaches that have been shown to promote recovery in those brain areas, clinicians can begin to take a neuroscience-based approach to psychotherapy. While it may not yet be clear which specific techniques should be used with which clients and when, clinicians can begin to apply neuroscience to their practice when they understand which brain regions are likely impacted by a client's disorder and which techniques therapeutically alter those brain regions. In other words, over time clinical neuroscience research may elucidate the *mechanisms* of psychotherapy approaches (that is, what causes psychotherapy to be effective). In this way, neuroscience can aid clinicians in better understanding their clients and can provide mental health professionals with guidance in creating client-centered treatment plans rooted in empirical science.

REFERENCES

THALAMUS REFERENCES

Balodis, I. M., Kober, H., Worhunsky, P. D., Stevens, M. C., Pearlson, G. D., Carroll, K. M., & Potenza, M. N. (2016). Neurofunctional reward processing changes in cocaine dependence during recovery. *Neuropsychopharmacology*, *41*(8), 2112–2121. https://doi.org/10.1038/npp.2016.11

Baxter, L. R., Schwartz, J. M., Bergman, K. S., Szuba, M. P., Guze, B. H., Mazziotta, J. C., Alazraki, A., Selin, C. E., Ferng, H.-K., Munford, P., & Phelps, M. E. (1992). Caudate glucose metabolic rate changes with both drug and behavior therapy for obsessive–compulsive disorder. *Archives of General Psychiatry*, *49*(9), 681–689. https://doi.org/10.1001/archpsyc.1992.01820090009002

Bergmann, U. (2008). The neurobiology of EMDR: Exploring the thalamus and neural integration. *Journal of EMDR Practice and Research*, *2*(4), 300–314. https://doi.org/10.1891/1933-3196.2.4.300

Bolkan, S. S., Stujenske, J. M., Parnaudeau, S., Spellman, T. J., Rauffenbart, C., & Abbas, A. I. (2017). Thalamic projections sustain prefrontal activity during working memory maintenance. *Nature Neuroscience*, *20*(7), 987–996. https://doi.org/10.1038/nn.4568

Child, N. D., & Benarroch, E. E. (2013). Anterior nucleus of the thalamus: Functional organization and clinical implications. *Neurology*, *81*(21), 1869–1876. https://doi.org/10.1212/01.wnl.0000436078.95856.56

Coulon, P., Budde, T., & Pape, H. C. (2012). The sleep relay—The role of the thalamus in central and decentral sleep regulation. *Pflügers Archiv - European Journal of Physiology*, *463*(1), 53–71. https://doi.org/10.1007/s00424-011-1014-6

De Gennaro, L., & Ferrara, M. (2003). Sleep spindles: An overview. *Sleep Medicine Reviews*, *7*(5), 423–440. https://doi.org/10.1053/smrv.2002.0252

De Lange, F. P., Koers, A., Kalkman, J. S., Bleijenberg, G., Hagoort, P., Van der Meer, J. W., & Toni, I. (2008). Increase in prefrontal cortical volume following cognitive behavioral therapy in patients with chronic fatigue syndrome. *Brain*, *131*(8), 2172–2180. https://doi.org/10.1093/brain/awn140

Du, M.-Y., Wu, Q.-Z., Yue, Q., Li, J., Liao, Y., Kuang, W.-H., Huang, X.-Q., Chan, R. C. K., Mechelli, A., & Gong, Q.-Y. (2012). Voxelwise meta-analysis of gray matter reduction in major depressive disorder. *Progress in Neuro-Psychopharmacology and Biological Psychiatry*, *36*(1), 11–16. https://doi.org/10.1016/j.pnpbp.2011.09.014

Dunsmoor, J. E., & Paz, R. (2015). Fear generalization and anxiety: Behavioral and neural mechanisms. *Biological Psychiatry*, *78*(5), 336–343. https://doi.org/10.1016/j.biopsych.2015.04.010

Duval, E. R., Javanbakht, A., & Liberzon, I. (2015). Neural circuits in anxiety and stress disorders: A focused review. *Therapeutics and Clinical Risk Management*, *11*, 115–126. https://doi.org/10.2147/TCRM.S48528

Etkin, A., & Wager, T. D. (2007). Functional neuroimaging of anxiety: A meta-analysis of emotional processing in PTSD, social anxiety disorder, and specific phobia. *American Journal of Psychiatry*, *164*(10), 1476–1488. https://doi.org/10.1176/appi.ajp.2007.07030504

Fogel, S. M., & Smith, C. T. (2011). The function of the sleep spindle: A physiological index of intelligence and a mechanism for sleep-dependent memory consolidation. *Neuroscience and Biobehavioral Reviews*, 35(5), 1154–1165. https://doi.org/10.1016/j.neubiorev.2010.12.003

Franklin, S. (2017). The peripheral and central nervous system. In *Conn's translational neuroscience* (pp. 113–129). Academic Press. https://doi.org/10.1016/B978-0-12-802381-5.00007-5

Furmark, T., Tillfors, M., Marteinsdottir, I., Fischer, H., Pissiota, A., Långström, B., & Fredrikson, M. (2002). Common changes in cerebral blood flow in patients with social phobia treated with citalopram or cognitive behavior therapy. *Archives of General Psychiatry*, 59(5), 425–433. https://doi.org/10.1001/archpsyc.59.5.425

Gais, S., Molle, M., Helms, K., & Born, J. (2002). Learning-dependent increases in spindle density. *Journal of Neuroscience*, 22(15), 6830-6834. https://doi.org/10.1523/JNEUROSCI.22-15-06830.2002

Giménez, M., Ortiz, H., Soriano-Mas, C., López-Solà, M., Farré, M., & Deus, J. (2014). Functional effects of chronic paroxetine versus placebo on the fear, stress and anxiety brain circuit in Social Anxiety Disorder: Initial validation of an imaging protocol for drug discovery. *European Neuropsychopharmacology*, 24(1), 105–116. https://doi.org/10.1016/j.euroneuro.2013.09.004

Goldman-Rakic, P. S. (1995). Cellular basis of working memory. *Neuron*, 14(3), 477–485. https://doi.org/10.1016/0896-6273(95)90304-6

Guillery, R. W., & Sherman, S. M. (2011). Branched thalamic afferents: What are the messages that they relay to the cortex? *Brain Research Reviews*, 66(1–2), 205–219. https://doi.org/10.1016/j.brainresrev.2010.08.001

Guo, Z. V., Inagaki, H. K., Daie, K., Druckmann, S., Gerfen, C. R., & Svoboda, K. (2017). Maintenance of persistent activity in a frontal thalamocortical loop. *Nature*, 545(7653), 181–186. https://doi.org/10.1038/nature22324

Haber, S. N., & Calzavara, R. (2009). The cortico-basal ganglia integrative network: The role of the thalamus. *Brain Research Bulletin*, 78(2–3), 69–74. https://doi.org/10.1016/j.brainresbull.2008.09.013

Halassa, M. M., Siegle, J. H., Ritt, J. T., Ting, J. T., Feng, G., & Moore, C. I. (2011). Selective optical drive of thalamic reticular nucleus generates thalamic bursts and cortical spindles. *Nature Neuroscience*, 14(9), 1118–1120. https://doi.org/10.1038/nn.2880

Herrero, M. T., Barcia, C., & Navarro, J. M. (2002). Functional anatomy of thalamus and basal ganglia. *Child's Nervous System*, 18(8), 386–404. https://doi.org/10.1007/s00381-002-0604-1

Huang, A. S., Mitchell, J. A., Haber, S. N., Alia-Klein, N., & Goldstein, R. Z. (2018). The thalamus in drug addiction: From rodents to humans. *Philosophical Transactions of the Royal Society of London. Series B, Biological Sciences*, 373(1742). https://doi.org/10.1098/rstb.2017.0028

Huber, M., Siol, T., Herholz, K., Lenz, O., Köhle, K., & Heiss, W. D. (2001). Activation of thalamo-cortical systems in post-traumatic flashbacks: A positron emission tomography study. *Traumatology*, 7(4), 131–141. https://doi.org/10.1177/153476560100700402

James, M. H., & Dayas, C. V. (2013). What about me. . .? The PVT: A role for the paraventricular thalamus (PVT) in drug-seeking behavior. *Frontiers in Behavioral Neuroscience*, 7, 18. https://doi.org/10.3389/fnbeh.2013.00018

Jan, J. E., Reiter, R. J., Wasdell, M. B., & Bax, M. (2009). The role of the thalamus in sleep, pineal melatonin production, and circadian rhythm sleep disorders. *Journal of Pineal Research*, 46(1), 1–7. https://doi.org/10.1111/j.1600-079X.2008.00628.x

Jia, Z., Wang, Y., Huang, X., Kuang, W., Wu, Q., & Lui, S. (2014). Impaired frontothalamic circuitry in suicidal patients with depression revealed by diffusion tensor imaging at 3.0 T. *Journal of Psychiatry and Neuroscience*, 39(3), 170–177. https://doi.org/10.1503/jpn.130023

Jones, E. G. (2007). *The thalamus*. Cambridge University Press.

Karim, H. T., Tudorascu, D. L., Butters, M. A., Walker, S., Aizenstein, H. J., & Andreescu, C. (2017). In the grip of worry: Cerebral blood flow changes during worry induction and reappraisal in late-life generalized anxiety disorder. *Translational Psychiatry, 7*(8), e1204–e1204. https://doi.org/10.1038/tp.2017.180

Kim, S. J., Lyoo, I. K., Lee, Y. S., Kim, J., Sim, M. E., Bae, S. J., . . . & Jeong, D. U. (2007). Decreased cerebral blood flow of thalamus in PTSD patients as a strategy to reduce re-experience symptoms. *Acta Psychiatrica Scandinavica, 116*(2), 145–153.

Lanius, R. A., Bluhm, R., Lanius, U., & Pain, C. (2006). A review of neuroimaging studies in PTSD: Heterogeneity of response to symptom provocation. *Journal of Psychiatric Research, 40*(8), 709–729. https://doi.org/10.1016/j.jpsychires.2005.07.007

Lanius, R. A., Williamson, P. C., Bluhm, R. L., Densmore, M., Boksman, K., Neufeld, R. W., Gati, S., & Menon, R. S. (2005). Functional connectivity of dissociative responses in posttraumatic stress disorder: A functional magnetic resonance imaging investigation. *Biological Psychiatry, 57*(8), 873–884. https://doi.org/10.1016/j.biopsych.2005.01.011

Lanius, R. A., Williamson, P. C., Densmore, M., Boksman, K., Gupta, M. A., Neufeld, R. W., Gati, J. S., & Menon, R. S. (2001). Neural correlates of traumatic memories in posttraumatic stress disorder: A functional MRI investigation. *American Journal of Psychiatry, 158*(11), 1920–1922. https://doi.org/10.1176/appi.ajp.158.11.1920

LeDoux, J. (1996). *Emotional networks and motor control: A fearful view. Progress in brain research.* Elsevier. https://doi.org/10.1016/S0079-6123(08)61880-4

Li, W., Liu, J., Skidmore, F., Liu, Y., Tian, J., & Li, K. (2010). White matter microstructure changes in the thalamus in Parkinson disease with depression: A diffusion tensor MR imaging study. *American Journal of Neuroradiology, 31*(10), 1861–1866. https://doi.org/10.3174/ajnr.A2195

Li, M., Wang, R., Zhao, M., Zhai, J., Liu, B., Yu, D., & Yuan, K. (2019). Abnormalities of thalamus volume and resting state functional connectivity in primary insomnia patients. *Brain Imaging and Behavior, 13*(5), 1193–1201. https://doi.org/10.1007/s11682-018-9932-y

Liberzon, I., Taylor, S. F., Fig, L. M., & Koeppe, R. A. (1996). Alteration of corticothalamic perfusion ratios during a PTSD flashback. *Depression and Anxiety, 4*(3), 146–150.

Liu, C.-H., Liu, C.-Z., Zhang, J., Yuan, Z., Tang, L.-R., Tie, C.-L., Fan, J. & Liu, Q.-Q. (2016). Reduced spontaneous neuronal activity in the insular cortex and thalamus in healthy adults with insomnia symptoms. *Brain Research, 1648*(A), 317–324. https://doi.org/10.1016/j.brainres.2016.07.024

Maingret, N., Girardeau, G., Todorova, R., Goutierre, M., & Zugaro, M. (2016). Hippocampo-cortical coupling mediates memory consolidation during sleep. *Nature Neuroscience, 19*(7), 959–964. https://doi.org/10.1038/nn.4304

Millan, E. Z., Ong, Z., & McNally, G. P. (2017). *Paraventricular thalamus: Gateway to feeding, appetitive motivation, and drug addiction. Progress in brain research.* Elsevier. https://doi.org/10.1016/bs.pbr.2017.07.006

Mohlman, J., & Gorman, J. M. (2005). The role of executive functioning in CBT: A pilot study with anxious older adults. *Behaviour Research and Therapy, 43*(4), 447–465. https://doi.org/10.1016/j.brat.2004.03.007

Nitschke, J. B., Sarinopoulos, I., Mackiewicz, K. L., Schaefer, H. S., & Davidson, R. J. (2006). Functional neuroanatomy of aversion and its anticipation. *NeuroImage, 29*(1), 106–116. https://doi.org/10.1016/j.neuroimage.2005.06.068

Normand, M. P., St-Hilaire, P., & Bastien, C. H. (2016). Sleep spindles characteristics in insomnia sufferers and their relationship with sleep misperception. *Neural Plasticity, 2016*, 6413473. https://doi.org/10.1155/2016/6413473

Otake, K., & Nakamura, Y. (1998). Single midline thalamic neurons projecting to both the ventral striatum and the prefrontal cortex in the rat. *Neuroscience, 86*(2), 635–649. https://doi.org/10.1016/s0306-4522(98)00062-1

Parnaudeau, S., Taylor, K., Bolkan, S. S., Ward, R. D., Balsam, P. D., & Kellendonk, C. (2015). Mediodorsal thalamus hypofunction impairs flexible goal-directed behavior. *Biological Psychiatry, 77*(5), 445–453. https://doi.org/10.1016/j.biopsych.2014.03.020

Parsons, M. P., Li, S., & Kirouac, G. J. (2007). Functional and anatomical connection between the paraventricular nucleus of the thalamus and dopamine fibers of the nucleus accumbens. *Journal of Comparative Neurology, 500*(6), 1050–1063. https://doi.org/10.1002/cne.21224

Penzo, M. A., Robert, V., Tucciarone, J., De Bundel, D., Wang, M., & Van Aelst, L. (2015). The paraventricular thalamus controls a central amygdala fear circuit. *Nature, 519*(7544), 455–459. https://doi.org/10.1038/nature13978

Peres, J. F., Newberg, A. B., Mercante, J. P., Simão, M., Albuquerque, V. E., Peres, M. J., & Nasello, A. G. (2007). Cerebral blood flow changes during retrieval of traumatic memories before and after psychotherapy: A SPECT study. *Psychological Medicine, 37*(10), 1481–1491. https://doi.org/10.1017/S003329170700997X

Porto, P. R., Oliveira, L., Mari, J., Volchan, E., Figueira, I., & Ventura, P. (2009). Does cognitive behavioral therapy change the brain? A systematic review of neuroimaging in anxiety disorders. *Journal of Neuropsychiatry and Clinical Neurosciences, 21*(2), 114–125. https://doi.org/10.1176/jnp.2009.21.2.114

Satterthwaite, T. D., Kable, J. W., Vandekar, L., Katchmar, N., Bassett, D. S., Baldassano, C. F., . . . & Wolf, D. H. (2015). Common and dissociable dysfunction of the reward system in bipolar and unipolar depression. *Neuropsychopharmacology, 40*(9), 2258–2268.

Schmitt, L. I., Wimmer, R. D., Nakajima, M., Happ, M., Mofakham, S., & Halassa, M. M. (2017). Thalamic amplification of cortical connectivity sustains attentional control. *Nature, 545*(7653), 219–223. https://doi.org/10.1038/nature22073

Schwartz, J. M., Stoessel, P. W., Baxter, L. R., Martin, K. M., & Phelps, M. E. (1996). Systematic changes in cerebral glucose metabolic rate after successful behavior modification treatment of obsessive–compulsive disorder. *Archives of General Psychiatry, 53*(2), 109–113. https://doi.org/10.1001/archpsyc.1996.01830020023004

Sforza, E., Montagna, P., Tinuper, P., Cortelli, P., Avoni, P., Ferrillo, F., Petersen, R., Gambetti, P., & Lugaresi, E. (1995). Sleep-wake cycle abnormalities in fatal familial insomnia. Evidence of the role of the thalamus in sleep regulation. *Electroencephalography and Clinical Neurophysiology, 94*(6), 398–405. https://doi.org/10.1016/0013-4694(94)00318-F

Snell, R. S. (2010). *Clinical neuroanatomy.* Lippincott Williams & Wilkins.

Spencer, S. J., Fox, J. C., & Day, T. A. (2004). Thalamic paraventricular nucleus lesions facilitate central amygdala neuronal responses to acute psychological stress. *Brain Research, 997*(2), 234–237. https://doi.org/10.1016/j.brainres.2003.10.054

Straube, T., Mentzel, H. J., & Miltner, W. H. (2007). Waiting for spiders: Brain activation during anticipatory anxiety in spider phobics. *NeuroImage, 37*(4), 1427–1436. https://doi.org/10.1016/j.neuroimage.2007.06.023

Vertes, R. P., & Hoover, W. B. (2008). Projections of the paraventricular and paratenial nuclei of the dorsal midline thalamus in the rat. *Journal of Comparative Neurology, 508*(2), 212–237. https://doi.org/10.1002/cne.21679

Watson, P., Pearson, D., Chow, M., Theeuwes, J., Wiers, R. W., Most, S. B., & Le Pelley, M. E. (2019). Capture and control: Working memory modulates attentional capture by reward-related stimuli. *Psychological Science, 30*(8), 1174–1185. https://doi.org/10.1177/0956797619855964

Wilensky, A. E., Schafe, G. E., Kristensen, M. P., & LeDoux, J. E. (2006). Rethinking the fear circuit: The central nucleus of the amygdala is required for the acquisition, consolidation, and expression of Pavlovian fear conditioning. *Journal of Neuroscience, 26*(48), 12387–12396. https://doi.org/10.1523/JNEUROSCI.4316-06.2006

Witteman, J., Post, H., Tarvainen, M., de Bruijn, A., Perna, Ede S., Ramaekers, J. G., & Wiers, R. W. (2015). Cue reactivity and its relation to craving and relapse in alcohol dependence: A combined laboratory and field study. *Psychopharmacology, 232*(20), 3685–3696. https://doi.org/10.1007/s00213-015-4027-6

Wolter, M., Huff, E., Speigel, T., Winters, B. D., & Leri, F. (2019). Cocaine, nicotine, and their conditioned contexts enhance consolidation of object memory in rats. *Learning and Memory, 26*(2), 46–55. https://doi.org/10.1101/lm.048579.118

Yan, X., Brown, A. D., Lazar, M., Cressman, V. L., Henn-Haase, C., & Neylan, T. C. (2013). Spontaneous brain activity in combat related PTSD. *Neuroscience Letters*, *547*, 1–5. https://doi.org/10.1016/j.neulet.2013.04.032

Yoon, S., Kim, J. E., Hwang, J., Kang, I., Jeon, S., & Im, J. J. (2017). Recovery from posttraumatic stress requires dynamic and sequential shifts in amygdalar connectivities. *Neuropsychopharmacology*, *42*(2), 454–461. https://doi.org/10.1038/npp.2016.136

Yoshimura, S., Okamoto, Y., Yoshino, A., Kobayakawa, M., Machino, A., & Yamawaki, S. (2014). Neural basis of anticipatory anxiety reappraisals. *PloS One*, *9*(7), e102836. https://doi.org/10.1371/journal.pone.0102836

Zhou, K., & Zhu, Y. (2019). The paraventricular thalamic nucleus: A key hub of neural circuits underlying drug addiction. *Pharmacological Research*, *142*, 70–76. https://doi.org/10.1016/j.phrs.2019.02.014

AMYGDALA REFERENCES

Abler, B., Erk, S., Herwig, U., & Walter, H. (2007). Anticipation of aversive stimuli activates extended amygdala in unipolar depression. *Journal of Psychiatric Research*, *41*(6), 511–522. https://doi.org/10.1016/j.jpsychires.2006.07.020

Abramowitz, J. S., Deacon, B. J., & Whiteside, S. P. (2019). *Exposure therapy for anxiety: Principles and practice*. Guilford Press.

AbuHasan, Q., & Reddy, V. (n.d.). *STATPearls: Neuroanatomy, amygdala* (W. Siddiqui, Ed.). Retrieved 9/20/2020 from https://www.statpearls.com/articlelibrary/viewarticle/17489/

Adhikari, A., Lerner, T. N., Finkelstein, J., Pak, S., Jennings, J. H., Davidson, T. J., Ferenczi, E., Gunaydin, L. A., Mirzabekov, J. J., Ye, L., Kim, S.-Y., Lei, A. & Deisseroth, K. (2015). Basomedial amygdala mediates top-down control of anxiety and fear. *Nature*, *527*(7577), 179–185. https://doi.org/10.1038/nature15698

Adolphs, R., Gosselin, F., Buchanan, T. W., Tranel, D., Schyns, P., & Damasio, A. R. (2005). A mechanism for impaired fear recognition after amygdala damage. *Nature*, *433*(7021), 68–72. https://doi.org/10.1038/nature03086

Åhs, F., Pissiota, A., Michelgård, A., Frans, O., Furmark, T., Appel, L., & Fredrikson, M. (2009). Disentangling the web of fear: Amygdala reactivity and functional connectivity in spider and snake phobia. *Psychiatry Research*, *172*(2), 103–108. https://doi.org/10.1016/j.pscychresns.2008.11.004

Amaral, D. G. (2002). The primate amygdala and the neurobiology of social behavior: Implications for understanding social anxiety. *Biological Psychiatry*, *51*(1), 11–17. https://doi.org/10.1016/s0006-3223(01)01307-5

Amunts, K., Kedo, O., Kindler, M., Pieperhoff, P., Mohlberg, H., Shah, N. J., Habel, U., Schneider, F., & Zilles, K. (2005). Cytoarchitectonic mapping of the human amygdala, hippocampal region and entorhinal cortex: Intersubject variability and probability maps. *Anatomy and Embryology*, *210*(5–6), 343–352. https://doi.org/10.1007/s00429-005-0025-5

Arshamian, A., Iannilli, E., Gerber, J. C., Willander, J., Persson, J., Seo, H.-S., Hummel, T., & Larsson, M. (2013). The functional neuroanatomy of odor evoked autobiographical memories cued by odors and words. *Neuropsychologia*, *51*(1), 123–131.

Baars, B. J., & Gage, N. M. (2010). *Cognition, brain, and consciousness: Introduction to cognitive neuroscience*. Academic Press.

Baczkowski, B. M., van Zutphen, L., Siep, N., Jacob, G. A., Domes, G., Maier, S., Sprenger, A., Senft, A., Willenborg, B., Tüscher, O., Arntz, A., & van de Ven, V. (2017). Deficient amygdala–prefrontal intrinsic connectivity after effortful emotion regulation in borderline personality disorder. *European Archives of Psychiatry and Clinical Neuroscience*, *267*(6), 551–565. https://doi.org/10.1007/s00406-016-0760-z

Badura-Brack, A., McDermott, T. J., Heinrichs-Graham, E., Ryan, T. J., Khanna, M. M., Pine, D. S., Bar-Haim, Y., & Wilson, T. W. (2018). Veterans with PTSD demonstrate amygdala hyperactivity while viewing threatening faces: A MEG study. *Biological Psychology, 132,* 228–232. https://doi .org/10.1016/j.biopsycho.2018.01.005

Baird, A. D., Wilson, S. J., Bladin, P. F., Saling, M. M., & Reutens, D. C. (2004). The amygdala and sexual drive: Insights from temporal lobe epilepsy surgery. *Annals of Neurology, 55*(1), 87–96. https:// doi.org/10.1002/ana.10997

Becker, B., Mihov, Y., Scheele, D., Kendrick, K. M., Feinstein, J. S., Matusch, A., Aydin, M., Reich, H., Urbach, H., Oros-Peusquens, A.-M., Shah, N. J., Kunz, W. S., Schlaepfer, T. E., Zilles, K., Maier, W., & Hurlemann, R. (2012). Fear processing and social networking in the absence of a functional amygdala. *Biological Psychiatry, 72*(1), 70–77. https://doi.org/10.1016/j.biopsych.2011.11.024

Birbaumer, N., Veit, R., Lotze, M., Erb, M., Hermann, C., Grodd, W., & Flor, H. (2005). Deficient fear conditioning in psychopathy: A functional magnetic resonance imaging study. *Archives of General Psychiatry, 62*(7), 799–805. https://doi.org/10.1001/archpsyc.62.7.799

Blair, R. J. R. (2006). *Subcortical brain systems in psychopathy: The amygdala and associated structures.* In C. J. Patrick (Ed.), *Handbook of psychopathy* (pp. 296–312). The Guilford Press.

Blair, R. J. R. (2012). Considering anger from a cognitive neuroscience perspective. *Wiley Interdisciplinary Reviews. Cognitive Science, 3*(1), 65–74. https://doi.org/10.1002/wcs.154

Brabec, J., Rulseh, A., Hoyt, B., Vizek, M., Horinek, D., Hort, J., & Petrovicky, P. (2010). Volumetry of the human amygdala—An anatomical study. *Psychiatry Research: Neuroimaging, 182*(1), 67–72. https://doi.org/10.1016/j.pscychresns.2009.11.005

Brashers-Krug, T., & Jorge, R. (2015). Bi-directional tuning of amygdala sensitivity in combat veterans investigated with fMRI. *PLOS ONE, 10*(6), e0130246. https://doi.org/10.1371/journal.pone .0130246

Breiter, H. C., & Rauch, S. L. (1996). Functional MRI and the study of OCD: From symptom provocation to cognitive-behavioral probes of cortico-striatal systems and the amygdala. *NeuroImage, 4*(3), S127–S138. https://doi.org/10.1006/nimg.1996.0063

Brinkmann, L., Buff, C., Neumeister, P., Tupak, S. V., Becker, M. P., Herrmann, M. J., & Straube, T. (2017). Dissociation between amygdala and bed nucleus of the stria terminalis during threat anticipation in female post-traumatic stress disorder patients. *Human Brain Mapping, 38*(4), 2190–2205. https://doi.org/10.1002/hbm.23513

Brunetti, M., Sepede, G., Mingoia, G., Catani, C., Ferretti, A., Merla, A., Del Gratta, C., Romani, G. L., & Babiloni, C. (2010). Elevated response of human amygdala to neutral stimuli in mild post traumatic stress disorder: Neural correlates of generalized emotional response. *Neuroscience, 168*(3), 670–679. https://doi.org/10.1016/j.neuroscience.2010.04.024

Buckley, T., Punkanen, M., & Ogden, P. (2018). The role of the body in fostering resilience: A Sensorimotor Psychotherapy perspective. *Body, Movement and Dance in Psychotherapy, 13*(4), 225–233. https://doi.org/10.1080/17432979.2018.1467344

Cadeddu, R., Ibba, M., Sadile, A., & Carboni, E. (2014). Antidepressants share the ability to increase catecholamine output in the bed nucleus of stria terminalis: A possible role in antidepressant therapy? *Psychopharmacology, 231*(9), 1925–1933. https://doi.org/10.1007/s00213-013-3335-y

Carr, L., Iacoboni, M., Dubeau, M. C., Mazziotta, J. C., & Lenzi, G. L. (2003). Neural mechanisms of empathy in humans: A relay from neural systems for imitation to limbic areas. *Proceedings of the National Academy of Sciences, 100*(9), 5497–5502. https://doi.org/10.1073/pnas.0935845100

Cheng, W., Rolls, E. T., Qiu, J., Xie, X., Lyu, W., Li, Y., Huang, C.-C., Yang, A. C., Tsai, S.-J., Lyu, F., Zhuang, K., Lin, C.-P., Xie, P., & Feng, J. (2018). Functional connectivity of the human amygdala in health and in depression. *Social Cognitive and Affective Neuroscience, 13*(6), 557–568. https:// doi.org/10.1093/scan/nsy032

Connolly, C. G., Ho, T. C., Blom, E. H., LeWinn, K. Z., Sacchet, M. D., Tymofiyeva, O., Simmons, A. N., & Yang, T. T. (2017). Resting-state functional connectivity of the amygdala and longitudinal changes in depression severity in adolescent depression. *Journal of Affective Disorders, 207,* 86–94. https://doi.org/10.1016/j.jad.2016.09.026

Cozzoli, D. K., Courson, J., Rostock, C., Campbell, R. R., Wroten, M. G., McGregor, H., Caruana, A. L., Miller, B. W., Hu, J.-H., Zhang, P. W., Xiao, B., Worley, P. F., Crabbe, J. C., Finn, D. A., & Szumlinski, K. K. (2016). Protein kinase C epsilon activity in the nucleus accumbens and central nucleus of the amygdala mediates binge alcohol consumption. *Biological Psychiatry, 79*(6), 443–451. https://doi.org/10.1016/j.biopsych.2015.01.019

Daldrup, T., Lesting, J., Meuth, P., Seidenbecher, T., & Pape, H. C. (2016). Neuronal correlates of sustained fear in the anterolateral part of the bed nucleus of stria terminalis. *Neurobiology of Learning and Memory, 131*, 137–146. https://doi.org/10.1016/j.nlm.2016.03.020

Davis, M., Walker, D. L., Miles, L., & Grillon, C. (2010). Phasic vs sustained fear in rats and humans: Role of the extended amygdala in fear vs anxiety. *Neuropsychopharmacology, 35*(1), 105–135. https://doi.org/10.1038/npp.2009.109

De Martino, B., Camerer, C. F., & Adolphs, R. (2010). Amygdala damage eliminates monetary loss aversion. *Proceedings of the National Academy of Sciences, 107*(8), 3788–3792.

De Raedt, R. (2006). Does neuroscience hold promise for the further development of behavior therapy? The case of emotional change after exposure in anxiety and depression. *Scandinavian Journal of Psychology, 47*(3), 225–236. https://doi.org/10.1111/j.1467-9450.2006.00511.x

Decety, J., & Jackson, P. L. (2004). The functional architecture of human empathy. *Behavioral and cognitive neuroscience reviews, 3*(2), 71–100.

Desbordes, G., Negi, L. T., Pace, T. W., Wallace, B. A., Raison, C. L., & Schwartz, E. L. (2012). Effects of mindful-attention and compassion meditation training on amygdala response to emotional stimuli in an ordinary, non-meditative state. *Frontiers in Human Neuroscience, 6*, 292. https://doi.org/10.3389/fnhum.2012.00292

Dichter, G. S., Gibbs, D., & Smoski, M. J. (2015). A systematic review of relations between resting-state functional-MRI and treatment response in major depressive disorder. *Journal of Affective Disorders, 172*, 8–17. https://doi.org/10.1016/j.jad.2014.09.028

Dilger, S., Straube, T., Mentzel, H. J., Fitzek, C., Reichenbach, J. R., Hecht, H., Krieschel, S., Gutberlet, I., Miltner, W. H. (2003). Brain activation to phobia-related pictures in spider phobic humans: An event-related functional magnetic resonance imaging study. *Neuroscience Letters, 348*(1), 29–32. https://doi.org/10.1016/s0304-3940(03)00647-5

Doll, A., Hölzel, B. K., Mulej Bratec, S. M., Boucard, C. C., Xie, X., Wohlschläger, A. M., & Sorg, C. (2016). Mindful attention to breath regulates emotions via increased amygdala–prefrontal cortex connectivity. *NeuroImage, 134*, 305–313. https://doi.org/10.1016/j.neuroimage.2016.03.041

Draaisma, D. (2000). *Metaphors of memory: A history of ideas about the mind.* University Press.

Dresler, T., Hahn, T., Plichta, M. M., Ernst, L. H., Tupak, S. V., Ehlis, A. C., Warrings, B., Deckert, J., & Fallgatter, A. J. (2011). Neural correlates of spontaneous panic attacks. *Journal of Neural Transmission, 118*(2), 263–269. https://doi.org/10.1007/s00702-010-0540-2

Dunbar, R. I. (2012). The social brain meets neuroimaging. *Trends in Cognitive Sciences, 16*(2), 101–102. https://doi.org/10.1016/j.tics.2011.11.013

Duvernoy, H. M. (2013). *The human hippocampus: an atlas of applied anatomy.* JF Bergmann-Verlag.

El Khoury-Malhame, M., Reynaud, E., Soriano, A., Michael, K., Salgado-Pineda, P., Zendjidjian, X., Gellato, C., Eric, F., Lefebvre, M.-N., Rouby, F., Samuelian, J.-C., Anton, J.-L., Blin, O., & Khalfa, S. (2011). Amygdala activity correlates with attentional bias in PTSD. *Neuropsychologia, 49*(7), 1969–1973. https://doi.org/10.1016/j.neuropsychologia.2011.03.025

Eren, İ., Tükel, R., Polat, A., Karaman, R., & Ünal, S. (2003). Evaluation of regional cerebral blood flow changes in panic disorder with Tc99m-HMPAO SPECT. *Psychiatry Research: Neuroimaging, 123*(2), 135–143. https://doi.org/10.1016/S0925-4927(03)00062-3

Etkin, A., & Wager, T. D. (2007). Functional neuroimaging of anxiety: A meta-analysis of emotional processing in PTSD, social anxiety disorder, and specific phobia. *American Journal of Psychiatry, 164*(10), 1476–1488. https://doi.org/10.1176/appi.ajp.2007.07030504

Felmingham, K. L., Falconer, E. M., Williams, L., Kemp, A. H., Allen, A., Peduto, A., & Bryant, R. A. (2014). Reduced amygdala and ventral striatal activity to happy faces in PTSD is associated with emotional numbing. *PLOS ONE, 9*(9), e103653. https://doi.org/10.1371/journal.pone.0103653

File, S. E., Gonzalez, L. E., & Gallant, R. (1998). Role of the basolateral nucleus of the amygdala in the formation of a phobia. *Neuropsychopharmacology, 19*(5), 397–405. https://doi.org/10.1016/S0893-133X(98)00035-9

Forster, G. L., Novick, A. M., Scholl, J. L., & Watt, M. J. (2012). The role of the amygdala in anxiety disorders. In B. Ferry (Ed.), *The Amygdala: A Discrete Multitasking Manager* (pp. 61–102). InTech. https://doi.org/10.5772/50323

Forster, G. L., Simons, R. M., & Baugh, L. A. (2017). Revisiting the role of the amygdala in posttraumatic stress disorder. In B. Ferry (Ed.), *The Amygdala: Where Emotions Shape Perception, Learning and Memories* (pp. 113–136). InTech. https://doi.org/10.5772/67585

Fulwiler, C. E., King, J. A., & Zhang, N. (2012). Amygdala-orbitofrontal resting-state functional connectivity is associated with trait anger. *NeuroReport, 23*(10), 606–610. https://doi.org/10.1097/WNR.0b013e3283551cfc

Garrido, M. I., Barnes, G. R., Sahani, M., & Dolan, R. J. (2012). Functional evidence for a dual route to amygdala. *Current Biology, 22*(2), 129–134. https://doi.org/10.1016/j.cub.2011.11.056

Gerritsen, L., Rijpkema, M., van Oostrom, I., Buitelaar, J., Franke, B., Fernández, G., & Tendolkar, I. (2012). Amygdala to hippocampal volume ratio is associated with negative memory bias in healthy subjects. *Psychological Medicine, 42*(2), 335–343. https://doi.org/10.1017/S003329171100122X

Goerlich-Dobre, K. S., Lamm, C., Pripfl, J., Habel, U., & Votinov, M. (2015). The left amygdala: A shared substrate of alexithymia and empathy. *NeuroImage, 122*, 20–32. https://doi.org/10.1016/j.neuroimage.2015.08.014

Gorno-Tempini, M. L., Pradelli, S., Serafini, M., Pagnoni, G., Baraldi, P., Porro, C., Nicoletti, R., Umità, C., & Nichelli, P. (2001). Explicit and incidental facial expression processing: An fMRI study. *NeuroImage, 14*(2), 465–473. https://doi.org/10.1006/nimg.2001.0811

Gotink, R. A., Meijboom, R., Vernooij, M. W., Smits, M., & Hunink, M. G. (2016). 8-week mindfulness based stress reduction induces brain changes similar to traditional long-term meditation practice– a systematic review. *Brain and Cognition, 108*, 32–41. https://doi.org/10.1016/j.bandc.2016.07.001

Grabenhorst, F., Báez-Mendoza, R., Genest, W., Deco, G., & Schultz, W. (2019). Primate amygdala neurons simulate decision processes of social partners. *Cell, 177*(4), 986–998.e15. https://doi.org/10.1016/j.cell.2019.02.042

Greenberg, T., Carlson, J. M., Cha, J., Hajcak, G., & Mujica-Parodi, L. R. (2013). Ventromedial prefrontal cortex reactivity is altered in generalized anxiety disorder during fear generalization. *Depression and Anxiety, 30*(3), 242–250. https://doi.org/10.1002/da.22016

Harmer, C. J., Mackay, C. E., Reid, C. B., Cowen, P. J., & Goodwin, G. M. (2006). Antidepressant drug treatment modifies the neural processing of nonconscious threat cues. *Biological Psychiatry, 59*(9), 816–820. https://doi.org/10.1016/j.biopsych.2005.10.015

Harper, M. (2012). Taming the amygdala: An EEG analysis of exposure therapy for the traumatized. *Traumatology, 18*(2), 61–74. https://doi.org/10.1177/1534765611429082

Hauner, K. K., Mineka, S., Voss, J. L., & Paller, K. A. (2012). Exposure therapy triggers lasting reorganization of neural fear processing. *Proceedings of the National Academy of Sciences, 109*(23), 9203–9208.

Hayano, F., Nakamura, M., Asami, T., Uehara, K., Yoshida, T., Roppongi, T., Otsuka, T., Inoue, T., & Hirayasu, Y. (2009). Smaller amygdala is associated with anxiety in patients with panic disorder. *Psychiatry and Clinical Neurosciences, 63*(3), 266–276. https://doi.org/10.1111/j.1440-1819.2009.01960.x

Hayes, J. P., LaBar, K. S., McCarthy, G., Selgrade, E., Nasser, J., & Dolcos, F. (2011). Reduced hippocampal and amygdala activity predicts memory distortions for trauma reminders in combat-related PTSD. *Journal of Psychiatric Research, 45*(5), 660–669. https://doi.org/10.1016/j.jpsychires.2010.10.007

Hayes, J. P., Vanelzakker, M. B., & Shin, L. M. (2012). Emotion and cognition interactions in PTSD: A review of neurocognitive and neuroimaging studies. *Frontiers in Integrative Neuroscience, 6,* 89. https://doi.org/10.3389/fnint.2012.00089

Hendler, T., Rotshtein, P., Yeshurun, Y., Weizmann, T., Kahn, I., Ben-Bashat, D., Malach, R., & Bleich, A. (2003). Sensing the invisible: Differential sensitivity of visual cortex and amygdala to traumatic context. *NeuroImage, 19*(3), 587–600. https://doi.org/10.1016/s1053-8119(03)00141-1

Hill, S. Y., De Bellis, M. D., Keshavan, M. S., Lowers, L., Shen, S., Hall, J., & Pitts, T. (2001). Right amygdala volume in adolescent and young adult offspring from families at high risk for developing alcoholism. *Biological Psychiatry, 49*(11), 894–905. https://doi.org/10.1016/S0006-3223(01)01088-5

Holmes, A. J., Lee, P. H., Hollinshead, M. O., Bakst, L., Roffman, J. L., Smoller, J. W., & Buckner, R. L. (2012). Individual differences in amygdala-medial prefrontal anatomy link negative affect, impaired social functioning, and polygenic depression risk. *Journal of Neuroscience, 32*(50), 18087–18100. https://doi.org/10.1523/JNEUROSCI.2531-12.2012

Hölzel, B. K., Hoge, E. A., Greve, D. N., Gard, T., Creswell, J. D., Brown, K. W., . . . & Lazar, S. W. (2013). Neural mechanisms of symptom improvements in generalized anxiety disorder following mindfulness training. *NeuroImage: Clinical, 2,* 448–458.

Hyde, L. W., Byrd, A. L., Votruba-Drzal, E., Hariri, A. R., & Manuck, S. B. (2014). Amygdala reactivity and negative emotionality: Divergent correlates of antisocial personality and psychopathy traits in a community sample. *Journal of Abnormal Psychology, 123*(1), 214–224. https://doi.org/10.1037/a0035467

Jalbrzikowski, M., Larsen, B., Hallquist, M. N., Foran, W., Calabro, F., & Luna, B. (2017). Development of white matter microstructure and intrinsic functional connectivity between the amygdala and ventromedial prefrontal cortex: Associations with anxiety and depression. *Biological Psychiatry, 82*(7), 511–521. https://doi.org/10.1016/j.biopsych.2017.01.008

Kim, D. K., Rhee, J. H., & Kang, S. W. (2014). Reorganization of the brain and heart rhythm during autogenic meditation. *Frontiers in Integrative Neuroscience, 7,* 109. https://doi.org/10.3389/fnint.2013.00109

Kohl, S., Baldermann, J. C., & Kuhn, J. (2016). The bed nucleus: A future hot spot in obsessive compulsive disorder research? *Molecular Psychiatry, 21*(8), 990–991. https://doi.org/10.1038/mp.2016.54

Lanius, R. A., Vermetten, E., Loewenstein, R. J., Brand, B., Schmahl, C., Bremner, J. D., & Spiegel, D. (2010). Emotion modulation in PTSD: Clinical and neurobiological evidence for a dissociative subtype. *American Journal of Psychiatry, 167*(6), 640–647. https://doi.org/10.1176/appi.ajp.2009.09081168

Lanteaume, L., Khalfa, S., Régis, J., Marquis, P., Chauvel, P., & Bartolomei, F. (2007). Emotion induction after direct intracerebral stimulations of human amygdala. *Cerebral Cortex, 17*(6), 1307–1313. https://doi.org/10.1093/cercor/bhl041

Laugharne, J., Kullack, C., Lee, C. W., McGuire, T., Brockman, S., Drummond, P. D., & Starkstein, S. (2016). Amygdala volumetric change following psychotherapy for posttraumatic stress disorder. *Journal of Neuropsychiatry and Clinical Neurosciences, 28*(4), 312–318. https://doi.org/10.1176/appi.neuropsych.16010006

LeDoux, J. (2007). The amygdala. *Current Biology, 17*(20), R868–R874. https://doi.org/10.1016/j.cub.2007.08.005

Leigh, R., Oishi, K., Hsu, J., Lindquist, M., Gottesman, R. F., Jarso, S., Crainiceanu, C., Mori, S., & Hillis, A. E. (2013). Acute lesions that impair affective empathy. *Brain, 136*(8), 2539–2549. https://doi.org/10.1093/brain/awt177

Lesting, J., Narayanan, R. T., Kluge, C., Sangha, S., Seidenbecher, T., & Pape, H. C. (2011). Patterns of coupled theta activity in amygdala-hippocampal-prefrontal cortical circuits during fear extinction. *PloS One, 6*(6), e21714. https://doi.org/10.1371/journal.pone.0021714

Leung, M. K., Lau, W. K. W., Chan, C. C. H., Wong, S. S. Y., Fung, A. L. C., & Lee, T. M. C. (2018). Meditation-induced neuroplastic changes in amygdala activity during negative affective processing. *Social Neuroscience, 13*(3), 277–288. https://doi.org/10.1080/17470919.2017.1311939

Li, G., Liu, P., Andari, E., Zhang, A., & Zhang, K. (2018). The role of amygdala in patients with euthymic bipolar disorder during resting state. *Frontiers in psychiatry*, 9, 445.

Likhtik, E., Stujenske, J. M., Topiwala, M. A., Harris, A. Z., & Gordon, J. A. (2014). Prefrontal entrainment of amygdala activity signals safety in learned fear and innate anxiety. *Nature Neuroscience*, 17(1), 106–113. https://doi.org/10.1038/nn.3582

Liu, J., Fang, J., Wang, Z., Rong, P., Hong, Y., Fan, Y., Wang, X., Park, J., Jin, Y., Liu, C., Zhu, B., & Kong, J. (2016). Transcutaneous vagus nerve stimulation modulates amygdala functional connectivity in patients with depression. *Journal of Affective Disorders*, 205, 319–326. https://doi.org/10.1016/j.jad.2016.08.003

Marchand, W. R. (2014). Neural mechanisms of mindfulness and meditation: Evidence from neuroimaging studies. *World Journal of Radiology*, 6(7), 471–479. https://doi.org/10.4329/wjr.v6.i7.471

Marsh, A. A., Finger, E. C., Fowler, K. A., Adalio, C. J., Jurkowitz, I. T., Schechter, J. C., Pine, D. S., Decety, J., & Blair, R. J. R. (2013). Empathic responsiveness in amygdala and anterior cingulate cortex in youths with psychopathic traits. *Journal of Child Psychology and Psychiatry, and Allied Disciplines*, 54(8), 900–910. https://doi.org/10.1111/jcpp.12063

McEwen, B. S. (2003). Mood disorders and allostatic load. *Biological Psychiatry*, 54(3), 200–207. https://doi.org/10.1016/s0006-3223(03)00177-x

McLaughlin, K. A., Busso, D. S., Duys, A., Green, J. G., Alves, S., Way, M., & Sheridan, M. A. (2014). Amygdala response to negative stimuli predicts PTSD symptom onset following a terrorist attack. *Depression and Anxiety*, 31(10), 834–842. https://doi.org/10.1002/da.22284

McNally, R. J. (2007). Mechanisms of exposure therapy: How neuroscience can improve psychological treatments for anxiety disorders. *Clinical Psychology Review*, 27(6), 750–759. https://doi.org/10.1016/j.cpr.2007.01.003

Milad, M. R., Orr, S. P., Lasko, N. B., Chang, Y., Rauch, S. L., & Pitman, R. K. (2008). Presence and acquired origin of reduced recall for fear extinction in PTSD: Results of a twin study. *Journal of Psychiatric Research*, 42(7), 515–520. https://doi.org/10.1016/j.jpsychires.2008.01.017

Mineka, S., & Thomas, C. (1999). *Mechanisms of change in exposure therapy for anxiety disorders.* In T. Dalgleish & M. J. Power (Eds.), *Handbook of cognition and emotion* (pp. 747–764). John Wiley & Sons Ltd. https://doi.org/10.1002/0470013494.ch35

Morey, R. A., Dolcos, F., Petty, C. M., Cooper, D. A., Hayes, J. P., LaBar, K. S., & McCarthy, G. (2009). The role of trauma-related distractors on neural systems for working memory and emotion processing in posttraumatic stress disorder. *Journal of Psychiatric Research*, 43(8), 809–817. https://doi.org/10.1016/j.jpsychires.2008.10.014

Murray, E. A., Izquierdo, A., & Malkova, L. (2009). *Amygdala function in positive reinforcement: Contributions from studies of nonhuman primates.* Guilford Press.

Murrough, J. W., Huang, Y., Hu, J., Henry, S., Williams, W., Gallezot, J. D., Bailey, C. R., Krystal, J. H., Carson, R. E., & Neumeister, A. (2011). Reduced amygdala serotonin transporter binding in posttraumatic stress disorder. *Biological Psychiatry*, 70(11), 1033–1038. https://doi.org/10.1016/j.biopsych.2011.07.003

Narayanan, N. S., Horst, N. K., & Laubach, M. (2006). Reversible inactivations of rat medial prefrontal cortex impair the ability to wait for a stimulus. *Neuroscience*, 139(3), 865–876. https://doi.org/10.1016/j.neuroscience.2005.11.072

Pagani, M., Högberg, G., Fernandez, I., & Siracusano, A. (2013). Correlates of EMDR therapy in functional and structural neuroimaging: A critical summary of recent findings. *Journal of EMDR Practice and Research*, 7(1), 29–38. https://doi.org/10.1891/1933-3196.7.1.29

Payne, P., Levine, P. A., & Crane-Godreau, M. A. (2015). Somatic experiencing: Using interoception and proprioception as core elements of trauma therapy. *Frontiers in Psychology*, 6, 93. https://doi.org/10.3389/fpsyg.2015.00093

Pelrine, E., Pasik, S. D., Bayat, L., Goldschmiedt, D., & Bauer, E. P. (2016). 5-HT2C receptors in the BNST are necessary for the enhancement of fear learning by selective serotonin reuptake inhibitors. *Neurobiology of learning and memory*, 136, 189–195.

Perlman, W. R., Webster, M. J., Kleinman, J. E., & Weickert, C. S. (2004). Reduced glucocorticoid and estrogen receptor alpha messenger ribonucleic acid levels in the amygdala of patients with major mental illness. *Biological Psychiatry*, 56(11), 844–852. https://doi.org/10.1016/j.biopsych.2004.09.006

Pessoa, L., & Adolphs, R. (2010). Emotion processing and the amygdala: From a "low road" to "many roads" of evaluating biological significance. *Nature Reviews Neuroscience*, 11(11), 773–783. https://doi.org/10.1038/nrn2920

Pfeifer, J. H., Iacoboni, M., Mazziotta, J. C., & Dapretto, M. (2008). Mirroring others' emotions relates to empathy and interpersonal competence in children. *NeuroImage*, 39(4), 2076–2085. https://doi.org/10.1016/j.neuroimage.2007.10.032

Pfleiderer, B., Zinkirciran, S., Arolt, V., Heindel, W., Deckert, J., & Domschke, K. (2007). fMRI amygdala activation during a spontaneous panic attack in a patient with panic disorder. *World Journal of Biological Psychiatry*, 8(4), 269–272. https://doi.org/10.1080/15622970701216673

Phan, K. L., Britton, J. C., Taylor, S. F., Fig, L. M., & Liberzon, I. (2006). Corticolimbic blood flow during nontraumatic emotional processing in posttraumatic stress disorder. *Archives of General Psychiatry*, 63(2), 184–192. https://doi.org/10.1001/archpsyc.63.2.184

Phelps, E. A., & LeDoux, J. E. (2005). Contributions of the amygdala to emotion processing: From animal models to human behavior. *Neuron*, 48(2), 175–187. https://doi.org/10.1016/j.neuron.2005.09.025

Rajmohan, V., & Mohandas, E. (2007). The limbic system. *Indian Journal of Psychiatry*, 49(2), 132–139. https://doi.org/10.4103/0019-5545.33264

Redlich, R., Bürger, C., Dohm, K., Grotegerd, D., Opel, N., Zaremba, D., Meinert, S., Förster, K., Repple, J., Schnelle, R., Wagenknecht, C., Zavorotnyy, M., Heindel, W., Kugel, H., Gerbaulet, M., Alferink, J., Arolt, V., Zwanzger, P., & Dannlowski, U. (2017). Effects of electroconvulsive therapy on amygdala function in major depression – a longitudinal functional magnetic resonance imaging study. *Psychological Medicine*, 47(12), 2166–2176. https://doi.org/10.1017/S0033291717000605

Roy, M. J., Costanzo, M. E., Blair, J. R., & Rizzo, A. A. (2014). Compelling evidence that exposure therapy for PTSD normalizes brain function. *Studies in Health Technology and Informatics*, 199, 61–65.

Salamon, E., Esch, T., & Stefano, G. B. (2005). Role of amygdala in mediating sexual and emotional behavior via coupled nitric oxide release. *Acta Pharmacologica Sinica*, 26(4), 389–395. https://doi.org/10.1111/j.1745-7254.2005.00083.x

Schade, S., & Paulus, W. (2016). D-cycloserine in neuropsychiatric diseases: A systematic review. *International Journal of Neuropsychopharmacology*, 19(4). https://doi.org/10.1093/ijnp/pyv102

Schafe, G. E., Atkins, C. M., Swank, M. W., Bauer, E. P., Sweatt, J. D., & LeDoux, J. E. (2000). Activation of ERK/MAP kinase in the amygdala is required for memory consolidation of Pavlovian fear conditioning. *Journal of Neuroscience*, 20(21), 8177–8187. https://doi.org/10.1523/JNEUROSCI.20-21-08177.2000

Shamay-Tsoory, S. G., Tomer, R., Berger, B. D., & Aharon-Peretz, J. (2003). Characterization of empathy deficits following prefrontal brain damage: the role of the right ventromedial prefrontal cortex. *Journal of cognitive neuroscience*, 15(3), 324–337.

Schneider, F., Weiss, U., Kessler, C., Müller-Gärtner, H. W., Posse, S., Salloum, J. B., Grodd, W., Himmelmann, F., Gaebel, W., & Birbaumer, N. (1999). Subcortical correlates of differential classical conditioning of aversive emotional reactions in social phobia. *Biological Psychiatry*, 45(7), 863–871. https://doi.org/10.1016/s0006-3223(98)00269-8

Schumann, C. M., Bauman, M. D., & Amaral, D. G. (2011). Abnormal structure or function of the amygdala is a common component of neurodevelopmental disorders. *Neuropsychologia*, 49(4), 745–759. https://doi.org/10.1016/j.neuropsychologia.2010.09.028

Shou, H., Yang, Z., Satterthwaite, T. D., Cook, P. A., Bruce, S. E., Shinohara, R. T., Rosenberg, B., & Sheline, Y. I. (2017). Cognitive behavioral therapy increases amygdala connectivity with the cognitive control network in both MDD and PTSD. *NeuroImage: Clinical*, 14, 464–470. https://doi.org/10.1016/j.nicl.2017.01.030

Siegle, G. J., Thompson, W., Carter, C. S., Steinhauer, S. R., & Thase, M. E. (2007). Increased amygdala and decreased dorsolateral prefrontal BOLD responses in unipolar depression: Related and independent features. *Biological Psychiatry, 61*(2), 198–209. https://doi.org/10.1016/j.biopsych.2006.05.048

Simon, D., Adler, N., Kaufmann, C., & Kathmann, N. (2014). Amygdala hyperactivation during symptom provocation in obsessive–compulsive disorder and its modulation by distraction. *NeuroImage: Clinical, 4*, 549–557. https://doi.org/10.1016/j.nicl.2014.03.011

Stamatakis, A. M., Sparta, D. R., Jennings, J. H., McElligott, Z. A., Decot, H., & Stuber, G. D. (2014). Amygdala and bed nucleus of the stria terminalis circuitry: Implications for addiction-related behaviors. *Neuropharmacology, 76*(B), 320–328. https://doi.org/10.1016/j.neuropharm.2013.05.046

Stein, M. B., & Leslie, W. D. (1996). A brain single photon-emission computed tomography (SPECT) study of generalized social phobia. *Biological Psychiatry, 39*(9), 825–828. https://doi.org/10.1016/0006-3223(95)00570-6

Stone, V. E., Baron-Cohen, S., Calder, A., Keane, J., & Young, A. (2003). Acquired theory of mind impairments in individuals with bilateral amygdala lesions. *Neuropsychologia, 41*(2), 209–220. https://doi.org/10.1016/s0028-3932(02)00151-3

Straube, T. (2016). Effects of psychotherapy on brain activation patterns in anxiety disorders. *Zeitschrift für Psychologie, 224*(2), 62–70. https://doi.org/10.1027/2151-2604/a000240

Suslow, T., Konrad, C., Kugel, H., Rumstadt, D., Zwitserlood, P., Schöning, S., Ohrmann, P., Bauer, J., Pyka, M., Kersting, A., Arolt, V., Heindel, W., & Dannlowski, U. (2010). Automatic mood-congruent amygdala responses to masked facial expressions in major depression. *Biological Psychiatry, 67*(2), 155–160. https://doi.org/10.1016/j.biopsych.2009.07.023

Swanson, L. W., & Petrovich, G. D. (1998). What is the amygdala? *Trends in Neurosciences, 21*(8), 323–331. https://doi.org/10.1016/s0166-2236(98)01265-x

Swartz, J. R., Wiggins, J. L., Carrasco, M., Lord, C., & Monk, C. S. (2013). Amygdala habituation and prefrontal functional connectivity in youth with autism spectrum disorders. *Journal of the American Academy of Child and Adolescent Psychiatry, 52*(1), 84–93. https://doi.org/10.1016/j.jaac.2012.10.012

Szeszko, P. R., Robinson, D., Alvir, J. M. J., Bilder, R. M., Lencz, T., Ashtari, M., Wu, H., & Bogerts, B. (1999). Orbital frontal and amygdala volume reductions in obsessive–compulsive disorder. *Archives of General Psychiatry, 56*(10), 913–919. https://doi.org/10.1001/archpsyc.56.10.913

Taren, A. A., Gianaros, P. J., Greco, C. M., Lindsay, E. K., Fairgrieve, A., Brown, K. W., Rosen, R. K., Ferris, J. L., Julson, E., Marsland, A. L., Bursley, J. K., Ramsburg, J., & Creswell, J. D. (2015). Mindfulness meditation training alters stress-related amygdala resting state functional connectivity: A randomized controlled trial. *Social Cognitive and Affective Neuroscience, 10*(12), 1758–1768. https://doi.org/10.1093/scan/nsv066

Tillfors, M., Furmark, T., Marteinsdottir, I., Fischer, H., Pissiota, A., Långström, B., & Fredrikson, M. (2001). Cerebral blood flow in subjects with social phobia during stressful speaking tasks: A PET study. *American Journal of Psychiatry, 158*(8), 1220–1226. https://doi.org/10.1176/appi.ajp.158.8.1220

Tottenham, N., Hare, T. A., Quinn, B. T., McCarry, T. W., Nurse, M., & Gilhooly, T. (2010). Prolonged institutional rearing is associated with atypically large amygdala volume and difficulties in emotion regulation. *Developmental Science, 13*(1), 46–61. https://doi.org/10.1111/j.1467-7687.2009.00852.x

Tuescher, O., Protopopescu, X., Pan, H., Cloitre, M., Butler, T., Goldstein, M., Root, J. C., Engelien, A., Yang, Y., Gorman, J., LeDoux, J., Silbersweig, D., & Stern, E. (2011). Differential activity of subgenual cingulate and brainstem in panic disorder and PTSD. *Journal of Anxiety Disorders, 25*(2), 251–257. https://doi.org/10.1016/j.janxdis.2010.09.010

Van der Kolk, B. A. (2015). *The body keeps the score: Brain, mind, and body in the healing of trauma.* Penguin Books.

Wackerhagen, C., Veer, I. M., Erk, S., Mohnke, S., Lett, T. A., Wüstenberg, T., Romanczuk-Seiferth, N. Y., Schwarz, K., Schweiger, J. I., Tost, H., Meyer-Lindenberg, A., Heinz, A., & Walter, H. (2019). Amygdala functional connectivity in major depression - disentangling markers of pathology, risk and resilience. *Psychological Medicine*, 50(16), 2740–2750. https://doi.org/10.1017/S0033291719002885

Walhovd, K. B., Fjell, A. M., Reinvang, I., Lundervold, A., Dale, A. M., Eilertsen, D. E., Quinn, B. T., Salat, D., Makris, N., & Fischl, B. (2005). Effects of age on volumes of cortex, white matter and subcortical structures. *Neurobiology of Aging*, 26(9), 1261–1270; discussion 1275. https://doi.org/10.1016/j.neurobiolaging.2005.05.020

Wang, X., Wang, Z., Liu, J., Chen, J., Liu, X., Nie, G., Byun, J.-S., Liang, Y., Park, J., Huang, R., Liu, M., Liu, B., & Kong, J. (2016). Repeated acupuncture treatments modulate amygdala resting state functional connectivity of depressive patients. *NeuroImage: Clinical*, 12, 746–752. https://doi.org/10.1016/j.nicl.2016.07.011

Watson, D. R., Bai, F., Barrett, S. L., Turkington, A., Rushe, T. M., Mulholland, C. C., & Cooper, S. J. (2012). Structural changes in the hippocampus and amygdala at first episode of psychosis. *Brain Imaging and Behavior*, 6(1), 49–60. https://doi.org/10.1007/s11682-011-9141-4

Weng, H. Y., Lapate, R. C., Stodola, D. E., Rogers, G. M., & Davidson, R. J. (2018). Visual attention to suffering after compassion training is associated with decreased amygdala responses. *Frontiers in Psychology*, 9, 771. https://doi.org/10.3389/fpsyg.2018.00771

Wessa, M., & Flor, H. (2007). Failure of extinction of fear responses in posttraumatic stress disorder: Evidence from second-order conditioning. *American Journal of Psychiatry*, 164(11), 1684–1692. https://doi.org/10.1176/appi.ajp.2007.07030525

Winter, L., Alam, M., Heissler, H. E., Saryyeva, A., Milakara, D., Jin, X., Heitland, I., Schwabe, K., Krauss, J. K., & Kahl, K. G. (2019). Neurobiological mechanisms of metacognitive therapy: An experimental paradigm: *Frontiers in Psychology*, 10, 660. https://doi.org/10.3389/fpsyg.2019.00660

Yassa, M. A., Hazlett, R. L., Stark, C. E., & Hoehn-Saric, R. (2012). Functional MRI of the amygdala and bed nucleus of the stria terminalis during conditions of uncertainty in generalized anxiety disorder. *Journal of Psychiatric Research*, 46(8), 1045–1052. https://doi.org/10.1016/j.jpsychires.2012.04.013

Young, K. D., Siegle, G. J., Bodurka, J., & Drevets, W. C. (2016). Amygdala activity during autobiographical memory recall in depressed and vulnerable individuals: Association with symptom severity and autobiographical overgenerality. *American Journal of Psychiatry*. 173(1), 78–89. https://doi.org/10.1176/appi.ajp.2015.15010119

Young, K. S., & Craske, M. G. (2018). The cognitive neuroscience of psychological treatment action in depression and anxiety. *Current Behavioral Neuroscience Reports*, 5(1), 13–25. https://doi.org/10.1007/s40473-018-0137-x

Zhu, X., Suarez-Jimenez, B., Lazarov, A., Helpman, L., Papini, S., Lowell, A., Durosky, A., Lindquist, M. A., Markowitz, J. C., Schneier, F., Wager, T. D., & Neria, Y. (2018). Exposure-based therapy changes amygdala and hippocampus resting-state functional connectivity in patients with posttraumatic stress disorder. *Depression and Anxiety*, 35(10), 974–984. https://doi.org/10.1002/da.22816

Zotev, V., Yuan, H., Misaki, M., Phillips, R., Young, K. D., Feldner, M. T., & Bodurka, J. (2016). Correlation between amygdala BOLD activity and frontal EEG asymmetry during real-time fMRI neurofeedback training in patients with depression. *NeuroImage: Clinical*, 11, 224–238. https://doi.org/10.1016/j.nicl.2016.02.003

HIPPOCAMPUS REFERENCES

Allen, K. M., Fung, S. J., & Shannon Weickert, C. (2016). Cell proliferation is reduced in the hippocampus in schizophrenia. *Australian & New Zealand Journal of Psychiatry*, 50(5), 473–480.

Amaral, D., & Lavenex, P. (2007). Hippocampal neuroanatomy. In P. Andersen, R. Morris, D. Amaral, T. Bliss & J. O'Keefe (Eds.), *The hippocampus book* (pp. 37–114). Oxford University Press.

Bird, C. M., & Burgess, N. (2008). The hippocampus and memory: Insights from spatial processing. *Nature Reviews Neuroscience*, 9(3), 182–194. https://doi.org/10.1038/nrn2335

Boldrini, M., Fulmore, C. A., Tartt, A. N., Simeon, L. R., Pavlova, I., Poposka, V., Rosoklija, G. B., Stankov, A., Arango, V., Dwork, A. J., & Hen, R. (2018). Human hippocampal neurogenesis persists throughout aging. *Cell Stem Cell*, 22(4), 589–599. https://doi.org/10.1016/j.stem.2018.03.015

Bossini, L., Casolaro, I., Santarnecchi, E., Caterini, C., Koukouna, D., Fernandez, I., & Fagiolini, A. (2012). Evaluation study of clinical and neurobiological efficacy of EMDR in patients suffering from post-traumatic stress disorder. *Rivista di Psichiatria*, 47(2), 12. https://doi.org/10.1708/2631.27051

Boukezzi, S., El Khoury-Malhame, M., Auzias, G., Reynaud, E., Rousseau, P. F., Richard, E., Zendjidjian, Z., Roques, J., Castelli, N., Correard, N., Guyon, V. Guyon, V., Gellato, C., Samuelian, J.-C., Cancel, A., Comte, M., Latinus, M., Guedj, E., & Khalfa, S. (2017). Grey matter density changes of structures involved in Posttraumatic Stress Disorder (PTSD) after recovery following Eye Movement Desensitization and Reprocessing (EMDR) therapy. *Psychiatry Research: Neuroimaging*, 266, 146–152. https://doi.org/10.1016/j.pscychresns.2017.06.009

Brown, T. I., Ross, R. S., Keller, J. B., Hasselmo, M. E., & Stern, C. E. (2010). Which way was I going? Contextual retrieval supports the disambiguation of well learned overlapping navigational routes. *Journal of Neuroscience*, 30(21), 7414–7422. https://doi.org/10.1523/JNEUROSCI.6021-09.2010

Campbell, S., & MacQueen, G. (2004). The role of the hippocampus in the pathophysiology of major depression. *Journal of Psychiatry and Neuroscience*, 29(6), 417–426.

Cha, J., Greenberg, T., Song, I., Blair Simpson, H., Posner, J., & Mujica-Parodi, L. R. (2016). Abnormal hippocampal structure and function in clinical anxiety and comorbid depression. *Hippocampus*, 26(5), 545–553. https://doi.org/10.1002/hipo.22566

Chang, B. S., & Lowenstein, D. H. (2003). Practice parameter: antiepileptic drug prophylaxis in severe traumatic brain injury: report of the Quality Standards Subcommittee of the American Academy of Neurology. *Neurology*, 60(1), 10–16.

da Silva, S. K., Wiener, C., Ghisleni, G., Oses, J. P., Jansen, K., Molina, M. L., Silva, R., & Souza, L. D. (2018). Effects of cognitive-behavioral therapy on neurotrophic factors in patients with major depressive disorder. *Brazilian Journal of Psychiatry*, 40(4), 361–366.

Dedovic, K., Duchesne, A., Andrews, J., Engert, V., & Pruessner, J. C. (2009). The brain and the stress axis: The neural correlates of cortisol regulation in response to stress. *NeuroImage*, 47(3), 864–871. https://doi.org/10.1016/j.neuroimage.2009.05.074

Eichenbaum, H. (2013). Memory on time. *Trends in cognitive sciences*, 17(2), 81–88. https://doi.org/10.1016/j.tics.2012.12.007

Eichenbaum, H. (2017). The role of the hippocampus in navigation is memory. *Journal of Neurophysiology*, 117(4), 1785–1796. https://doi.org/10.1152/jn.00005.2017

Eichenbaum, H., & Cohen, N. J. (1993). *Memory, amnesia, and the hippocampal system*. MIT Press.

Epstein, R. A., Patai, E. Z., Julian, J. B., & Spiers, H. J. (2017). The cognitive map in humans: Spatial navigation and beyond. *Nature Neuroscience*, 20(11), 1504–1513. https://doi.org/10.1038/nn.4656

Foltran, R. B., & Diaz, S. L. (2016). BDNF isoforms: A round trip ticket between neurogenesis and serotonin? *Journal of neurochemistry*, 138(2), 204–221. https://doi.org/10.1111/jnc.13658

Garavan, H., Kaufman, J. N., & Hester, R. (2008). Acute effects of cocaine on the neurobiology of cognitive control. *Philosophical Transactions of the Royal Society of London. Series B, Biological Sciences*, 363(1507), 3267–3276. https://doi.org/10.1098/rstb.2008.0106

Giap, B. T., Jong, C. N., Ricker, J. H., Cullen, N. K., & Zafonte, R. D. (2000). The hippocampus: Anatomy, pathophysiology, and regenerative capacity. *Journal of Head Trauma Rehabilitation*, 15(3), 875–894. https://doi.org/10.1097/00001199-200006000-00003

Goodman, J., & Packard, M. G. (2016). Memory systems and the addicted brain. *Frontiers in Psychiatry*, 7, 24. https://doi.org/10.3389/fpsyt.2016.00024

Goto, Y., & Grace, A. A. (2008). Limbic and cortical information processing in the nucleus accumbens. *Trends in Neurosciences*, 31(11), 552–558. https://doi.org/10.1016/j.tins.2008.08.002

Gourgouvelis, J., Yielder, P., Clarke, S. T., Behbahani, H., & Murphy, B. A. (2018). Exercise leads to better clinical outcomes in those receiving medication plus cognitive behavioral therapy for major depressive disorder. *Frontiers in Psychiatry*, 9, 37. https://doi.org/10.3389/fpsyt.2018.00037

Gu, H., Salmeron, B. J., Ross, T. J., Geng, X., Zhan, W., Stein, E. A., & Yang, Y. (2010). Mesocortico-limbic circuits are impaired in chronic cocaine users as demonstrated by resting-state functional connectivity. *NeuroImage*, 53(2), 593–601. https://doi.org/10.1016/j.neuroimage.2010.06.066

Gulick, D., & Gould, T. J. (2008). Interactive effects of ethanol and nicotine on learning in C57BL/6J mice depend on both dose and duration of treatment. *Psychopharmacology*, 196(3), 483–495. https://doi.org/10.1007/s00213-007-0982-x

Gurvits, T. V., Shenton, M. E., Hokama, H., Ohta, H., Lasko, N. B., Gilbertson, M. W., . . . & Pitman, R. K. (1996). Magnetic resonance imaging study of hippocampal volume in chronic, combat-related posttraumatic stress disorder. *Biological psychiatry*, 40(11), 1091–1099.

Halliday, G. (2017). Pathology and hippocampal atrophy in Alzheimer's disease. *The Lancet Neurology*, 16(11), 862–864.

Hamelink, C., Hampson, A., Wink, D. A., Eiden, L. E., & Eskay, R. L. (2005). Comparison of cannabidiol, antioxidants, and diuretics in reversing binge ethanol-induced neurotoxicity. *Journal of Pharmacology and Experimental Therapeutics*, 314(2), 780–788. https://doi.org/10.1124/jpet.105.085779

Hamilton, G. F., & Rhodes, J. S. (2015). Exercise regulation of cognitive function and neuroplasticity in the healthy and diseased brain. *Progress in Molecular Biology and Translational Science*, 135, 381–406. https://doi.org/10.1016/bs.pmbts.2015.07.004

Harrison, P. J. (2004). The hippocampus in schizophrenia: A review of the neuropathological evidence and its pathophysiological implications. *Psychopharmacology*, 174(1), 151–162. https://doi.org/10.1007/s00213-003-1761-y

Hashimoto, M., Kazui, H., Matsumoto, K., Nakano, Y., Yasuda, M., & Mori, E. (2005). Does donepezil treatment slow the progression of hippocampal atrophy in patients with Alzheimer's disease?. *American Journal of Psychiatry*, 162(4), 676–682.

Hayes, J. P., LaBar, K. S., McCarthy, G., Selgrade, E., Nasser, J., Dolcos, F., & Morey, R. A. (2011). Reduced hippocampal and amygdala activity predicts memory distortions for trauma reminders in combat-related PTSD. *Journal of Psychiatric Research*, 45(5), 660–669. https://doi.org/10.1016/j.jpsychires.2010.10.007

Henckens, M. J., Hermans, E. J., Pu, Z., Joëls, M., & Fernández, G. (2009). Stressed memories: How acute stress affects memory formation in humans. *Journal of Neuroscience*, 29(32), 10111–10119. https://doi.org/10.1523/JNEUROSCI.1184-09.2009

Joëls, M. (2008). Functional actions of corticosteroids in the hippocampus. *European Journal of Pharmacology*, 583(2–3), 312–321. https://doi.org/10.1016/j.ejphar.2007.11.064

Kelley, B. J., Yeager, K. R., Pepper, T. H., & Beversdorf, D. Q. (2005). Cognitive impairment in acute cocaine withdrawal. *Cognitive and Behavioral Neurology*, 18(2), 108–112. https://doi.org/10.1097/01.wnn.0000160823.61201.20

Khantzian, E. J. (1985). The self-medication hypothesis of addictive disorders: Focus on heroin and cocaine dependence. *American Journal of Psychiatry*, 142(11), 1259–1264. https://doi.org/10.1176/ajp.142.11.1259

Khodagholy, D., Gelinas, J. N., & Buzsáki, G. (2017). Learning-enhanced coupling between ripple oscillations in association cortices and hippocampus. *Science*, 358(6361), 369–372. https://doi.org/10.1126/science.aan6203

Kim, E. J., Pellman, B., & Kim, J. J. (2015). Stress effects on the hippocampus: A critical review. *Learning and Memory, 22*(9), 411–416. https://doi.org/10.1101/lm.037291.114

Kolb, B., & Whishaw, I. Q. (2009). *Fundamentals of human neuropsychology.* Macmillan.

Kuruba, R., Hattiangady, B., & Shetty, A. K. (2009). Hippocampal neurogenesis and neural stem cells in temporal lobe epilepsy. *Epilepsy and Behavior, 14*(1), 65–73. https://doi.org/10.1016/j.yebeh.2008.08.020

Kutlu, M. G., & Gould, T. J. (2016). Effects of drugs of abuse on hippocampal plasticity and hippocampus-dependent learning and memory: Contributions to development and maintenance of addiction. *Learning and Memory, 23*(10), 515–533. https://doi.org/10.1101/lm.042192.116

Lee, J. L., Nader, K., & Schiller, D. (2017). An update on memory reconsolidation updating. *Trends in cognitive sciences, 21*(7), 531–545. https://doi.org/10.1016/j.tics.2017.04.006

Le Merre, P., Esmaeili, V., Charrière, E., Galan, K., Salin, P. A., Petersen, C. C. H., & Crochet, S. (2018). Reward-based learning drives rapid sensory signals in the medial prefrontal cortex and dorsal hippocampus necessary for goal-directed behavior. *Neuron, 97*(1), 83–91.E5. https://doi.org/10.1016/j.neuron.2017.11.031

Lindauer, R. J., Olff, M., van Meijel, E. P., Carlier, I. V., & Gersons, B. P. (2006). Cortisol, learning, memory, and attention in relation to smaller hippocampal volume in police officers with post-traumatic stress disorder. *Biological Psychiatry, 59*(2), 171–177. https://doi.org/10.1016/j.biopsych.2005.06.033

Loprinzi, P. D., & Frith, E. (2019). A brief primer on the mediational role of BDNF in the exercise-memory link. *Clinical Physiology and Functional Imaging, 39*(1), 9–14.

Maguire, E. A., Burgess, N., Donnett, J. G., Frackowiak, R. S. J., Frith, C. D., & O'Keefe, J. (1998). Knowing where and getting there: A Human Navigation Network. *Science, 280*(5365), 921–924. https://doi.org/10.1126/science.280.5365.921

Maguire, E. A., Gadian, D. G., Johnsrude, I. S., Good, C. D., Ashburner, J., Frackowiak, R. S., & Frith, C. D. (2000). Navigation-related structural change in the hippocampi of taxi drivers. *Proceedings of the National Academy of Sciences of the United States of America, 97*(8), 4398–4403. https://doi.org/10.1073/pnas.070039597

Mah, L., Szabuniewicz, C., & Fiocco, A. J. (2016). Can anxiety damage the brain? *Current Opinion in Psychiatry, 29*(1), 56–63. https://doi.org/10.1097/YCO.0000000000000223

McEwen, B. S., & Magarinos, A. M. (2001). Stress and hippocampal plasticity: Implications for the pathophysiology of affective disorders. *Human Psychopharmacology: Clinical and Experimental, 16*(S1), S7–S19. https://doi.org/10.1002/hup.266

McEwen, B. S., & Stellar, E. (1993). Stress and the individual: mechanisms leading to disease. *Archives of Internal Medicine, 153*(18), 2093–2101. https://doi.org/10.1001/archinte.1993.00410180039004

Meeter, M., Myers, C. E., & Gluck, M. A. (2005). Integrating incremental learning and episodic memory models of the hippocampal region. *Psychological Review, 112*(3), 560–585. https://doi.org/10.1037/0033-295X.112.3.560

Miller, W. R., & Rollnick, S. (2012). *Motivational interviewing: Helping people change.* Guilford Press.

Milne, A. M., MacQueen, G. M., & Hall, G. B. (2012). Abnormal hippocampal activation in patients with extensive history of major depression: An fMRI study. *Journal of Psychiatry & Neuroscience, 37*(1), 28. https://doi.org/10.1503/jpn.110004

Morris, R. G. M., Garrud, P., Rawlins, J. N. P., & O'Keefe, J. (1982). Place navigation impaired in rats with hippocampal lesions. *Nature, 297*(5868), 681–683. https://doi.org/10.1038/297681a0

Moser, E. I., Kropff, E., & Moser, M. B. (2008). Place cells, grid cells, and the brain's spatial representation system. *Annu. Rev. Neurosci., 31*, 69–89.

Najavits, L. (2001). *Seeking safety: A treatment manual for PTSD and substance abuse.* Guilford Press.

Noble, E. E., Billington, C. J., Kotz, C. M., & Wang, C. (2011). The lighter side of BDNF. *American Journal of Physiology: Regulatory, Integrative and Comparative Physiology, 300*(5), R1053-R1069. https://doi.org/10.1152/ajpregu.00776.2010

North, A., Swant, J., Salvatore, M. F., Gamble-George, J., Prins, P., Butler, B., Mittal, M. K., Heltsley, R., Clark, J. T., & Khoshbouei, H. (2013). Chronic methamphetamine exposure produces a delayed, long-lasting memory deficit. *Synapse*, *67*(5), 245–257. https://doi.org/10.1002/syn.21635

O'Keefe, J., & Dostrovsky, J. (1971). The hippocampus as a spatial map. Preliminary evidence from unit activity in the freely-moving rat. *Brain Research*, *34*(1), 171–175. https://doi.org/10.1016/0006-8993(71)90358-1

O'Keefe, J., & Nadel, L. (1978). *The hippocampus as a cognitive map*. Oxford University Press.

O'Mara, S. (2005). The subiculum: What it does, what it might do, and what neuroanatomy has yet to tell us. *Journal of Anatomy*, *207*(3), 271–282. https://doi.org/10.1111/j.1469-7580.2005.00446.x

Postle, B. R. (2016). The hippocampus, memory, and consciousness. In S. Laureys, O. Gosseries, & G. Tononi (Eds.), *The Neurology of Consciousness* (2nd ed., pp. 349–363). Academic Press.

Pozzulo, J., Pica, E., & Sheahan, C. (Eds.). (2020). *Memory and Sexual Misconduct: Psychological Research for Criminal Justice*. Routledge.

Pruessner, J. C., Dedovic, K., Khalili-Mahani, N., Engert, V., Pruessner, M., Buss, C., Renwick, R., Dagher, A., Meaney, M. J., & Lupien, S. (2008). Deactivation of the limbic system during acute psychosocial stress: Evidence from positron emission tomography and functional magnetic resonance imaging studies. *Biological Psychiatry*, *63*(2), 234–240. https://doi.org/10.1016/j.biopsych.2007.04.041

Ragland, J. D., Layher, E., Hannula, D. E., Niendam, T. A., Lesh, T. A., Solomon, M., . . . & Ranganath, C. (2017). Impact of schizophrenia on anterior and posterior hippocampus during memory for complex scenes. *NeuroImage: Clinical*, *13*, 82–88.

Ritchey, M., Dolcos, F., Eddington, K. M., Strauman, T. J., & Cabeza, R. (2011). Neural correlates of emotional processing in depression: Changes with cognitive behavioral therapy and predictors of treatment response. *Journal of Psychiatric Research*, *45*(5), 577–587. https://doi.org/10.1016/j.jpsychires.2010.09.007

Roddy, D. W., Farrell, C., Doolin, K., Roman, E., Tozzi, L., Frodl, T., . . . & O'Hanlon, E. (2019). The hippocampus in depression: more than the sum of its parts? Advanced hippocampal substructure segmentation in depression. *Biological Psychiatry*, *85*(6), 487–497.

Roozendaal, B. (2002). Stress and memory: Opposing effects of glucocorticoids on memory consolidation and memory retrieval. *Neurobiology of Learning and Memory*, *78*(3), 578–595. https://doi.org/10.1006/nlme.2002.4080

Sahay, A., & Hen, R. (2007). Adult hippocampal neurogenesis in depression. *Nature Neuroscience*, *10*(9), 1110–1115. https://doi.org/0.1038/nn1969

Sala, M., Perez, J., Soloff, P., Di Nemi, S. U., Caverzasi, E., Soares, J. C., & Brambilla, P. (2004). Stress and hippocampal abnormalities in psychiatric disorders. *European Neuropsychopharmacology*, *14*(5), 393–405. https://doi.org/10.1016/j.euroneuro.2003.12.005

Sapolsky, R. M. (2001). Depression, antidepressants, and the shrinking hippocampus. *Proceedings of the National Academy of Sciences*, *98*(22), 12320–12322. https://doi.org/10.1073/pnas.231475998

Saunders, R. C., Rosene, D. L., & Van Hoesen, G. W. (1988). Comparison of the efferents of the amygdala and the hippocampal formation in the rhesus monkey: II. Reciprocal and non-reciprocal connections. *Journal of Comparative Neurology*, *271*(2), 185–207. https://doi.org/10.1002/cne.902710203

Sawangjit, A., Oyanedel, C. N., Niethard, N., Salazar, C., Born, J., & Inostroza, M. (2018). The hippocampus is crucial for forming non-hippocampal long-term memory during sleep. *Nature*, *564*(7734), 109–113. https://doi.org/10.1038/s41586-018-0716-8

Scheff, S. W., Price, D. A., Schmitt, F. A., & Mufson, E. J. (2006). Hippocampal synaptic loss in early Alzheimer's disease and mild cognitive impairment. *Neurobiology of aging*, *27*(10), 1372-1384.

Segal, M., Richter-Levin, G., & Maggio, N. (2010). Stress-induced dynamic routing of hippocampal connectivity: A hypothesis. *Hippocampus*, *20*(12), 1332–1338. https://doi.org/10.1002/hipo.20751

Sheline, Y. I. (2000). 3D MRI studies of neuroanatomic changes in unipolar major depression: The role of stress and medical comorbidity. *Biological Psychiatry*, *48*(8), 791–800. https://doi.org/10.1016/s0006-3223(00)00994-x

Shin, L. M., & Liberzon, I. (2010). The neurocircuitry of fear, stress, and anxiety disorders. *Neuropsychopharmacology*, 35(1), 169–191. https://doi.org/10.1038/npp.2009.83

Shorvon, S. (2010). *Handbook of epilepsy treatment*. John Wiley & Sons.

Sloviter, R. S. (2005). The neurobiology of temporal lobe epilepsy: Too much information, not enough knowledge. *Comptes Rendus Biologies*, 328(2), 143–153. https://doi.org/10.1016/j.crvi.2004.10.010

Squire, L. R. (1992). Memory and the hippocampus: A synthesis from findings with rats, monkeys, and humans. *Psychological Review*, 99(2), 195–231. https://doi.org/10.1037/0033-295x.99.2.195

Squire, L. R., & Schacter, D. L. (2002). *The neuropsychology of memory*. Guilford Press.

Steinvorth, S., Levine, B., & Corkin, S. (2005). Medial temporal lobe structures are needed to re-experience remote autobiographical memories: Evidence from HM and WR. *Neuropsychologia*, 43(4), 479–496.

Stoianov, I. P., Pennartz, C. M. A., Lansink, C. S., & Pezzulo, G. (2018). Model-based spatial navigation in the hippocampus-ventral striatum circuit: A computational analysis. *PLOS Computational Biology*, 14(9), e1006316. https://doi.org/10.1371/journal.pcbi.1006316

Szeszko, P. R., Lehrner, A., & Yehuda, R. (2018). Glucocorticoids and hippocampal structure and function in PTSD. *Harvard Review of Psychiatry*, 26(3), 142–157.

Teyler, T. J., & Discenna, P. (1984). The topological anatomy of the hippocampus: A clue to its function. *Brain Research Bulletin*, 12(6), 711–719. https://doi.org/10.1016/0361-9230(84)90152-7

Tollenaar, M. S., Elzinga, B. M., Spinhoven, P., & Everaerd, W. (2009). Autobiographical memory after acute stress in healthy young men. *Memory*, 17(3), 301–310. https://doi.org/10.1080/09658210802665845

Tubridy, S., & Davachi, L. (2011). Medial temporal lobe contributions to episodic sequence encoding. *Cerebral Cortex*, 21(2), 272–280. https://doi.org/10.1093/cercor/bhq092

van Ast, V. A., Cornelisse, S., Meeter, M., Joëls, M., & Kindt, M. (2013). Time-dependent effects of cortisol on the contextualization of emotional memories. *Biological Psychiatry*, 74(11), 809–816. https://doi.org/10.1016/j.biopsych.2013.06.022

Wang, Y., Cui, H., Wang, W., Zhao, B., & Lai, J. (2012). The region-specific activation of Ca^{2+}/calmodulin dependent protein kinase II and extracellular signal-regulated kinases in hippocampus following chronic alcohol exposure. *Brain Research Bulletin*, 89(5–6), 191–196. https://doi.org/10.1016/j.brainresbull.2012.08.007

Weller, J., & Budson, A. (2018). Current understanding of Alzheimer's disease diagnosis and treatment. *F1000Research*, 7.

Wilkinson, D. S., Turner, J. R., Blendy, J. A., & Gould, T. J. (2013). Genetic background influences the effects of withdrawal from chronic nicotine on learning and high-affinity nicotinic acetylcholine receptor binding in the dorsal and ventral hippocampus. *Psychopharmacology*, 225(1), 201–208. https://doi.org/10.1007/s00213-012-2808-8

Wingenfeld, K., & Wolf, O. T. (2014). Stress, memory, and the hippocampus. In *The Hippocampus in Clinical Neuroscience* (Vol. 34, pp. 109–120). Karger Publishers. https://doi.org/10.1159/000356423

Woodward, M. L., Gicas, K. M., Warburton, D. E., White, R. F., Rauscher, A., Leonova, O., . . . & Lang, D. J. (2018). Hippocampal volume and vasculature before and after exercise in treatment-resistant schizophrenia. *Schizophrenia research*, 202, 158–165.

Wu, A., Ying, Z., & Gomez-Pinilla, F. (2008). Docosahexaenoic acid dietary supplementation enhances the effects of exercise on synaptic plasticity and cognition. *Neuroscience*, 155(3), 751–759. https://doi.org/0.1016/j.neuroscience.2008.05.061

Xiong, G. L., & Doraiswamy, P. M. (2009). Does meditation enhance cognition and brain plasticity? *Annals of the New York Academy of Sciences*, 1172(1), 63.

Zeeuws, I., & Soetens, E. (2007). Verbal memory performance improved via an acute administration of D-amphetamine. *Human Psychopharmacology*, 22(5), 279–287. https://doi.org/10.1002/hup.848

Zheng, J., Anderson, K. L., Leal, S. L., Shestyuk, A., Gulsen, G., Mnatsakanyan, L., Vadera, S.,

Hsu, F. P. K., Yassa, M. A., Knight, R. T., & Lin, J. J. (2017). Amygdala-hippocampal dynamics during salient information processing. *Nature Communications*, 8, 14413. https://doi.org/10.1038/ncomms14413

INSULA REFERENCES

Alvarez, R. P., Kirlic, N., Misaki, M., Bodurka, J., Rhudy, J. L., Paulus, M. P., & Drevets, W. C. (2015). Increased anterior insula activity in anxious individuals is linked to diminished perceived control. *Translational psychiatry*, 5(6), e591. https://doi.org/10.1038/tp.2015.84

Avery, J. A., Drevets, W. C., Moseman, S. E., Bodurka, J., Barcalow, J. C., & Simmons, W. K. (2014). Major depressive disorder is associated with abnormal interoceptive activity and functional connectivity in the insula. *Biological Psychiatry*, 76(3), 258–266. https://doi.org/10.1016/j.biopsych.2013.11.027

Bar-Anan, Y., Wilson, T. D., & Gilbert, D. T. (2009). The feeling of uncertainty intensifies affective reactions. *Emotion*, 9(1), 123–127. https://doi.org/doi.org/10.1037/a0014607

Barrett, L. F., & Simmons, W. K. (2015). Interoceptive predictions in the brain. *Nature Reviews Neuroscience*, 16(7), 419. https://doi.org/doi.org/10.1038/nrn3950

Beauregard M., Paquette V., & Lévesque J. (2006). Dysfunction in the neural circuitry of emotional self-regulation in major depressive disorder. *Neuroreport*, 17, 843–846. https://doi.org/10.1097/01.wnr.0000220132.32091.9f

Borsook, D., Linnman, C., Faria, V., Strassman, A. M., Becerra, L., & Elman, I. (2016). Reward deficiency and anti-reward in pain chronification. *Neuroscience & Biobehavioral Reviews*, 68, 282–297.

Brewer, J. A., Worhunsky, P. D., Gray, J. R., Tang, Y. Y., Weber, J., & Kober, H. (2011). Meditation experience is associated with differences in default mode network activity and connectivity. *Proceedings of the National Academy of Sciences*, 108(50), 20254–20259. https://doi.org/10.1073/pnas.1112029108

Brooks, J. O., III, Wang, P. W., Bonner, J. C., Rosen, A. C., Hoblyn, J. C., Hill, S. J., & Ketter, T. A. (2009). Decreased prefrontal, anterior cingulate, insula, and ventral striatal metabolism in medication-free depressed outpatients with bipolar disorder. *Journal of psychiatric research*, 43(3), 181–188. https://doi.org/10.1016/j.jpsychires.2008.04.015

Brown, R. P., Gerbarg, P. L., & Muench, F. (2013). Breathing practices for treatment of psychiatric and stress-related medical conditions. *Psychiatric Clinics of North America*, 36(1), 121–140. https://doi.org/10.1016/j.psc.2013.01.001

Bruce, S. E., Buchholz, K. R., Brown, W. J., Yan, L., Durbin, A., & Sheline, Y. I. (2013). Altered emotional interference processing in the amygdala and insula in women with post-traumatic stress disorder. *NeuroImage: Clinical*, 2, 43–49. https://doi.org/10.1016/j.nicl.2012.11.003

Carlson, J. M., & Mujica-Parodi, L. R. (2010). A disposition to reappraise decreases anterior insula reactivity during anxious anticipation. *Biological Psychology*, 85(3), 383–385. https://doi.org/10.1016/j.biopsycho.2010.08.010

Cauda, F., D'agata, F., Sacco, K., Duca, S., Geminiani, G., & Vercelli, A. (2011). Functional connectivity of the insula in the resting brain. *NeuroImage*, 55(1), 8–23. https://doi.org/10.1016/j.neuroimage.2010.11.049

Chang, L. J., Yarkoni, T., Khaw, M. W., & Sanfey, A. G. (2013). Decoding the role of the insula in human cognition: Functional parcellation and large-scale reverse inference. *Cerebral Cortex*, 23(3), 739–749. https://doi.org/10.1093/cercor/bhs065

Chattopadhyay, S., Tait, R., Simas, T., van Nieuwenhuizen, A., Hagan, C. C., Holt, R. J., Graham, J., Sahakian, B. J., Wilkinson, P. O., Goodyer, I. M., & Suckling, J. (2017). Cognitive behavioral therapy lowers elevated functional connectivity in depressed adolescents. *EBiomedicine*, 17, 216–222. https://doi.org/10.1016/j.ebiom.2017.02.010

Christianson, J. P., Benison, A. M., Jennings, J., Sandsmark, E. K., Amat, J., Kaufman, R. D., Baratta,

M. V., Paul, E. D., Campeau, S., Watkins, L. R., Barth, D. S., & Maier, S. F. (2008). The sensory insular cortex mediates the stress-buffering effects of safety signals but not behavioral control. *Journal of Neuroscience*, 28(50), 13703–13711. https://doi.org/10.1523/JNEUROSCI.4270-08.2008

Contreras, M., Ceric, F., & Torrealba, F. (2007). Inactivation of the interoceptive insula disrupts drug craving and malaise induced by lithium. *Science*, 318(5850), 655–658. https://doi.org/10.1126/science.1145590

Craig, A. D. (2002). How do you feel? Interoception: The sense of the physiological condition of the body. *Nature Reviews. Neuroscience*, 3(8), 655–666. https://doi.org/10.1038/nrn894

Craig, A. D. (2009). How do you feel—Now? The anterior insula and human awareness. *Nature Reviews. Neuroscience*, 10(1).

Craig, A. D. (2010). Once an island, now the focus of attention. *Brain Structure and Function*, 214(5–6), 395–396. https://doi.org/10.1007/s00429-010-0270-0

Craig, A. D. (2011). Significance of the insula for the evolution of human awareness of feelings from the body. *Annals of the New York Academy of Sciences*, 1225, 72–82. https://doi.org/10.1111/j.1749-6632.2011.05990.x

Critchley, H. D., Wiens, S., Rotshtein, P., Öhman, A., & Dolan, R. J. (2004). Neural systems supporting interoceptive awareness. *Nature Neuroscience*, 7(2), 189–195. https://doi.org/10.1038/nn1176

de Divitiis, O., Somma, T., Turgut, M., & Cappabianca, P. (2018). *Role of the insula in human cognition and motivation*. In M. Turgut, C. Yurttas, & R. S. Tubbs (Eds.), *Island of Reil (Insula) in the Human Brain*, (pp. 147–149). Springer. https://doi.org/10.1007/978-3-319-75468-0_15

Dunn, R. T., Kimbrell, T. A., Ketter, T. A., Frye, M. A., Willis, M. W., Luckenbaugh, D. A., & Post, R. M. (2002). Principal components of the Beck Depression Inventory and regional cerebral metabolism in unipolar and bipolar depression. *Biological Psychiatry*, 51(5), 387–399. https://doi.org/10.1016/s0006-3223(01)01244-6

Duval, E. R., Joshi, S. A., Russman Block, S. R., Abelson, J. L., & Liberzon, I. (2018). Insula activation is modulated by attention shifting in social anxiety disorder. *Journal of Anxiety Disorders*, 56, 56–62. https://doi.org/10.1016/j.janxdis.2018.04.004

Ebisch, S. J., Gallese, V., Willems, R. M., Mantini, D., Groen, W. B., Romani, G. L., Buitelaar, J. K., & Bekkering, H. (2011). Altered intrinsic functional connectivity of anterior and posterior insula regions in high-functioning participants with autism spectrum disorder. *Human Brain Mapping*, 32(7), 1013–1028. https://doi.org/10.1002/hbm.21085

Eisenberger, N. I., Lieberman, M. D., & Williams, K. D. (2003). Does rejection hurt? An fMRI study of social exclusion. *Science*, 302(5643), 290–292.

Engel, K. R., Obst, K., Bandelow, B., Dechent, P., Gruber, O., Zerr, I., Ulrich, K., & Wedekind, D. (2016). Functional MRI activation in response to panic-specific, non-panic aversive, and neutral pictures in patients with panic disorder and healthy controls. *European Archives of Psychiatry and Clinical Neuroscience*, 266(6), 557–566. https://doi.org/10.1007/s00406-015-0653-6

Fazeli, S., & Büchel, C. (2018). Pain-related expectation and prediction error signals in the anterior insula are not related to aversiveness. *Journal of Neuroscience*, 38(29), 6461–6474. https://doi.org/10.1523/JNEUROSCI.0671-18.2018

Fitzgerald, P. B., Laird, A. R., Maller, J., & Daskalakis, Z. J. (2008). A meta-analytic study of changes in brain activation in depression. *Human Brain Mapping*, 29(6), 683–695. https://doi.org/10.1002/hbm.20426

Frewen, P. A., & Lanius, R. A. (2015). *Healing the traumatized self: Consciousness, neuroscience, and treatment*. W. W. Norton & Company.

Frewen, P. A., Pain, C., Dozois, D. J., & Lanius, R. A. (2006). Alexithymia in PTSD: psychometric and FMRI studies. *Annals of the New York Academy of Sciences*, 1071(1), 397–400. https://doi.org/10.1196/annals.1364.029

Fusar-Poli, P., Howes, O., & Borgwardt, S. (2009). Johann Cristian Reil on the 200th anniversary of the first description of the insula (1809).

Garavan, H. (2010). Insula and drug cravings. *Brain Structure and Function*, *214*(5–6), 593–601. https://doi.org/10.1007/s00429-010-0259-8

Garfinkel, S. N., & Liberzon, I. (2009). Neurobiology of PTSD: A review of neuroimaging findings. *Psychiatric Annals*, *39*(6), 370–381. https://doi.org/10.3928/00485713-20090527-01

Gasquoine, P. G. (2014). Contributions of the insula to cognition and emotion. *Neuropsychology Review*, *24*(2), 77–87. https://doi.org/10.1007/s11065-014-9246-9

Gu, X., Liu, X., Van Dam, N. T., Hof, P. R., & Fan, J. (2013). Cognition–emotion integration in the anterior insular cortex. *Cerebral Cortex*, *23*(1), 20–27. https://doi.org/10.1093/cercor/bhr367

Hamilton, J. P., Furman, D. J., Chang, C., Thomason, M. E., Dennis, E., & Gotlib, I. H. (2011). Default-mode and task-positive network activity in major depressive disorder: Implications for adaptive and maladaptive rumination. *Biological Psychiatry*, *70*(4), 327–333. https://doi.org/10.1016/j.biopsych.2011.02.003

Herbert, B. M., & Pollatos, O. (2012). The body in the mind: On the relationship between interoception and embodiment. *Topics in Cognitive Science*, *4*(4), 692–704. https://doi.org/10.1111/j.1756-8765.2012.01189.x

Hopper, J. W., Frewen, P. A., Van der Kolk, B. A., & Lanius, R. A. (2007). Neural correlates of re-experiencing, avoidance, and dissociation in PTSD: Symptom dimensions and emotion dysregulation in responses to script-driven trauma imagery. *Journal of Traumatic Stress*, *20*(5), 713–725. https://doi.org/10.1002/jts.20284

Isnard, J., Magnin, M., Jung, J., Mauguière, F., & Garcia-Larrea, L. (2011). Does the insula tell our brain that we are in pain? *Pain: The Journal of the International Association for the Study of Pain*, *152*(4), 946–951. https://doi.org/10.1016/j.pain.2010.12.025

Johnson, D. C., Thom, N. J., Stanley, E. A., Haase, L., Simmons, A. N., Shih, P. A. B., Thompson, W. K., Potterat, E. G., Minor, T. R., & Paulus, M. P. (2014). Modifying resilience mechanisms in at-risk individuals: A controlled study of mindfulness training in Marines preparing for deployment. *American Journal of Psychiatry*, *171*(8), 844–853. https://doi.org/10.1176/appi.ajp.2014.13040502

Johnstone, T., van Reekum, C. M., Urry, H. L., Kalin, N. H., & Davidson, R. J. (2007). Failure to regulate: Counterproductive recruitment of top-down prefrontal-subcortical circuitry in major depression. *Journal of Neuroscience*, *27*(33), 8877–8884. https://doi.org/10.1523/JNEUROSCI.2063-07.2007

Kabat-Zinn, J. (2003). Mindfulness-based stress reduction (MBSR). *Constructivism in the Human Sciences*, *8*(2), 73.

Kang, Y., Williams, L. E., Clark, M. S., Gray, J. R., & Bargh, J. A. (2011). Physical temperature effects on trust behavior: The role of insula. *Social Cognitive and Affective Neuroscience*, *6*(4), 507–515. https://doi.org/10.1093/scan/nsq077

Karnath, H. O., & Baier, B. (2010). Right insula for our sense of limb ownership and self-awareness of actions. *Brain Structure and Function*, *214*(5–6), 411–417. https://doi.org/10.1007/s00429-010-0250-4

Klumpp, H., Angstadt, M., & Phan, K. L. (2012). Insula reactivity and connectivity to anterior cingulate cortex when processing threat in generalized social anxiety disorder. *Biological Psychology*, *89*(1), 273–276. https://doi.org/10.1016/j.biopsycho.2011.10.010

Klumpp, H., Fitzgerald, D. A., & Phan, K. L. (2013). Neural predictors and mechanisms of cognitive behavioral therapy on threat processing in social anxiety disorder. *Progress in Neuro-Psychopharmacology and Biological Psychiatry*, *45*, 83–91. https://doi.org/10.1016/j.pnpbp.2013.05.004

Klumpp, H., Post, D., Angstadt, M., Fitzgerald, D. A., & Phan, K. L. (2013). Anterior cingulate cortex and insula response during indirect and direct processing of emotional faces in generalized social anxiety disorder. *Biology of Mood and Anxiety Disorders*, *3*(1), 7. https://doi.org/10.1186/2045-5380-3-7

Koch, S. B., van Zuiden, M., Nawijn, L., Frijling, J. L., Veltman, D. J., & Olff, M. (2016). Aberrant resting-state brain activity in posttraumatic stress disorder: A meta-analysis and systematic review. *Depression and Anxiety*, *33*(7), 592–605. https://doi.org/10.1002/da.22478

Kutlu, M. G., Burke, D., Slade, S., Hall, B. J., Rose, J. E., & Levin, E. D. (2013). Role of insular cortex D1 and D2 dopamine receptors in nicotine self-administration in rats. *Behavioural Brain Research*, *256*, 273–278. https://doi.org/10.1016/j.bbr.2013.08.005

Lanius, R. A., Frewen, P. A., Tursich, M., Jetly, R., & McKinnon, M. C. (2015). Restoring large-scale brain networks in PTSD and related disorders: A proposal for neuroscientifically-informed treatment interventions. *European Journal of Psychotraumatology*, *6*(1), 27313. https://doi.org/10.3402/ejpt.v6.27313

LeDoux, J. E., & Brown, R. (2017). A higher-order theory of emotional consciousness. *Proceedings of the National Academy of Sciences*, *114*(10), E2016–E2025.

Levine, P. A. (1997). *Waking the tiger: Healing trauma: The innate capacity to transform overwhelming experiences*. North Atlantic Books.

Lipka, J., Hoffmann, M., Miltner, W. H., & Straube, T. (2014). Effects of cognitive-behavioral therapy on brain responses to subliminal and supraliminal threat and their functional significance in specific phobia. *Biological Psychiatry*, *76*(11), 869–877. https://doi.org/10.1016/j.biopsych.2013.11.008

Lutz, A., McFarlin, D. R., Perlman, D. M., Salomons, T. V., & Davidson, R. J. (2013). Altered anterior insula activation during anticipation and experience of painful stimuli in expert meditators. *NeuroImage*, *64*, 538–546. https://doi.org/10.1016/j.neuroimage.2012.09.030

MacDonald, G., & Leary, M. R. (2005). Why does social exclusion hurt? The relationship between social and physical pain. *Psychological bulletin*, *131*(2), 202.

Mayberg, H. S., Liotti, M., Brannan, S. K., McGinnis, S., Mahurin, R. K., Jerabek, P. A., Silva, J. A., Tekell, J. L., Martin, C. C., Lancaster, J. L., & Fox, P. T. (1999). Reciprocal limbic-cortical function and negative mood: converging PET findings in depression and normal sadness. *American Journal of Psychiatry*, *156*(5), 675–682. https://doi.org/10.1176/ajp.156.5.675

Menon, V., & Uddin, L. Q. (2010). Saliency, switching, attention and control: A network model of insula function. *Brain Structure and Function*, *214*(5–6), 655–667. https://doi.org/10.1007/s00429-010-0262-0

Modinos, G., Renken, R., Ormel, J., & Aleman, A. (2011). Self-reflection and the psychosis-prone brain: An fMRI study. *Neuropsychology*, *25*(3), 295. https://doi.org/10.1037/a0021747

Najavits, L. (2002). *Seeking safety: A treatment manual for PTSD and substance abuse*. Guilford Publications.

Namkung, H., Kim, S. H., & Sawa, A. (2017). The insula: An underestimated brain area in clinical neuroscience, psychiatry, and neurology. *Trends in Neurosciences*, *40*(4), 200–207. https://doi.org/10.1016/j.tins.2017.02.002

Napadow, V., Sheehan, J. D., Kim, J., LaCount, L. T., Park, K., Kaptchuk, T. J., Rosen, B. R., & Kuo, B. (2013). The brain circuitry underlying the temporal evolution of nausea in humans. *Cerebral Cortex*, *23*(4), 806–813. https://doi.org/10.1093/cercor/bhs073

Naqvi, N. H., & Bechara, A. (2009). The hidden island of addiction: The insula. *Trends in Neurosciences*, *32*(1), 56–67. https://doi.org/10.1016/j.tins.2008.09.009

Naqvi, N. H., & Bechara, A. (2010). The insula and drug addiction: An interoceptive view of pleasure, urges, and decision-making. *Brain Structure and Function*, *214*(5–6), 435–450. https://doi.org/10.1007/s00429-010-0268-7

Naqvi, N. H., Gaznick, N., Tranel, D., & Bechara, A. (2014). The insula: A critical neural substrate for craving and drug seeking under conflict and risk. *Annals of the New York Academy of Sciences*, *1316*, 53–70. https://doi.org/10.1111/nyas.12415

Naqvi, N. H., Rudrauf, D., Damasio, H., & Bechara, A. (2007). Damage to the insula disrupts addiction to cigarette smoking. *Science*, *315*(5811), 531–534. https://doi.org/10.1126/science.1135926

Nicholson, A. A., Sapru, I., Densmore, M., Frewen, P. A., Neufeld, R. W., Théberge, J., McKinnon, M. C., & Lanius, R. A. (2016). Unique insula subregion resting-state functional connectivity with amygdala complexes in posttraumatic stress disorder and its dissociative subtype. *Psychiatry Research: Neuroimaging*, *250*, 61–72. https://doi.org/10.1016/j.pscychresns.2016.02.002

Palaniyappan, L., & Liddle, P. F. (2012). Does the salience network play a cardinal role in psychosis? An emerging hypothesis of insular dysfunction. *Journal of Psychiatry and Neuroscience*, *37*(1), 17–27. https://doi.org/10.1503/jpn.100176

Penfield, W., & Faulk, M. E., Jr. (1955). The insula: Further observations on its function. *Brain*, *78*(4), 445–470. https://doi.org/10.1093/brain/78.4.445

Puhl, M., Lapidus, R., Simmons, W. K., Lignieres, A., Feinstein, J., Paulus, M., & Khalsa, S. (2018). S18. Interoceptive prediction signals in the anterior insula. *Biological Psychiatry*, *83*(9), S353–S354. https://doi.org/10.1016/j.biopsych.2018.02.909

Ramautar, J. R., Slagter, H. A., Kok, A., & Ridderinkhof, K. R. (2006). Probability effects in the stop-signal paradigm: The insula and the significance of failed inhibition. *Brain Research*, *1105*(1), 143–154. https://doi.org/10.1016/j.brainres.2006.02.091

Reiss, S., Peterson, R. A., Gursky, D. M., & McNally, R. J. (1986). Anxiety sensitivity, anxiety frequency and the prediction of fearfulness. *Behaviour Research and Therapy*, *24*(1), 1–8. https://doi.org/10.1016/0005-7967(86)90143-9

Rizzolatti, G., Fabbri-Destro, M., & Cattaneo, L. (2009). Mirror neurons and their clinical relevance. *Nature Clinical Practice. Neurology*, *5*(1), 24–34. https://doi.org/10.1038/ncpneuro0990

Rizzolatti, G., Fogassi, L., & Gallese, V. (2001). Neurophysiological mechanisms underlying the understanding and imitation of action. *Nature Reviews Neuroscience*, *2*(9), 661–670. https://doi.org/10.1038/35090060

Rosso, I. M., Weiner, M. R., Crowley, D. J., Silveri, M. M., Rauch, S. L., & Jensen, J. E. (2014). Insula and anterior cingulate GABA levels in posttraumatic stress disorder: Preliminary findings using magnetic resonance spectroscopy. *Depression and Anxiety*, *31*(2), 115–123. https://doi.org/10.1002/da.22155

Santarnecchi, E., D'Arista, S., Egiziano, E., Gardi, C., Petrosino, R., Vatti, G., Reda, M., & Rossi, A. (2014). Interaction between neuroanatomical and psychological changes after mindfulness-based training. *PloS ONE*, *9*(10), e108359. https://doi.org/10.1371/journal.pone.0108359

Schlamann, M., Naglatzki, R., de Greiff, A., Forsting, M., & Gizewski, E. R. (2010). Autogenic training alters cerebral activation patterns in fMRI. *International Journal of Clinical and Experimental Hypnosis*, *58*(4), 444–456. https://doi.org/10.1080/00207144.2010.499347

Segerdahl, A. R., Mezue, M., Okell, T. W., Farrar, J. T., & Tracey, I. (2015). The dorsal posterior insula subserves a fundamental role in human pain. *Nature Neuroscience*, *18*(4), 499. https://doi.org/10.1038/nn.3969

Shah, S. G., Klumpp, H., Angstadt, M., Nathan, P. J., & Phan, K. L. (2009). Amygdala and insula response to emotional images in patients with generalized social anxiety disorder. *Journal of Psychiatry and Neuroscience*, *34*(4), 296–302.

Shura, R. D., Hurley, R. A., & Taber, K. H. (2014). Insular cortex: Structural and functional neuroanatomy. *Journal of Neuropsychiatry and Clinical Neurosciences*, *26*(4), 276–282. https://doi.org/10.1176/appi.neuropsych.260401

Simmons, A. N., Matthews, S. C., Paulus, M. P., & Stein, M. B. (2008). Intolerance of uncertainty correlates with insula activation during affective ambiguity. *Neuroscience Letters*, *430*(2), 92–97. https://doi.org/10.1016/j.neulet.2007.10.030

Simmons, A. N., Stein, M. B., Strigo, I. A., Arce, E., Hitchcock, C., & Paulus, M. P. (2011). Anxiety positive subjects show altered processing in the anterior insula during anticipation of negative stimuli. *Human Brain Mapping*, *32*(11), 1836–1846. https://doi.org/10.1002/hbm.21154

Simmons, A., Strigo, I. A., Matthews, S. C., Paulus, M. P., & Stein, M. B. (2009). Initial evidence of a failure to activate right anterior insula during affective set shifting in posttraumatic stress disorder. *Psychosomatic Medicine*, *71*(4), 373–377. https://doi.org/10.1097/PSY.0b013e3181a56ed8

Simmons, W. K., Avery, J. A., Barcalow, J. C., Bodurka, J., Drevets, W. C., & Bellgowan, P. (2013). Keeping the body in mind: Insula functional organization and functional connectivity integrate interoceptive, exteroceptive, and emotional awareness. *Human Brain Mapping*, *34*(11), 2944–2958. https://doi.org/10.1002/hbm.22113

Simmons, W. K., Burrows, K., Avery, J. A., Kerr, K. L., Bodurka, J., Savage, C. R., & Dre-vets, W. C. (2016). Depression-related increases and decreases in appetite: Dissociable patterns of aberrant activity in reward and interoceptive neurocircuitry. *American Journal of Psychiatry*, *173*(4), 418–428. https://doi.org/10.1176/appi.ajp.2015.15020162

Singer, T., Critchley, H. D., & Preuschoff, K. (2009). A common role of insula in feelings, empathy and uncertainty. *Trends in Cognitive Sciences*, *13*(8), 334–340. https://doi.org/10.1016/j.tics.2009.05.001

Sliz, D., & Hayley, S. (2012). Major depressive disorder and alterations in insular cortical activity: A review of current functional magnetic imaging research. *Frontiers in Human Neuroscience*, *6*, 323. https://doi.org/10.3389/fnhum.2012.00323

Stein, M. B., Simmons, A. N., Feinstein, J. S., & Paulus, M. P. (2007). Increased amygdala and insula activation during emotion processing in anxiety-prone subjects. *American Journal of Psychiatry*, *164*(2), 318–327. https://doi.org/10.1176/ajp.2007.164.2.318

Tapper, K. (2018). Mindfulness and craving: Effects and mechanisms. *Clinical Psychology Review*, *59*, 101–117. https://doi.org/10.1016/j.cpr.2017.11.003

Uddin, L. Q., & Menon, V. (2009). The anterior insula in autism: Under-connected and under-exam-ined. *Neuroscience and Biobehavioral Reviews*, *33*(8), 1198–1203. https://doi.org/10.1016/j.neubiorev.2009.06.002

Uddin, L. Q., Nomi, J. S., Hébert-Seropian, B., Ghaziri, J., & Boucher, O. (2017). Structure and func-tion of the human insula. *Journal of Clinical Neurophysiology*, *34*(4), 300–306. https://doi.org/10.1097/WNP.0000000000000377

Wager, T. D., & Barrett, L. F. (2017). From affect to control: Functional specialization of the insula in motivation and regulation. *BioRxiv*, 102368.

Wicker, B., Keysers, C., Plailly, J., Royet, J. P., Gallese, V., & Rizzolatti, G. (2003). Both of us disgusted in my insula: The common neural basis of seeing and feeling disgust. *Neuron*, *40*(3), 655–664. https://doi.org/10.1016/s0896-6273(03)00679-2

Wright, P., He, G., Shapira, N. A., Goodman, W. K., & Liu, Y. (2004). Disgust and the insula: fMRI responses to pictures of mutilation and contamination. *NeuroReport*, *15*(15), 2347–2351. https://doi.org/10.1097/00001756-200410250-00009

Wylie, K. P., & Tregellas, J. R. (2010). The role of the insula in schizophrenia. *Schizophrenia Research*, *123*(2–3), 93–104. https://doi.org/10.1016/j.schres.2010.08.027

Yan, X., Brown, A. D., Lazar, M., Cressman, V. L., Henn-Haase, C., Neylan, T. C., Shalev, A., Wolkow-itz, O. M., Hamilton, S. P., Yehuda, R., Sodickson, D. K., Weiner, M. W., & Marmar, C. R. (2013). Spontaneous brain activity in combat related PTSD. *Neuroscience Letters*, *547*, 1–5. https://doi.org/10.1016/j.neulet.2013.04.032

Yao, S., Becker, B., Geng, Y., Zhao, Z., Xu, X., Zhao, W., Ren, P., & Kendrick, K. M. (2016). Voluntary control of anterior insula and its functional connections is feedback-independent and increases pain empathy. *NeuroImage*, *130*, 230–240. https://doi.org/10.1016/j.neuroimage.2016.02.035

Yao, Z., Wang, L., Lu, Q., Liu, H., & Teng, G. (2009). Regional homogeneity in depression and its rela-tionship with separate depressive symptom clusters: A resting-state fMRI study. *Journal of Affec-tive Disorders*, *115*(3), 430–438. https://doi.org/10.1016/j.jad.2008.10.013

Zaki, J., Davis, J. I., & Ochsner, K. N. (2012). Overlapping activity in anterior insula during interocep-tion and emotional experience. *NeuroImage*, *62*(1), 493–499. https://doi.org/10.1016/j.neuroimage.2012.05.012

NUCLEUS ACCUMBENS REFERENCES

Acevedo, B. P., Aron, A., Fisher, H. E., & Brown, L. L. (2012). Neural correlates of long-term intense romantic love. *Social Cognitive and Affective Neuroscience*, *7*(2), 145–159. https://doi.org/10.1093/scan/nsq092

Baumann, B., Danos, P., Krell, D., Diekmann, S., Leschinger, A., Stauch, R., Wurthmann, C., Bernstein,

H.-G., & Bogerts, B. (1999). Reduced volume of limbic system-affiliated basal ganglia in mood disorders: Preliminary data from a postmortem study. *Journal of Neuropsychiatry and Clinical Neurosciences*, 11(1), 71–78. https://doi.org/10.1176/jnp.11.1.71

Bewernick, B. H., Hurlemann, R., Matusch, A., Kayser, S., Grubert, C., Hadrysiewicz, B., Axmacher, N., Lemke, M., Cooper-Mahkorn, D., Cohen, M. X., Brockmann, H., Lenartz, D., Sturm, V., & Schlaepfer, T. E. (2010). Nucleus accumbens deep brain stimulation decreases ratings of depression and anxiety in treatment-resistant depression. *Biological Psychiatry*, 67(2), 110–116. https://doi.org/10.1016/j.biopsych.2009.09.013

Boehme, S., Ritter, V., Tefikow, S., Stangier, U., Strauss, B., Miltner, W. H., & Straube, T. (2014). Brain activation during anticipatory anxiety in social anxiety disorder. *Social Cognitive and Affective Neuroscience*, 9(9), 1413–1418. https://doi.org/10.1093/scan/nst129

Boileau, I., Assaad, J. M., Pihl, R. O., Benkelfat, C., Leyton, M., Diksic, M., Tremblay, R. E., & Dagher, A. (2003). Alcohol promotes dopamine release in the human nucleus accumbens. *Synapse*, 49(4), 226–231. https://doi.org/10.1002/syn.10226

Bremner, J. D., Narayan, M., Anderson, E. R., Staib, L. H., Miller, H. L., & Charney, D. S. (2000). Hippocampal volume reduction in major depression. *American Journal of Psychiatry*, 157(1), 115–118. https://doi.org/10.1176/ajp.157.1.115

Buckholtz, J. W., Treadway, M. T., Cowan, R. L., Woodward, N. D., Benning, S. D., Li, R., Ansari, M. S., Baldwin, R. M., Schwartzman, A. N., Shelby, E. S., Smith, C. E., Cole, D., Kessler, R. M., & Zald, D. H. (2010). Mesolimbic dopamine reward system hypersensitivity in individuals with psychopathic traits. *Nature Neuroscience*, 13(4), 419–421. https://doi.org/10.1038/nn.2510

Buhle, J. T., Silvers, J. A., Wager, T. D., Lopez, R., Onyemekwu, C., Kober, H., Weber, J., & Ochsner, K. N. (2014). Cognitive reappraisal of emotion: A meta-analysis of human neuroimaging studies. *Cerebral Cortex*, 24(11), 2981–2990. https://doi.org/10.1093/cercor/bht154

Burkett, J. P., & Young, L. J. (2012). The behavioral, anatomical and pharmacological parallels between social attachment, love and addiction. *Psychopharmacology*, 224(1), 1–26. https://doi.org/10.1007/s00213-012-2794-x

Burkhouse, K. L., Gorka, S. M., Klumpp, H., Kennedy, A. E., Karich, S., Francis, J., Ajilore, O., Craske, M. G., Langenecker, S. A., Shankman, S. A., Hajcak, G., & Phan, K. L. (2018). Neural responsiveness to reward as an index of depressive symptom change following cognitive-behavioral therapy and selective serotonin reuptake inhibitor treatment. *Journal of Clinical Psychiatry*, 79(4). https://doi.org/10.4088/JCP.17m11836

Burkhouse, K. L., Kujawa, A., Kennedy, A. E., Shankman, S. A., Langenecker, S. A., Phan, K. L., & Klumpp, H. (2016). Neural reactivity to reward as a predictor of cognitive behavioral therapy response in anxiety and depression. *Depression and Anxiety*, 33(4), 281–288. https://doi.org/10.1002/da.22482

Cardinal, R. N., Parkinson, J. A., Hall, J., & Everitt, B. J. (2002). Emotion and motivation: The role of the amygdala, ventral striatum, and prefrontal cortex. *Neuroscience and Biobehavioral Reviews*, 26(3), 321–352. https://doi.org/10.1016/s0149-7634(02)00007-6

Chen, C. H., Suckling, J., Ooi, C., Fu, C. H., Williams, S. C., Walsh, N. D., Mitterschiffthaler, M. T., Pich, E. M., & Bullmore, E. (2008). Functional coupling of the amygdala in depressed patients treated with antidepressant medication. *Neuropsychopharmacology*, 33(8), 1909–1918. https://doi.org/10.1038/sj.npp.1301593

Dafny, N., & Rosenfeld, G. C. (2017). Neurobiology of drugs of abuse. In P. M. Conn (Ed.), *Conn's translational neuroscience* (pp. 715–722). Academic Press.

Dani, J. A., & Heinemann, S. (1996). Molecular and cellular aspects of nicotine abuse. *Neuron*, 16(5), 905–908. https://doi.org/10.1016/s0896-6273(00)80112-9

Day, J. J., & Carelli, R. M. (2007). The nucleus accumbens and Pavlovian reward learning. *Neuroscientist: A Review Journal Bringing Neurobiology, Neurology and Psychiatry*, 13(2), 148–159. https://doi.org/10.1177/1073858406295854

Di Chiara, G., & Imperato, A. (1988). Drugs abused by humans preferentially increase synaptic dopamine concentrations in the mesolimbic system of freely moving rats. *Proceedings of the National Academy of Sciences of the United States of America, 85*(14), 5274–5278. https://doi.org/10.1073/pnas.85.14.5274

Drevets, W. C., Videen, T. O., Price, J. L., Preskorn, S. H., Carmichael, S. T., & Raichle, M. E. (1992). A functional anatomical study of unipolar depression. *Journal of Neuroscience, 12*(9), 3628–3641. https://doi.org/10.1523/JNEUROSCI.12-09-03628.1992

Du, L., Liu, H., Du, W., Chao, F., Zhang, L., Wang, K., Huang, C., Gao, Y., & Tang, Y. (2018). Stimulated left DLPFC-nucleus accumbens functional connectivity predicts the anti-depression and anti-anxiety effects of rTMS for depression. *Translational Psychiatry, 7*(11), 3. https://doi.org/10.1038/s41398-017-0005-6

Engelmann, J. B., Meyer, F., Fehr, E., & Ruff, C. C. (2015). Anticipatory anxiety disrupts neural valuation during risky choice. *Journal of Neuroscience, 35*(7), 3085–3099. https://doi.org/10.1523/JNEUROSCI.2880-14.2015

Ericson, M., Chau, P., Clarke, R. B., Adermark, L., & Söderpalm, B. (2011). Rising taurine and ethanol concentrations in nucleus accumbens interact to produce dopamine release after ethanol administration. *Addiction Biology, 16*(3), 377–385. https://doi.org/10.1111/j.1369-1600.2010.00245.x

Fisher, H. E., Brown, L. L., Aron, A., Strong, G., & Mashek, D. (2010). Reward, addiction, and emotion regulation systems associated with rejection in love. *Journal of Neurophysiology, 104*(1), 51–60. https://doi.org/10.1152/jn.00784.2009

Fisher, H. E., Xu, X., Aron, A., & Brown, L. L. (2016). Intense, passionate, romantic love: A natural addiction? How the fields that investigate romance and substance abuse can inform each other. *Frontiers in Psychology, 7*, 687. https://doi.org/10.3389/fpsyg.2016.00687

Gold, B. P., Mas-Herrero, E., Zeighami, Y., Benovoy, M., Dagher, A., & Zatorre, R. J. (2019). Musical reward prediction errors engage the nucleus accumbens and motivate learning. *Proceedings of the National Academy of Sciences of the United States of America, 116*(8), 3310–3315. https://doi.org/10.1073/pnas.1809855116

Goto, Y., & Grace, A. A. (2008). Limbic and cortical information processing in the nucleus accumbens. *Trends in Neurosciences, 31*(11), 552–558. https://doi.org/10.1016/j.tins.2008.08.002

Greening, S. G., Osuch, E. A., Williamson, P. C., & Mitchell, D. G. (2014). The neural correlates of regulating positive and negative emotions in medication-free major depression. *Social Cognitive and Affective Neuroscience, 9*(5), 628–637. https://doi.org/10.1093/scan/nst027

Groenewegen, H. J., Wright, C. I., Beijer, A. V., & Voorn, P. (1999). Convergence and segregation of ventral striatal inputs and outputs. *Annals of the New York Academy of Sciences, 877*, 49–63. https://doi.org/10.1111/j.1749-6632.1999.tb09260.x

Grubert, C., Hurlemann, R., Bewernick, B. H., Kayser, S., Hadrysiewicz, B., Axmacher, N., Sturm, V., & Schlaepfer, T. E. (2011). Neuropsychological safety of nucleus accumbens deep brain stimulation for major depression: Effects of 12-month stimulation. *World Journal of Biological Psychiatry, 12*(7), 516–527. https://doi.org/10.3109/15622975.2011.583940

Günther, V., Ihme, K., Kersting, A., Hoffmann, K. T., Lobsien, D., & Suslow, T. (2018). Volumetric associations between amygdala, nucleus accumbens, and socially anxious tendencies in healthy women. *Neuroscience, 374*, 25–32. https://doi.org/10.1016/j.neuroscience.2018.01.034

Hannestad, J., Taylor, W. D., McQuoid, D. R., Payne, M. E., Krishnan, K. R., Steffens, D. C., & Macfall, J. R. (2006). White matter lesion volumes and caudate volumes in late-life depression. *International Journal of Geriatric Psychiatry, 21*(12), 1193–1198. https://doi.org/10.1002/gps.1640

Heller, A. S., Johnstone, T., Shackman, A. J., Light, S. N., Peterson, M. J., Kolden, G. G., Kalin, N. H., & Davidson, R. J. (2009). Reduced capacity to sustain positive emotion in major depression reflects diminished maintenance of fronto-striatal brain activation. *Proceedings of the National Academy of Sciences of the United States of America, 106*(52), 22445–22450. https://doi.org/10.1073/pnas.0910651106

Husain, M. M., McDonald, W. M., Doraiswamy, P. M., Figiel, G. S., Na, C., Escalona, P. R., Boyko, O. B., Nemeroff, C. B., & Krishnan, K. R. (1991). A magnetic resonance imaging study of putamen nuclei in major depression. *Psychiatry Research*, *40*(2), 95–99. https://doi.org/10.1016/0925 -4927(91)90001-7

Hyman, S. E. (1996). Addiction to cocaine and amphetamine. *Neuron*, *16*(5), 901–904. https://doi .org/10.1016/s0896-6273(00)80111-7

Idris, Z., & Abdullah, J. M. (2017). *Neurosurgery notes for the graduate students*. Penerbit USM.

Ikemoto, S. (2010). Brain reward circuitry beyond the mesolimbic dopamine system: A neurobiological theory. *Neuroscience and Biobehavioral Reviews*, *35*(2), 129–150. https://doi.org/10.1016/j .neubiorev.2010.02.001

Jayaram-Lindström, N., Guterstam, J., Häggkvist, J., Ericson, M., Malmlöf, T., Schilström, B., Halldin, C., Cervenka, S., Saijo, T., Nordström, A.-L., & Franck, J. (2017). Naltrexone modulates dopamine release following chronic, but not acute amphetamine administration: A translational study. *Translational Psychiatry*, *7*(4), e1104. https://doi.org/10.1038/tp.2017.79

Johnston, S. J., Boehm, S. G., Healy, D., Goebel, R., & Linden, D. E. (2010). Neurofeedback: A promising tool for the self-regulation of emotion networks. *NeuroImage*, *49*(1), 1066–1072. https://doi .org/10.1016/j.neuroimage.2009.07.056

Kerfoot, E. C., & Williams, C. L. (2018). Contributions of the nucleus accumbens shell in mediating the enhancement in memory following noradrenergic activation of either the amygdala or hippocampus. *Frontiers in Pharmacology*, *9*, 47. https://doi.org/10.3389/fphar.2018.00047

Kilts, C. D., Kelsey, J. E., Knight, B., Ely, T. D., Bowman, F. D., Gross, R. E., Selvig, A., Gordon, A., Newport, D. J., & Nemeroff, C. B. (2006). The neural correlates of social anxiety disorder and response to pharmacotherapy. *Neuropsychopharmacology*, *31*(10), 2243–2253. https://doi.org/10 .1038/sj.npp.1301053

Koob, G. F., Maldonado, R., & Stinus, L. (1992). Neural substrates of opiate withdrawal. *Trends in Neurosciences*, *15*(5), 186–191. https://doi.org/10.1016/0166-2236(92)90171-4

Korponay, C., Kosson, D. S., Decety, J., Kiehl, K. A., & Koenigs, M. (2017). Brain volume correlates with duration of abstinence from substance abuse in a region-specific and substance-specific manner. *Biological Psychiatry: Cognitive Neuroscience and Neuroimaging*, *2*(7), 626–635. https://doi .org/10.1016/j.bpsc.2017.03.011

Krishnan, K. R., McDonald, W. M., Escalona, P. R., Doraiswamy, P. M., Na, C., Husain, M. M., Figiel, G. S., Boyko, O. B., Ellinwood, E. H., & Nemeroff, C. B. (1992). Magnetic resonance imaging of the caudate nuclei in depression. Preliminary observations. *Archives of General Psychiatry*, *49*(7), 553–557. https://doi.org/10.1001/archpsyc.1992.01820070047007

Kühn, S., Schubert, F., & Gallinat, J. (2011). Structural correlates of trait anxiety: Reduced thickness in medial orbitofrontal cortex accompanied by volume increase in nucleus accumbens. *Journal of Affective Disorders*, *134*(1–3), 315–319. https://doi.org/10.1016/j.jad.2011.06.003

Laine, T. P., Ahonen, A., Torniainen, P., Heikkilä, J., Pyhtinen, J., Räsänen, P., Niemelä, O., & Hillbom, M. (1999). Dopamine transporters increase in human brain after alcohol withdrawal. *Molecular Psychiatry*, *4*(2), 189–91, 104. https://doi.org/10.1038/sj.mp.4000514

Lee, L. T., Tsai, H. C., Chi, M. H., Chang, W. H., Chen, K. C., Lee, I. H., Chen, P. S., Yao, W. J., Chiu, N. T., & Yang, Y. K. (2015). Lower availability of striatal dopamine transporter in generalized anxiety disorder: A preliminary two-ligand SPECT study. *International Clinical Psychopharmacology*, *30*(3), 175–178. https://doi.org/10.1097/YIC.0000000000000067

Levita, L., Hoskin, R., & Champi, S. (2012). Avoidance of harm and anxiety: A role for the nucleus accumbens. *NeuroImage*, *62*(1), 189–198. https://doi.org/10.1016/j.neuroimage.2012.04.059

Linden, D. E., Habes, I., Johnston, S. J., Linden, S., Tatineni, R., Subramanian, L., Sorger, B., Healy, D., & Goebel, R. (2012). Real-time self-regulation of emotion networks in patients with depression. *PLOS ONE*, *7*(6), e38115. https://doi.org/10.1371/journal.pone.0038115

Linden, D., & Lancaster, T. (2011). Functional magnetic resonance imaging (FMRI)-based neurofeedback as a new treatment tool for depression. *European Psychiatry*, *26*(Suppl. 2), 937–937. https:// doi.org/10.1016/S0924-9338(11)72642-6

Luigjes, J. V., Van Den Brink, W., Feenstra, M. V., Van Den Munckhof, P., Schuurman, P. R., Schippers, R., Mazaheri, A., De Vries, T. J., & Denys, D. (2012). Deep brain stimulation in addiction: A review of potential brain targets. *Molecular Psychiatry*, *17*(6), 572–583. https://doi.org/10.1038/mp.2011.114

Macpherson, T., & Hikida, T. (2019). Role of basal ganglia neurocircuitry in the pathology of psychiatric disorders. *Psychiatry and Clinical Neurosciences*, *73*(6), 289–301. https://doi.org/10.1111/pcn.12830

Malone, D. A., Jr., Dougherty, D. D., Rezai, A. R., Carpenter, L. L., Friehs, G. M., Eskandar, E. N., Rauch, S. L., Rasmussen, S. A., Machado, A. G., Kubu, C. S., Tyrka, A. R., Price, L. H., Stypulkowski, P. H., Giftakis, J. E., Rise, M. T., Malloy, P. F., Salloway, S. P., & Greenberg, B. D. (2009). Deep brain stimulation of the ventral capsule/ventral striatum for treatment-resistant depression. *Biological Psychiatry*, *65*(4), 267–275. https://doi.org/10.1016/j.biopsych.2008.08.029

Mantione, M., Nieman, D. H., Figee, M., & Denys, D. (2014). Cognitive-behavioural therapy augments the effects of deep brain stimulation in obsessive–compulsive disorder. *Psychological Medicine*, *44*(16), 3515–3522. https://doi.org/10.1017/S0033291714000956

Mayberg, H. S., Brannan, S. K., Tekell, J. L., Silva, J. A., Mahurin, R. K., McGinnis, S., & Jerabek, P. A. (2000). Regional metabolic effects of fluoxetine in major depression: Serial changes and relationship to clinical response. *Biological Psychiatry*, *48*(8), 830–843. https://doi.org/10.1016/s0006-3223(00)01036-2

McCabe, C., Mishor, Z., Cowen, P. J., & Harmer, C. J. (2010). Diminished neural processing of aversive and rewarding stimuli during selective serotonin reuptake inhibitor treatment. *Biological psychiatry*, *67*(5), 439–445.

Mccutcheon, J. E., Ebner, S. R., Loriaux, A. L., & Roitman, M. F. (2012). Encoding of aversion by dopamine and the nucleus accumbens. *Frontiers in Neuroscience*, *6*, 137. https://doi.org/10.3389/fnins.2012.00137

Mehler, D. M. A., Sokunbi, M. O., Habes, I., Barawi, K., Subramanian, L., Range, M., Evans, J., Hood, K., Lührs, M., Keedwell, P., Goebel, R., & Linden, D. E. J. (2018). Targeting the affective brain—A randomized controlled trial of real-time fMRI neurofeedback in patients with depression. *Neuropsychopharmacology*, *43*(13), 2578–2585. https://doi.org/10.1038/s41386-018-0126-5

Mehta, N. D., Stevens, J. S., Li, Z., Gillespie, C. F., Fani, N., Michopoulos, V., & Felger, J. C. (2020). Inflammation, reward circuitry and symptoms of anhedonia and PTSD in trauma-exposed women. *Social Cognitive and Affective Neuroscience*, *15*(10), 1046–1055. https://doi.org/10.1093/scan/nsz100

Melis, M., Spiga, S., & Diana, M. (2005). The dopamine hypothesis of drug addiction: Hypodopaminergic state. *International Review of Neurobiology*, *63*, 101–154. https://doi.org/10.1016/S0074-7742(05)63005-X

Nauczyciel, C., Robic, S., Dondaine, T., Verin, M., Robert, G., Drapier, D., Naudet, F., & Millet, B. (2013). The nucleus accumbens: A target for deep brain stimulation in resistant major depressive disorder. *Journal of Molecular Psychiatry*, *1*(1), 17. https://doi.org/10.1186/2049-9256-1-17

Oathes, D. J., Patenaude, B., Schatzberg, A. F., & Etkin, A. (2015). Neurobiological signatures of anxiety and depression in resting-state functional magnetic resonance imaging. *Biological Psychiatry*, *77*(4), 385–393. https://doi.org/10.1016/j.biopsych.2014.08.006

O'Connor, M. F., Wellisch, D. K., Stanton, A. L., Eisenberger, N. I., Irwin, M. R., & Lieberman, M. D. (2008). Craving love? Enduring grief activates brain's reward center. *NeuroImage*, *42*(2), 969–972. https://doi.org/10.1016/j.neuroimage.2008.04.256

O'Donnell, P., Lavín, A., Enquist, L. W., Grace, A. A., & Card, J. P. (1997). Interconnected parallel circuits between rat nucleus accumbens and thalamus revealed by retrograde transsynaptic transport of pseudorabies virus. *Journal of Neuroscience*, *17*(6), 2143–2167. https://doi.org/10.1523/JNEUROSCI.17-06-02143.1997

Oishi, Y., Xu, Q., Wang, L., Zhang, B. J., Takahashi, K., Takata, Y., Luo, Y.-J., Cherasse, Y., Schiffmann, S. N., De Kerchove d'Exaerde, A., Urade, Y., Qu, W.-M., Huang, Z.-L., & Lazarus, M. (2017). Slow-wave sleep is controlled by a subset of nucleus accumbens core neurons in mice. *Nature Communications*, *8*(1), 734. https://doi.org/10.1038/s41467-017-00781-4

Pierce, R. C., & Vassoler, F. M. (2013). Deep brain stimulation for the treatment of addiction: Basic and clinical studies and potential mechanisms of action. *Psychopharmacology, 229*(3), 487–491. https://doi.org/10.1007/s00213-013-3214-6

Pohlack, S. T., Nees, F., Ruttorf, M., Schad, L. R., & Flor, H. (2012). Activation of the ventral striatum during aversive contextual conditioning in humans. *Biological Psychology, 91*(1), 74–80. https://doi .org/10.1016/j.biopsycho.2012.04.004

Rocha, A., & Kalivas, P. W. (2010). Role of the prefrontal cortex and nucleus accumbens in reinstating methamphetamine seeking. *European Journal of Neuroscience, 31*(5), 903–909. https://doi.org/10 .1111/j.1460-9568.2010.07134.x

Russo, S. J., & Nestler, E. J. (2013). The brain reward circuitry in mood disorders. *Nature Reviews Neuroscience, 14*(9), 609–625. https://doi.org/10.1038/nrn3381

Saal, D., Dong, Y., Bonci, A., & Malenka, R. C. (2003). Drugs of abuse and stress trigger a common synaptic adaptation in dopamine neurons. *Neuron, 37*(4), 577–582. https://doi.org/10.1016/s0896 -6273(03)00021-7

Salamone, J. D. (1994). The involvement of nucleus accumbens dopamine in appetitive and aversive moti- vation. *Behavioural Brain Research, 61*(2), 117–133. https://doi.org/10.1016/0166-4328(94)90153-8

Salgado, S., & Kaplitt, M. G. (2015). The nucleus accumbens: A comprehensive review. *Stereotactic and Functional Neurosurgery, 93*(2), 75–93. https://doi.org/10.1159/000368279

Satterthwaite, T. D., Kable, J. W., Vandekar, L., Katchmar, N., Bassett, D. S., Baldassano, C. F., Ruparel, K., Elliott, M. A., Sheline, Y. I., Gur, R. C., Gur, R. E., Davatzikos, C., Liebenluft, E., Thase, M. E., & Wolf, D. H. (2015). Common and dissociable dysfunction of the reward system in bipolar and unipolar depression. *Neuropsychopharmacology, 40*(9), 2258–2268. https://doi.org/10 .1038/npp.2015.75

Schultz, D. H., Ito, T., Solomyak, L. I., Chen, R. H., Mill, R. D., Anticevic, A., & Cole, M. W. (2019). Global connectivity of the fronto-parietal cognitive control network is related to depression symptoms in the general population. *Network Neuroscience, 3*(1), 107–123. https://doi.org/10.1162/netn_a_00056

Scofield, M. D., Heinsbroek, J. A., Gipson, C. D., Kupchik, Y. M., Spencer, S., Smith, A. C. W., Roberts- Wolfe, D., & Kalivas, P. W. (2016). The nucleus accumbens: Mechanisms of addiction across drug classes reflect the importance of glutamate homeostasis. *Pharmacological Reviews, 68*(3), 816–871. https://doi.org/10.1124/pr.116.012484

Scott, D. J., Stohler, C. S., Egnatuk, C. M., Wang, H., Koeppe, R. A., & Zubieta, J. K. (2007). Individual differences in reward responding explain placebo-induced expectations and effects. *Neuron, 55*(2), 325–336. https://doi.org/10.1016/j.neuron.2007.06.028

Sekine, Y., Iyo, M., Ouchi, Y., Matsunaga, T., Tsukada, H., Okada, H., Yoshikawa, E., Futatsubashi, M., Takei, N., & Mori, N. (2001). Methamphetamine-related psychiatric symptoms and reduced brain dopamine transporters studied with PET. *American Journal of Psychiatry, 158*(8), 1206– 1214. https://doi.org/10.1176/appi.ajp.158.8.1206

Seminowicz, D. A., Remeniuk, B., Krimmel, S. R., Smith, M. T., Barrett, F. S., Wulff, A. B., Furman, A. J., Geuter, S., Lindquist, M. A., Irwin, M. R., & Finan, P. H. (2019). Pain-related nucleus accumbens function: Modulation by reward and sleep disruption. *Pain, 160*(5), 1196–1207. https:// doi.org/10.1097/j.pain.0000000000001498

Seshadri, K. G. (2016). The neuroendocrinology of love. *Indian Journal of Endocrinology and Metabo- lism, 20*(4), 558–563. https://doi.org/10.4103/2230-8210.183479

Sripada, C., Angstadt, M., Liberzon, I., McCabe, K., & Phan, K. L. (2013). Aberrant reward center response to partner reputation during a social exchange game in generalized social phobia. *Depres- sion and Anxiety, 30*(4), 353–361. https://doi.org/10.1002/da.22091

Stoy, M., Schlagenhauf, F., Sterzer, P., Bermpohl, F., Hägele, C., Suchotzki, K., Schmack, K., Wrase, J., Ricken, R., Knutson, B., Adli, M., Bauer, M., Heinz, A., & Ströhle, A. (2012). Hypoactivity of ventral striatum towards incentive stimuli in unmedicated depressed patients normalizes after treatment with escitalopram. *Journal of Psychopharmacology, 26*(5), 677–688. https://doi.org/10 .1177/0269881111416686

Sturm, V., Lenartz, D., Koulousakis, A., Treuer, H., Herholz, K., Klein, J. C., & Klosterkötter, J. (2003). The nucleus accumbens: A target for deep brain stimulation in obsessive–compulsive- and anxiety-disorders. *Journal of Chemical Neuroanatomy*, 26(4), 293–299. https://doi.org/10.1016/j.jchemneu .2003.09.003

Tanda, G., Pontieri, F. E., & Di Chiara, G. (1997). Cannabinoid and heroin activation of mesolimbic dopamine transmission by a common μ1 opioid receptor mechanism. *Science*, 276(5321), 2048– 2050. https://doi.org/10.1126/science.276.5321.2048

Voges, J., Müller, U., Bogerts, B., Münte, T., & Heinze, H. J. (2013). Deep brain stimulation surgery for alcohol addiction. *World Neurosurgery*, 80(3–4), S28.e21–S28.e31. https://doi.org/10.1016/j.wneu .2012.07.011

Volkow, N. D., Chang, L., Wang, G. J., Fowler, J. S., Franceschi, D., Sedler, M., Gatley, S. J., Miller, E., Hitzemann, R., Ding, Y.-S., & Logan, J. (2001). Loss of dopamine transporters in methamphet-amine abusers recovers with protracted abstinence. *Journal of Neuroscience*, 21(23), 9414–9418. https://doi.org/10.1523/JNEUROSCI.21-23-09414.2001

Volkow, N. D., Fowler, J. S., Wang, G. J., & Swanson, J. M. (2004). Dopamine in drug abuse and addiction: Results from imaging studies and treatment implications. *Molecular Psychiatry*, 9(6), 557–569. https://doi.org/10.1038/sj.mp.4001507

Volkow, N. D., Wang, G. J., Kollins, S. H., Wigal, T. L., Newcorn, J. H., Telang, F.,Fowler, J. S., Zhu, W., Logan, J., Ma, Y., Pradhan, K., Wong, C., & Swanson, J. M. (2009). Evaluating dopamine reward pathway in ADHD: Clinical implications. *JAMA*, 302(10), 1084–1091. https://doi.org/10 .1001/jama.2009.1308

Volman, S. F., Lammel, S., Margolis, E. B., Kim, Y., Richard, J. M., Roitman, M. F., & Lobo, M. K. (2013). New insights into the specificity and plasticity of reward and aversion encoding in the mesolimbic system. *Journal of Neuroscience*, 33(45), 17569–17576.

Wager, T. D., Davidson, M. L., Hughes, B. L., Lindquist, M. A., & Ochsner, K. N. (2008). Prefrontal-subcortical pathways mediating successful emotion regulation. *Neuron*, 59(6), 1037–1050. https:// doi.org/10.1016/j.neuron.2008.09.006

Wang, T. R., Moosa, S., Dallapiazza, R. F., Elias, W. J., & Lynch, W. J. (2018). Deep brain stimulation for the treatment of drug addiction. *Neurosurgical Focus*, 45(2), E11. https://doi.org/10.3171/2018 .5.FOCUS18163

Wang, Z., Wang, X., Liu, J., Chen, J., Liu, X., Nie, G., Jorgenson, K., Sohn, K. C., Huang, R., Liu, M., Liu, B., & Kong, J. (2017). Acupuncture treatment modulates the corticostriatal reward circuitry in major depressive disorder. *Journal of Psychiatric Research*, 84, 18–26. https://doi.org/10.1016/j .jpsychires.2016.09.014

Wittmann, A., Schlagenhauf, F., Guhn, A., Lueken, U., Elle, M., Stoy, M., Liebscher, C., Bermpohl, F., Fydrich, T., Pfleiderer, B., Bruhn, H., Gerlach, A. L., Straube, B., Wittchen, H.-U., Arolt, V., Heinz, A., Kircher, T., & Ströhle, A. (2018). Effects of cognitive behavioral therapy on neural processing of agoraphobia-specific stimuli in panic disorder and agoraphobia. *Psychotherapy and Psychosomat-ics*, 87(6), 350–365. https://doi.org/10.1159/000493146

Wu, J. C., Buchsbaum, M. S., Hershey, T. G., Hazlett, E., Sicotte, N., & Johnson, J. C. (1991). PET in generalized anxiety disorder. *Biological Psychiatry*, 29(12), 1181–1199. https://doi.org/10 .1016/0006-3223(91)90326-h

Yager, L. M., Garcia, A. F., Wunsch, A. M., & Ferguson, S. M. (August 2015). The ins and outs of the striatum: Role in drug addiction. *Neuroscience*, 301, 529–541. https://doi.org/10.1016/j .neuroscience.2015.06.033

ANTERIOR CINGULATE CORTEX REFERENCES

Anand, A., Li, Y., Wang, Y., Gardner, K., & Lowe, M. J. (2007). Reciprocal effects of antidepressant treatment on activity and connectivity of the mood regulating circuit: An FMRI study. *Journal of*

Neuropsychiatry and Clinical Neurosciences, 19(3), 274–282. https://doi.org/10.1176/jnp.2007.19
.3.274

Anand, A., Li, Y., Wang, Y., Wu, J., Gao, S., Bukhari, L., Mathews, V. P., Kalnin, A., & Lowe, M. J. (2005).
Activity and connectivity of brain mood regulating circuit in depression: A functional magnetic resonance study. *Biological Psychiatry, 57*(10), 1079–1088. https://doi.org/10.1016/j.biopsych.2005.02.021

Apps, M. A., Rushworth, M. F., & Chang, S. W. (2016). The anterior cingulate gyrus and social cognition: Tracking the motivation of others. *Neuron, 90*(4), 692–707. https://doi.org/10.1016/j.neuron
.2016.04.018

Aupperle, R. L., Allard, C. B., Simmons, A. N., Flagan, T., Thorp, S. R., Norman, S. B., Paulus, M P., &
Stein, M. B. (2013). Neural responses during emotional processing before and after cognitive trauma
therapy for battered women. *Psychiatry Research, 214*(1), 48–55. https://doi.org/10.1016/j.pscychresns
.2013.05.001

Benes, F. M. (1993). Relationship of cingulate cortex to schizophrenia and other psychiatric disorders.
In B. A. Vogt & M. S. Gabriel, *Neurobiology of cingulate cortex and limbic thalamus* (pp. 581–
605). Birkhäuser Verlag.

Bloom, P. (2017). Empathy and its discontents. *Trends in Cognitive Sciences, 21*(1), 24–31. https://doi
.org/10.1016/j.tics.2016.11.004

Boccia, M., Piccardi, L., Cordellieri, P., Guariglia, C., & Giannini, A. M. (2015). EMDR therapy for
PTSD after motor vehicle accidents: Meta-analytic evidence for specific treatment. *Frontiers in
Human Neuroscience, 9*, 213. https://doi.org/10.3389/fnhum.2015.00213

Bornovalova, M. A., Gratz, K. L., Daughters, S. B., Hunt, E. D., & Lejuez, C. W. (2012). Initial RCT
of a distress tolerance treatment for individuals with substance use disorders. *Drug and Alcohol
Dependence, 122*(1–2), 70–76. https://doi.org/10.1016/j.drugalcdep.2011.09.012

Brown, V. M., LaBar, K. S., Haswell, C. C., Gold, A. L., Mid-Atlantic MIRECC Workgroup, McCarthy, G., & Morey, R. A. (2014). Altered resting-state functional connectivity of basolateral and
ventromedial amygdala complexes in posttraumatic stress disorder. *Neuropsychopharmacology,
39*(2), 351–359. https://doi.org/10.1038/npp.2013.197

Bush, G., Luu, P., & Posner, M. I. (2000). Cognitive and emotional influences in anterior cingulate cortex. *Trends in Cognitive Sciences, 4*(6), 215–222. https://doi.org/10.1016/s1364-6613(00)01483-2

Cannon, R., Congedo, M., Lubar, J., & Hutchens, T. (2009). Differentiating a network of executive
attention: LORETA neurofeedback in anterior cingulate and dorsolateral prefrontal cortices. *International Journal of Neuroscience, 119*(3), 404–441. https://doi.org/10.1080/00207450802480325

Chong, T. T. J., Apps, M., Giehl, K., Sillence, A., Grima, L. L., & Husain, M. (2017). Neurocomputa-
tional mechanisms underlying subjective valuation of effort costs. *PLOS Biology, 15*(2), e1002598.
https://doi.org/10.1371/journal.pbio.1002598

Clausen, A. N., Francisco, A. J., Thelen, J., Bruce, J., Martin, L. E., McDowd, J., Simmons, W. K.,
& Aupperle, R. L. (2017). PTSD and cognitive symptoms relate to inhibition-related prefrontal
activation and functional connectivity. *Depression and Anxiety, 34*(5), 427–436. https://doi.org/10
.1002/da.22613

Corrigan, F. M. (2004). Psychotherapy as assisted homeostasis: Activation of emotional processing
mediated by the anterior cingulate cortex. *Medical Hypotheses, 63*(6), 968–973. https://doi.org/10
.1016/j.mehy.2004.06.009

Critchley, H. D., Mathias, C. J., Josephs, O., O'Doherty, J., Zanini, S., Dewar, B. K., Cipolotti, L., Shal-
lice, T., & Dolan, R. J. (2003). Human cingulate cortex and autonomic control: Converging neuroimaging and clinical evidence. *Brain, 126*(10), 2139–2152. https://doi.org/10.1093/brain/awg216

de Cates, A. N., Rees, K., Jollant, F., Perry, B., Bennett, K., Joyce, K., Leyden, E., Harmer, C., Hawton,
K., van Heeringen, K., & Broome, M. R. (2017). Are neurocognitive factors associated with repe-
tition of self-harm? A systematic review. *Neuroscience and Biobehavioral Reviews, 72*, 261–277.
https://doi.org/10.1016/j.neubiorev.2016.10.032

Devinsky, O., Morrell, M. J., & Vogt, B. A. (1995). Contributions of anterior cingulate cortex to
behaviour. *Brain, 118*(1), 279–306. https://doi.org/10.1093/brain/118.1.279

Dickie, E. W., Brunet, A., Akerib, V., & Armony, J. L. (2011). Neural correlates of recovery from post-traumatic stress disorder: A longitudinal fMRI investigation of memory encoding. *Neuropsychologia*, *49*(7), 1771–1778. https://doi.org/10.1016/j.neuropsychologia.2011.02.055

Disner, S. G., Beevers, C. G., Haigh, E. A., & Beck, A. T. (2011). Neural mechanisms of the cognitive model of depression. *Nature Reviews Neuroscience*, *12*(8), 467–477. https://doi.org/10.1038/nrn3027

Dong, G., Huang, J., & Du, X. (2011). Enhanced reward sensitivity and decreased loss sensitivity in Internet addicts: An fMRI study during a guessing task. *Journal of Psychiatric Research*, *45*(11), 1525–1529. https://doi.org/10.1016/j.jpsychires.2011.06.017

Elton, A., Dove, S., Spencer, C. N., Robinson, D. L., & Boettiger, C. A. (2019). Naltrexone acutely enhances connectivity between the ventromedial prefrontal cortex and a left frontoparietal network. *Alcoholism, Clinical and Experimental Research*, *43*(5), 965–978. https://doi.org/10.1111/acer.13999

Ende, G., Cackowski, S., Van Eijk, J., Sack, M., Demirakca, T., Kleindienst, N., Bohus, M., Sobanski, E., Krause-Utz, A., & Schmahl, C. (2016). Impulsivity and aggression in female BPD and ADHD patients: Association with ACC glutamate and GABA concentrations. *Neuropsychopharmacology*, *41*(2), 410–418. https://doi.org/10.1038/npp.2015.153

Ersche, K. D., Turton, A. J., Pradhan, S., Bullmore, E. T., & Robbins, T. W. (2010). Drug addiction endophenotypes: Impulsive versus sensation-seeking personality traits. *Biological Psychiatry*, *68*(8), 770–773. https://doi.org/10.1016/j.biopsych.2010.06.015

Etkin, A., & Schatzberg, A. F. (2011). Common abnormalities and disorder-specific compensation during implicit regulation of emotional processing in generalized anxiety and major depressive disorders. *American Journal of Psychiatry*, *168*(9), 968–978. https://doi.org/10.1176/appi.ajp.2011.10091290

Etkin, A., & Wager, T. D. (2007). Functional neuroimaging of anxiety: A meta-analysis of emotional processing in PTSD, social anxiety disorder, and specific phobia. *American Journal of Psychiatry*, *164*(10), 1476–1488. https://doi.org/10.1176/appi.ajp.2007.07030504

Felmingham, K., Kemp, A., Williams, L., Das, P., Hughes, G., Peduto, A., & Bryant, R. (2007). Changes in anterior cingulate and amygdala after cognitive behavior therapy of posttraumatic stress disorder. *Psychological Science*, *18*(2), 127–129. https://doi.org/10.1111/j.1467-9280.2007.01860.x

Forman, S. D., Dougherty, G. G., Casey, B. J., Siegle, G. J., Braver, T. S., Barch, D. M., Stenger, V. A., Wick-Hull, C., Pisarov, L. A., & Lorensen, E. (2004). Opiate addicts lack error-dependent activation of rostral anterior cingulate. *Biological Psychiatry*, *55*(5), 531–537. https://doi.org/10.1016/j.biopsych.2003.09.011

Fu, C. H., Williams, S. C., Cleare, A. J., Brammer, M. J., Walsh, N. D., Kim, J., Andrew, C. M., Pich, E. M., Williams, P. M., Reed, L. J., Mitterschiffthaler, M. T., Suckling, J., & Bullmore, E. T. (2004). Attenuation of the neural response to sad faces in major depression by antidepressant treatment: A prospective, event-related functional magnetic resonance imaging study. *Archives of General Psychiatry*, *61*(9), 877–889. https://doi.org/10.1001/archpsyc.61.9.877

Garrison, K. A., & Potenza, M. N. (2014). Neuroimaging and biomarkers in addiction treatment. *Current Psychiatry Reports*, *16*(12), 513. https://doi.org/10.1007/s11920-014-0513-5

Ghahremani, D. G., Tabibnia, G., Monterosso, J., Hellemann, G., Poldrack, R. A., & London, E. D. (2011). Effect of modafinil on learning and task-related brain activity in methamphetamine-dependent and healthy individuals. *Neuropsychopharmacology*, *36*(5), 950–959. https://doi.org/10.1038/npp.2010.233

Giuliani, N. R., Drabant, E. M., Bhatnagar, R., & Gross, J. J. (2011). Emotion regulation and brain plasticity: Expressive suppression use predicts anterior insula volume. *NeuroImage*, *58*(1), 10–15. https://doi.org/10.1016/j.neuroimage.2011.06.028

Godlewska, B. R., Browning, M., Norbury, R., Cowen, P. J., & Harmer, C. J. (2016). Early changes in emotional processing as a marker of clinical response to SSRI treatment in depression. *Translational Psychiatry*, *6*(11), e957. https://doi.org/10.1038/tp.2016.130

Goldapple, K., Segal, Z., Garson, C., Lau, M., Bieling, P., Kennedy, S., & Mayberg, H. (2004). Modulation of cortical-limbic pathways in major depression: Treatment-specific effects of cognitive behavior therapy. *Archives of General Psychiatry*, 61(1), 34–41. https://doi.org/10.1001/archpsyc.61.1.34

Goldstein, R. Z., Alia-Klein, N., Tomasi, D., Carrillo, J. H., Maloney, T., Woicik, P. A., Wang, R., Telang, F., & Volkow, N. D. (2009). Anterior cingulate cortex hypoactivations to an emotionally salient task in cocaine addiction. *Proceedings of the National Academy of Sciences*, 106(23), 9453–9458.

Goldstein, R. Z., & Volkow, N. D. (2011a). Dysfunction of the prefrontal cortex in addiction: Neuroimaging findings and clinical implications. *Nature Reviews Neuroscience*, 12(11), 652–669. https://doi.org/10.1038/nrn3119

Goldstein, R. Z., & Volkow, N. D. (2011b). Oral methylphenidate normalizes cingulate activity and decreases impulsivity in cocaine addiction during an emotionally salient cognitive task. *Neuropsychopharmacology*, 36(1), 366–367. https://doi.org/10.1038/npp.2010.145

Goldstein, R. Z., Woicik, P. A., Maloney, T., Tomasi, D., Alia-Klein, N., Shan, J., Honorio, J., Samaras, D., Wang, R., Telang, F., . . . Wang, G. J., & Volkow, N. D. (2010). Oral methylphenidate normalizes cingulate activity in cocaine addiction during a salient cognitive task. *Proceedings of the National Academy of Sciences*, 107(38), 16667–16672.

Halari, R., Simic, M., Pariante, C. M., Papadopoulos, A., Cleare, A., Brammer, M., Fombonne, E., & Rubia, K. (2009). Reduced activation in lateral prefrontal cortex and anterior cingulate during attention and cognitive control functions in medication-naive adolescents with depression compared to controls. *Journal of Child Psychology and Psychiatry, and Allied Disciplines*, 50(3), 307–316. https://doi.org/10.1111/j.1469-7610.2008.01972.x

Hamilton, J. P., Glover, G. H., Hsu, J. J., Johnson, R. F., & Gotlib, I. H. (2011). Modulation of subgenual anterior cingulate cortex activity with real-time neurofeedback. *Human Brain Mapping*, 32(1), 22–31. https://doi.org/10.1002/hbm.20997

Heilbronner, S. R., & Hayden, B. Y. (2016). Dorsal anterior cingulate cortex: A bottom-up view. *Annual Review of Neuroscience*, 39, 149–170. https://doi.org/10.1146/annurev-neuro-070815-013952

Helpman, L., Marin, M. F., Papini, S., Zhu, X., Sullivan, G. M., Schneier, F., Neria, M., Shvil, E., Aragon, M. J. M., Markowitz, J. C., Lindquist, M. A., Wager, T. D., Milad, M. R., & Neria, Y. (2016). Neural changes in extinction recall following prolonged exposure treatment for PTSD: A longitudinal fMRI study. *NeuroImage: Clinical*, 12, 715–723. https://doi.org/10.1016/j.nicl.2016.10.007

Hermann, A., Keck, T., & Stark, R. (2014). Dispositional cognitive reappraisal modulates the neural correlates of fear acquisition and extinction. *Neurobiology of Learning and Memory*, 113, 115–124. https://doi.org/10.1016/j.nlm.2014.03.008

Holsen, L. M., Lee, J. H., Spaeth, S. B., Ogden, L. A., Klibanski, A., Whitfield-Gabrieli, S., Sloan, R. P., & Goldstein, J. M. (2012). Brain hypoactivation, autonomic nervous system dysregulation, and gonadal hormones in depression: A preliminary study. *Neuroscience Letters*, 514(1), 57–61. https://doi.org/10.1016/j.neulet.2012.02.056

Hopper, J. W., Frewen, P. A., Van der Kolk, B. A., & Lanius, R. A. (2007). Neural correlates of reexperiencing, avoidance, and dissociation in PTSD: Symptom dimensions and emotion dysregulation in responses to script-driven trauma imagery. *Journal of Traumatic Stress*, 20(5), 713–725. https://doi.org/10.1002/jts.20284

Iannaccone, R., Hauser, T. U., Staempfli, P., Walitza, S., Brandeis, D., & Brem, S. (2015). Conflict monitoring and error processing: New insights from simultaneous EEG–fMRI. *NeuroImage*, 105, 395–407. https://doi.org/10.1016/j.neuroimage.2014.10.028

Janes, A. C., Pizzagalli, D. A., Richardt, S., deB Frederick, B. deB., Chuzi, S., Pachas, G., Culhane, M. A., Holmes, A. J., Fava, M., Evins, A. E., & Kaufman, M. J. (2010). Brain reactivity to smoking cues prior to smoking cessation predicts ability to maintain tobacco abstinence. *Biological Psychiatry*, 67(8), 722–729. https://doi.org/10.1016/j.biopsych.2009.12.034

Jumah, F. R., & Dossani, R. H. (2019). *STATPearls: Neuroanatomy, Cingulate Cortex*. Retrieved 3/18/2021 from https://www.ncbi.nlm.nih.gov/books/NBK537077/

Kanske, P., Heissler, J., Schönfelder, S., & Wessa, M. (2012). Neural correlates of emotion regulation deficits in remitted depression: The influence of regulation strategy, habitual regulation use, and emotional valence. *NeuroImage, 61*(3), 686–693. https://doi.org/10.1016/j.neuroimage.2012.03 .089

King, A. P., Block, S. R., Sripada, R. K., Rauch, S., Giardino, N., Favorite, T., Angstadt, M., Kessler, D., Welsh, R., & Liberzon, I. (2016). Altered default mode network (DMN) resting state functional connectivity following a mindfulness-based exposure therapy for posttraumatic stress disorder (PTSD) in combat veterans of Afghanistan and Iraq. *Depression and Anxiety, 33*(4), 289–299. https://doi.org/10.1002/da.22481

Klimecki, O., & Singer, T. (2013). Empathy from the Perspective of Social Neuroscience. In J. Armony & P. Vuilleumier (Eds.), *The Cambridge Handbook of Human Affective Neuroscience* (pp. 533–550). Cambridge University Press. https://doi.org/10.1017/CBO9780511843716.029

Koenen, K. C. (2006). Developmental epidemiology of PTSD: Self-regulation as a central mechanism. *Annals of the New York Academy of Sciences, 1071*, 255–266. https://doi.org/10.1196/annals.1364 .020

Kohn, N., Eickhoff, S. B., Scheller, M., Laird, A. R., Fox, P. T., & Habel, U. (2014). Neural network of cognitive emotion regulation: An ALE meta-analysis and MACM analysis. *NeuroImage, 87*, 345– 355. https://doi.org/10.1016/j.neuroimage.2013.11.001

Konova, A. B., Moeller, S. J., & Goldstein, R. Z. (2013). Common and distinct neural targets of treatment: Changing brain function in substance addiction. *Neuroscience and Biobehavioral Reviews, 37*(10 Pt 2), 2806–2817. https://doi.org/10.1016/j.neubiorev.2013.10.002

Koso, M., & Hansen, S. (2006). Executive function and memory in posttraumatic stress disorder: A study of Bosnian War veterans. *European Psychiatry, 21*(3), 167–173. https://doi.org/10.1016/j .eurpsy.2005.06.004

Kutlu, M. G., Burke, D., Slade, S., Hall, B. J., Rose, J. E., & Levin, E. D. (2013). Role of insular cortex D1 and D2 dopamine receptors in nicotine self-administration in rats. *Behavioural Brain Research, 256*, 273–278. https://doi.org/10.1016/j.bbr.2013.08.005

Ladouceur, C. D., Slifka, J. S., Dahl, R. E., Birmaher, B., Axelson, D. A., & Ryan, N. D. (2012). Altered error-related brain activity in youth with major depression. *Developmental Cognitive Neuroscience, 2*(3), 351–362. https://doi.org/10.1016/j.dcn.2012.01.005

Larson, M. J., Fair, J. E., Good, D. A., & Baldwin, S. A. (2010). Empathy and error processing. *Psychophysiology, 47*(3), 415–424. https://doi.org/10.1111/j.1469-8986.2009.00949.x

Levkovitz, Y., Sheer, A., Harel, E. V., Katz, L. N., Most, D., Zangen, A., & Isserles, M. (2011). Differential effects of deep TMS of the prefrontal cortex on apathy and depression. *Brain Stimulation, 4*(4), 266–274. https://doi.org/10.1016/j.brs.2010.12.004

Liotti, M., & Mayberg, H. S. (2001). The role of functional neuroimaging in the neuropsychology of depression. *Journal of Clinical and Experimental Neuropsychology, 23*(1), 121–136. https://doi .org/10.1076/jcen.23.1.121.1223

Lippelt, D. P., Hommel, B., & Colzato, L. S. (2014). Focused attention, open monitoring and loving kindness meditation: Effects on attention, conflict monitoring, and creativity–A review. *Frontiers in Psychology, 5*, 1083. https://doi.org/10.3389/fpsyg.2014.01083

Lown, B. A. (2016). A social neuroscience-informed model for teaching and practising compassion in health care. *Medical Education, 50*(3), 332–342. https://doi.org/10.1111/medu.12926

Ma, N., Liu, Y., Li, N., Wang, C. X., Zhang, H., Jiang, X. F., Xu, H.-S., Fu, X.-M., Hu, X., & Zhang, D.-R. (2010). Addiction related alteration in resting-state brain connectivity. *NeuroImage, 49*(1), 738–744. https://doi.org/10.1016/j.neuroimage.2009.08.037

Margulies, D. S., Kelly, A. M., Uddin, L. Q., Biswal, B. B., Castellanos, F. X., & Milham, M. P. (2007). Mapping the functional connectivity of anterior cingulate cortex. *NeuroImage, 37*(2), 579–588. https://doi.org/10.1016/j.neuroimage.2007.05.019

Mayberg, H. S., Lozano, A. M., Voon, V., McNeely, H. E., Seminowicz, D., Hamani, C., Schwalb, J. M.,

& Kennedy, S. H. (2005). Deep brain stimulation for treatment-resistant depression. *Neuron, 45*(5), 651–660. https://doi.org/10.1016/j.neuron.2005.02.014

Melcher, T., Falkai, P., & Gruber, O. (2008). Functional brain abnormalities in psychiatric disorders: Neural mechanisms to detect and resolve cognitive conflict and interference. *Brain Research Reviews, 59*(1), 96–124. https://doi.org/10.1016/j.brainresrev.2008.06.003

Melloni, M., Lopez, V., & Ibanez, A. (2014). Empathy and contextual social cognition. *Cognitive, Affective and Behavioral Neuroscience, 14*(1), 407–425. https://doi.org/10.3758/s13415-013-0205-3

Naqvi, N. H., & Bechara, A. (2010). The insula and drug addiction: An interoceptive view of pleasure, urges, and decision-making. *Brain Structure and Function, 214*(5–6), 435–450. https://doi.org/10.1007/s00429-010-0268-7

Nicholson, A. A., Rabellino, D., Densmore, M., Frewen, P. A., Paret, C., Kluetsch, R., . . . & Lanius, R. A. (2017). The neurobiology of emotion regulation in posttraumatic stress disorder: Amygdala downregulation via real-time fMRI neurofeedback. *Human Brain Mapping, 38*(1), 541–560.

O'Connell, R. G., Dockree, P. M., Bellgrove, M. A., Kelly, S. P., Hester, R., Garavan, H., Robertson, I. H., & Foxe, J. J. (2007). The role of cingulate cortex in the detection of errors with and without awareness: A high-density electrical mapping study. *European Journal of Neuroscience, 25*(8), 2571–2579. https://doi.org/10.1111/j.1460-9568.2007.05477.x

Pantazatos, S. P., Yttredahl, A., Rubin-Falcone, H., Kishon, R., Oquendo, M. A., Mann, J. J., & Miller, J. M. (2020). Depression-related anterior cingulate prefrontal resting state connectivity normalizes following cognitive behavioral therapy. *European Psychiatry, 63*(1).

Patel, R., Spreng, R. N., Shin, L. M., & Girard, T. A. (2012). Neurocircuitry models of posttraumatic stress disorder and beyond: A meta-analysis of functional neuroimaging studies. *Neuroscience and Biobehavioral Reviews, 36*(9), 2130–2142. https://doi.org/10.1016/j.neubiorev.2012.06.003

Philippi, C. L., Motzkin, J. C., Pujara, M. S., & Koenigs, M. (2015). Subclinical depression severity is associated with distinct patterns of functional connectivity for subregions of anterior cingulate cortex. *Journal of Psychiatric Research, 71*, 103–111. https://doi.org/10.1016/j.jpsychires.2015.10.005

Pizzagalli, D., Pascual-Marqui, R. D., Nitschke, J. B., Oakes, T. R., Larson, C. L., Abercrombie, H. C., Schaefer, S. M., Koger, J. V., Benca, R. M., & Davidson, R. J. (2001). Anterior cingulate activity as a predictor of degree of treatment response in major depression: Evidence from brain electrical tomography analysis. *American Journal of Psychiatry, 158*(3), 405–415. https://doi.org/10.1176/appi.ajp.158.3.405

Potenza, M. N., Sofuoglu, M., Carroll, K. M., & Rounsaville, B. J. (2011). Neuroscience of behavioral and pharmacological treatments for addictions. *Neuron, 69*(4), 695–712. https://doi.org/10.1016/j.neuron.2011.02.009

Rauch, S. L., Jenike, M. A., Alpert, N. M., Baer, L., Breiter, H. C., Savage, C. R., & Fischman, A. J. (1994). Regional cerebral blood flow measured during symptom provocation in obsessive–compulsive disorder using oxygen 15-labeled carbon dioxide and positron emission tomography. *Archives of General Psychiatry, 51*(1), 62–70. https://doi.org/10.1001/archpsyc.1994.03950010062008

Ridderinkhof, K. R., Ullsperger, M., Crone, E. A., & Nieuwenhuis, S. (2004). The role of the medial frontal cortex in cognitive control. *Science, 306*(5695), 443–447. https://doi.org/10.1126/science.1100301

Roiser, J. P., Elliott, R., & Sahakian, B. J. (2012). Cognitive mechanisms of treatment in depression. *Neuropsychopharmacology, 37*(1), 117–136. https://doi.org/10.1038/npp.2011.183

Rosso, I. M., Weiner, M. R., Crowley, D. J., Silveri, M. M., Rauch, S. L., & Jensen, J. E. (2014). Insula and anterior cingulate GABA levels in posttraumatic stress disorder: Preliminary findings using magnetic resonance spectroscopy. *Depression and Anxiety, 31*(2), 115–123. https://doi.org/10.1002/da.22155

Rousseau, P. F., El Khoury-Malhame, M., Reynaud, E., Zendjidjian, X., Samuelian, J. C., & Khalfa, S.

(2019). Neurobiological correlates of EMDR therapy effect in PTSD. *European Journal of Trauma and Dissociation*, 3(2), 103–111. https://doi.org/10.1016/j.ejtd.2018.07.001

Roy, M. J., Costanzo, M. E., Blair, J. R., & Rizzo, A. A. (2014). Compelling evidence that exposure therapy for PTSD normalizes brain function. *Studies in Health Technology and Informatics*, 199, 61–65.

Sander, I. D., & Scherer, K. R. (2010). *Oxford companion to emotion and the affective sciences*. Oxford University Press.

Sanders, G. S., Gallup, G. G., Heinsen, H., Hof, P. R., & Schmitz, C. (2002). Cognitive deficits, schizophrenia, and the anterior cingulate cortex. *Trends in Cognitive Sciences*, 6(5), 190–192. https://doi.org/10.1016/s1364-6613(02)01892-2

Shang, J., Fu, Y., Ren, Z., Zhang, T., Du, M., Gong, Q., Lui, S., & Zhang, W. (2014). The common traits of the ACC and PFC in anxiety disorders in the DSM-5: Meta-analysis of voxel-based morphometry studies. *PloS ONE*, 9(3), e93432. https://doi.org/10.1371/journal.pone.0093432

Solomon, R. M., & Rando, T. A. (2012). Treatment of grief and mourning through EMDR: Conceptual considerations and clinical guidelines. *European Review of Applied Psychology*, 62(4), 231–239. https://doi.org/10.1016/j.erap.2012.09.002

Sripada, R. K., King, A. P., Garfinkel, S. N., Wang, X., Sripada, C. S., Welsh, R. C., & Liberzon, I. (2012). Altered resting-state amygdala functional connectivity in men with posttraumatic stress disorder. *Journal of Psychiatry and Neuroscience*, 37(4), 241–249. https://doi.org/10.1503/jpn.110069

Strom, T. Q., Leskela, J., James, L. M., Thuras, P. D., Voller, E., Weigel, R., Yutsis, M., Knaylis, A., Lindberg, J., & Holz, K. B. (2012). An exploratory examination of risk-taking behavior and PTSD symptom severity in a veteran sample. *Military Medicine*, 177(4), 390–396. https://doi.org/10.7205/milmed-d-11-00133

Tang, Y. Y., Posner, M. I., Rothbart, M. K., & Volkow, N. D. (2015). Circuitry of self-control and its role in reducing addiction. *Trends in cognitive sciences*, 19(8), 439–444.

Tang, Y. Y., & Tang, R. (2013). Ventral-subgenual anterior cingulate cortex and self-transcendence. *Frontiers in Psychology*, 4, 1000. https://doi.org/10.3389/fpsyg.2013.01000

Thomaes, K., Dorrepaal, E., Draijer, N., Jansma, E. P., Veltman, D. J., & van Balkom, A. J. (2014). Can pharmacological and psychological treatment change brain structure and function in PTSD? A systematic review. *Journal of Psychiatric Research*, 50, 1–15. https://doi.org/10.1016/j.jpsychires.2013.11.002

To, W. T., De Ridder, D., Menovsky, T., Hart, J., & Vanneste, S. (2017). The role of the dorsal Anterior cingulate Cortex (dACC) in a cognitive and emotional counting Stroop task: Two cases. *Restorative Neurology and Neuroscience*, 35(3), 333–345. https://doi.org/10.3233/RNN-170730

Vanderhasselt, M. A., Baeken, C., Van Schuerbeek, P., Luypaert, R., & De Raedt, R. (2013). Inter-individual differences in the habitual use of cognitive reappraisal and expressive suppression are associated with variations in prefrontal cognitive control for emotional information: An event related fMRI study. *Biological Psychology*, 92(3), 433–439. https://doi.org/10.1016/j.biopsycho.2012.03.005

Veer, I. M., Beckmann, C. F., Van Tol, M. J., Ferrarini, L., Milles, J., Veltman, D. J., Aleman, A., van Buchem, M. A., van der Wee, N. J., & Rombouts, S. A. R. B. (2010). Whole brain resting-state analysis reveals decreased functional connectivity in major depression. *Frontiers in Systems Neuroscience*, 4, Article 41. https://doi.org/10.3389/fnsys.2010.00041

Vogt, B. A., Nimchinsky, E. A., Vogt, L. J., & Hof, P. R. (1995). Human cingulate cortex: Surface features, flat maps, and cytoarchitecture. *Journal of Comparative Neurology*, 359(3), 490–506. https://doi.org/10.1002/cne.903590310

Wei, Z., Yang, N., Liu, Y., Yang, L., Wang, Y., Han, L., Zha, R., Huang, R., Zhang, P., Zhou, Y., & Zhang, X. (2016). Resting-state functional connectivity between the dorsal anterior cingulate cortex and thalamus is associated with risky decision-making in nicotine addicts. *Scientific Reports*, 6, 21778. https://doi.org/10.1038/srep21778

Weiss, N. H., Tull, M. T., Viana, A. G., Anestis, M. D., & Gratz, K. L. (2012). Impulsive behaviors as an emotion regulation strategy: Examining associations between PTSD, emotion dysregulation, and impulsive behaviors among substance dependent inpatients. *Journal of Anxiety Disorders, 26*(3), 453–458. https://doi.org/10.1016/j.janxdis.2012.01.007

Wessel, J. R., Danielmeier, C., & Ullsperger, M. (2011). Error awareness revisited: Accumulation of multimodal evidence from central and autonomic nervous systems. *Journal of Cognitive Neuroscience, 23*(10), 3021–3036. https://doi.org/10.1162/jocn.2011.21635

Wexler, B. E., Gottschalk, C. H., Fulbright, R. K., Prohovnik, I., Lacadie, C. M., Rounsaville, B. J., & Gore, J. C. (2001). GoreFunctional magnetic resonance imaging of cocaine craving. *American Journal of Psychiatry, 158*(1), 86–95. https://doi.org/10.1176/appi.ajp.158.1.86

Yang, Z., Oathes, D. J., Linn, K. A., Bruce, S. E., Satterthwaite, T. D., Cook, P. A., Satchell, E. K., Shou, H., & Sheline, Y. I. (2018). Cognitive behavioral therapy is associated with enhanced cognitive control network activity in major depression and posttraumatic stress disorder. *Biological Psychiatry: Cognitive Neuroscience and Neuroimaging, 3*(4), 311–319. https://doi.org/10.1016/j.bpsc.2017.12.006

Yoshimura, S., Okamoto, Y., Onoda, K., Matsunaga, M., Okada, G., Kunisato, Y., Yoshino, A., Ueda, K., Suzuki, S., & Yamawaki, S. (2014). Cognitive behavioral therapy for depression changes medial prefrontal and ventral anterior cingulate cortex activity associated with self-referential processing. *Social Cognitive and Affective Neuroscience, 9*(4), 487–493. https://doi.org/10.1093/scan/nst009

Yücel, M., Wood, S. J., Fornito, A., Riffkin, J., Velakoulis, D., & Pantelis, C. (2003). Anterior cingulate dysfunction: Implications for psychiatric disorders? *Journal of Psychiatry and Neuroscience, 28*(5), 350–354.

Zilverstand, A., Parvaz, M. A., Moeller, S. J., & Goldstein, R. Z. (2016). Cognitive interventions for addiction medicine: Understanding the underlying neurobiological mechanisms. In *Progress in Brain Research, 224*, 285–304. https://doi.org/10.1016/bs.pbr.2015.07.019

Zilverstand, A., Sorger, B., Slaats-Willemse, D., Kan, C. C., Goebel, R., & Buitelaar, J. K. (2017). fMRI neurofeedback training for increasing anterior cingulate cortex activation in adult attention deficit hyperactivity disorder. An exploratory randomized, single-blinded study. *PloS ONE, 12*(1), e0170795. https://doi.org/10.1371/journal.pone.0170795

Zweerings, J., Pflieger, E. M., Mathiak, K. A., Zvyagintsev, M., Kacela, A., Flatten, G., & Mathiak, K. (2018). Impaired voluntary control in PTSD: Probing self-regulation of the ACC with real-time fMRI. *Frontiers in Psychiatry, 9*, 219. https://doi.org/10.3389/fpsyt.2018.00219

VENTROMEDIAL PREFRONTAL CORTEX REFERENCES

Addis, D. R., Wong, A. T., & Schacter, D. L. (2007). Remembering the past and imagining the future: Common and distinct neural substrates during event construction and elaboration. *Neuropsychologia, 45*(7), 1363–1377. https://doi.org/10.1016/j.neuropsychologia.2006.10.016

Akiki, T. J., Averill, C. L., & Abdallah, C. G. (2017). A network-based neurobiological model of PTSD: Evidence from structural and functional neuroimaging studies. *Current Psychiatry Reports, 19*(11), 81. https://doi.org/10.1007/s11920-017-0840-4

An, J., Wang, L., Li, K., Zeng, Y., Su, Y., Jin, Z., Yu, Z., & Si, T. (2017). Differential effects of antidepressant treatment on long-range and short-range functional connectivity strength in patients with major depressive disorder. *Scientific Reports, 7*(1), 10214. https://doi.org/10.1038/s41598-017-10575-9

Anand, A., Li, Y., Wang, Y., Gardner, K., & Lowe, M. J. (2007). Reciprocal effects of antidepressant treatment on activity and connectivity of the mood regulating circuit: An fMRI study. *Journal of Neuropsychiatry and Clinical Neurosciences, 19*(3), 274–282. https://doi.org/10.1176/jnp.2007.19.3.274

Andrewes, D. G., & Jenkins, L. M. (2019). The role of the amygdala and the ventromedial prefrontal cortex in emotional regulation: Implications for post-traumatic stress disorder. *Neuropsychology Review, 29*(2), 220–243. https://doi.org/10.1007/s11065-019-09398-4

Ball, T. M., Knapp, S. E., Paulus, M. P., & Stein, M. B. (2017). Brain activation during fear extinction predicts exposure success. *Depression and Anxiety, 34*(3), 257–266. https://doi.org/10.1002/da.22583

Beer, J. S., John, O. P., Scabini, D., & Knight, R. T. (2006). Orbitofrontal cortex and social behavior: Integrating self-monitoring and emotion-cognition interactions. *Journal of Cognitive Neuroscience, 18*(6), 871–879. https://doi.org/10.1162/jocn.2006.18.6.871

Benoit, R. G., Szpunar, K. K., & Schacter, D. L. (2014). Ventromedial prefrontal cortex supports effective future simulation by integrating distributed knowledge. *Proceedings of the National Academy of Sciences, 111*(46), 16550–16555.

Bhanji, J., Smith, D. V., & Delgado, M. (2019, July 17). A brief anatomical sketch of human ventromedial prefrontal cortex. https://doi.org/10.31234/osf.io/zdt7f

Bonnici, H. M., & Maguire, E. A. (2018). Two years later – Revisiting autobiographical memory representations in vmPFC and hippocampus. *Neuropsychologia, 110*, 159–169. https://doi.org/10.1016/j.neuropsychologia.2017.05.014

Brody, A. L., Saxena, S., Mandelkern, M. A., Fairbanks, L. A., Ho, M. L., & Baxter, L. R. (2001). Brain metabolic changes associated with symptom factor improvement in major depressive disorder. *Biological Psychiatry, 50*(3), 171–178. https://doi.org/10.1016/s0006-3223(01)01117-9

Calancie, O. G., Khalid-Khan, S., Booij, L., & Munoz, D. P. (2018). Eye movement desensitization and reprocessing as a treatment for PTSD: Current neurobiological theories and a new hypothesis. *Annals of the New York Academy of Sciences, 1426*(1), 127–145. https://doi.org/10.1111/nyas.13882

Cao, X., Liu, Z., Xu, C., Li, J., Gao, Q., Sun, N., Xu, Y., Ren, Y., Yang, C., & Zhang, K. (2012). Disrupted resting-state functional connectivity of the hippocampus in medication-naïve patients with major depressive disorder. *Journal of Affective Disorders, 141*(2–3), 194–203. https://doi.org/10.1016/j.jad.2012.03.002

Campbell, K. L., Madore, K. P., Benoit, R. G., Thakral, P. P., & Schacter, D. L. (2018). Increased hippocampus to ventromedial prefrontal connectivity during the construction of episodic future events. *Hippocampus, 28*(2), 76–80.

Carlson, N. R. (2013). *Physiology of behavior* (11th ed). Pearson.

Chester, D. S., Lynam, D. R., Milich, R., & DeWall, C. N. (2017). Physical aggressiveness and gray matter deficits in ventromedial prefrontal cortex. *Cortex, 97*, 17–22. https://doi.org/10.1016/j.cortex.2017.09.024

Connolly, C. G., Ho, T. C., Blom, E. H., LeWinn, K. Z., Sacchet, M. D., Tymofiyeva, O., Simmons, A. N., & Yang, T. T. (2017). Resting-state functional connectivity of the amygdala and longitudinal changes in depression severity in adolescent depression. *Journal of Affective Disorders, 207*, 86–94. https://doi.org/10.1016/j.jad.2016.09.026

Creswell, J. D., Way, B. M., Eisenberger, N. I., & Lieberman, M. D. (2007). Neural correlates of dispositional mindfulness during affect labeling. *Psychosomatic Medicine, 69*(6), 560–565. https://doi.org/10.1097/PSY.0b013e3180f6171f

D'Argembeau, A. (2013). On the role of the ventromedial prefrontal cortex in self-processing: The valuation hypothesis. *Frontiers in Human Neuroscience, 7*, 372. https://doi.org/10.3389/fnhum.2013.00372

D'Argembeau, A., Stawarczyk, D., Majerus, S., Collette, F., Van der Linden, M., Feyers, D., Maquet, P., & Salmon, E. (2010). The neural basis of personal goal processing when envisioning future events. *Journal of Cognitive Neuroscience, 22*(8), 1701–1713. https://doi.org/10.1162/jocn.2009.21314

Davidson, R. J., Putnam, K. M., & Larson, C. L. (2000). Dysfunction in the neural circuitry of emotion regulation—A possible prelude to violence. *Science, 289*(5479), 591–594. https://doi.org/10.1126/science.289.5479.591

Decety, J., Skelly, L., Yoder, K. J., & Kiehl, K. A. (2014). Neural processing of dynamic emotional facial

expressions in psychopaths. *Social Neuroscience, 9*(1), 36–49. https://doi.org/10.1080/17470919
.2013.866905

Dickie, E. W., Brunet, A., Akerib, V., & Armony, J. L. (2008). An fMRI investigation of memory encoding in PTSD: Influence of symptom severity. *Neuropsychologia, 46*(5), 1522–1531. https://doi.org/10.1016/j.neuropsychologia.2008.01.007

Di Simplicio, M., Norbury, R., & Harmer, C. J. (2012). Short-term antidepressant administration reduces negative self-referential processing in the medial prefrontal cortex in subjects at risk for depression. *Molecular Psychiatry, 17*(5), 503–510. https://doi.org/10.1038/mp.2011.16

Drevets, W. C. (1998). Functional neuroimaging studies of depression: The anatomy of melancholia. *Annual Review of Medicine, 49*, 341–361. https://doi.org/10.1146/annurev.med.49.1.341

Ersner-Hershfield, H., Wimmer, G. E., & Knutson, B. (2009). Saving for the future self: Neural measures of future self-continuity predict temporal discounting. *Social Cognitive and Affective Neuroscience, 4*(1), 85–92. https://doi.org/10.1093/scan/nsn042

Euston, D. R., Gruber, A. J., & McNaughton, B. L. (2012). The role of medial prefrontal cortex in memory and decision making. *Neuron, 76*(6), 1057–1070. https://doi.org/10.1016/j.neuron.2012.12.002

Evans, K. C., Simon, N. M., Dougherty, D. D., Hoge, E. A., Worthington, J. J., Chow, C., Kaufman, R. E., Gold, A. L., Fischman, A. J., Pollack, M. H., & Rauch, S. L. (2009). A PET study of tiagabine treatment implicates ventral medial prefrontal cortex in generalized social anxiety disorder. *Neuropsychopharmacology, 34*(2), 390–398. https://doi.org/10.1038/npp.2008.69

Farooq, R. K., Asghar, K., Kanwal, S., & Zulqernain, A. (2017). Role of inflammatory cytokines in depression: Focus on interleukin-1β. *Biomedical Reports, 6*(1), 15–20. https://doi.org/10.3892/br.2016.807

Felger, J. C., Li, Z., Haroon, E., Woolwine, B. J., Jung, M. Y., Hu, X., & Miller, A. H. (2016). Inflammation is associated with decreased functional connectivity within corticostriatal reward circuitry in depression. *Molecular Psychiatry, 21*(10), 1358–1365. https://doi.org/10.1038/mp.2015.168

Fitzgerald, J. M., DiGangi, J. A., & Phan, K. L. (2018). Functional neuroanatomy of emotion and its regulation in PTSD. *Harvard Review of Psychiatry, 26*(3), 116–128. https://doi.org/10.1097/HRP.0000000000000185

Fonzo, G. A., Goodkind, M. S., Oathes, D. J., Zaiko, Y. V., Harvey, M., Peng, K. K., Weiss, M. E., Thompson, A. L., Zack, S. E., Mills-Finnerty, C. E., Rosenberg, B. M., Edelstein, R., Wright, R. N., Kole, C. A., Lindley, S. E., Arnow, B. A., Jo, B., Gross, J. J., Rothbaum, B. O., & Etkin, A. (2017). Selective effects of psychotherapy on frontopolar cortical function in PTSD. *American Journal of Psychiatry, 174*(12), 1175–1184. https://doi.org/10.1176/appi.ajp.2017.16091073

Franklin, G., Carson, A. J., & Welch, K. A. (2016). Cognitive behavioural therapy for depression: Systematic review of imaging studies. *Acta Neuropsychiatrica, 28*(2), 61–74. https://doi.org/10.1017/neu.2015.41

Furman, D. J., Hamilton, J. P., & Gotlib, I. H. (2011). Frontostriatal functional connectivity in major depressive disorder. *Biology of Mood and Anxiety Disorders, 1*(1), 11. https://doi.org/10.1186/2045-5380-1-11

Gage, N., & Baars, B. (2018). *Fundamentals of Cognitive Neuroscience: A Beginner's Guide.* Academic Press.

Greenberg, T., Carlson, J. M., Cha, J., Hajcak, G., & Mujica-Parodi, L. R. (2013). Ventromedial prefrontal cortex reactivity is altered in generalized anxiety disorder during fear generalization. *Depression and Anxiety, 30*(3), 242–250. https://doi.org/10.1002/da.22016

Greicius, M. D., Flores, B. H., Menon, V., Glover, G. H., Solvason, H. B., Kenna, H., Reiss, A. L., & Schatzberg, A. F. (2007). Resting-state functional connectivity in major depression: Abnormally increased contributions from subgenual cingulate cortex and thalamus. *Biological Psychiatry, 62*(5), 429–437. https://doi.org/10.1016/j.biopsych.2006.09.020

Grimm, S., Boesiger, P., Beck, J., Schuepbach, D., Bermpohl, F., Walter, M., Ernst, J., Hell, D., Boeker, H., & Northoff, G. (2009). Altered negative BOLD responses in the default-mode network during emotion processing in depressed subjects. *Neuropsychopharmacology, 34*(4), 932–943. https://doi.org/10.1038/npp.2008.81

Guo, C. C., Hyett, M. P., Nguyen, V. T., Parker, G. B., & Breakspear, M. J. (2016). Distinct neuro-biological signatures of brain connectivity in depression subtypes during natural viewing of emotionally salient films. *Psychological Medicine, 46*(7), 1535–1545. https://doi.org/10.1017/S0033291716000179

Harenski, C. L., Harenski, K. A., Shane, M. S., & Kiehl, K. A. (2010). Aberrant neural processing of moral violations in criminal psychopaths. *Journal of Abnormal Psychology, 119*(4), 863–874. https://doi.org/10.1037/a0020979

Hayes, J. P., VanElzakker, M. B., & Shin, L. M. (2012). Emotion and cognition interactions in PTSD: A review of neurocognitive and neuroimaging studies. *Frontiers in Integrative Neuroscience, 6,* 89. https://doi.org/10.3389/fnint.2012.00089

Herrmann, M. J., Katzorke, A., Busch, Y., Gromer, D., Polak, T., Pauli, P., & Deckert, J. (2017). Medial prefrontal cortex stimulation accelerates therapy response of exposure therapy in acrophobia. *Brain Stimulation, 10*(2), 291–297. https://doi.org/10.1016/j.brs.2016.11.007

Herzog, J. I., Niedtfeld, I., Rausch, S., Thome, J., Mueller-Engelmann, M., Steil, R., Priebe, K., Bohus, M., & Schmahl, C. (2019). Increased recruitment of cognitive control in the presence of traumatic stimuli in complex PTSD. *European Archives of Psychiatry and Clinical Neuroscience, 269*(2), 147–159. https://doi.org/10.1007/s00406-017-0822-x

Hiser, J., & Koenigs, M. (2018). The multifaceted role of the ventromedial prefrontal cortex in emotion, decision making, social cognition, and psychopathology. *Biological Psychiatry, 83*(8), 638–647. https://doi.org/10.1016/j.biopsych.2017.10.030

Hofmann, S. G., Papini, S., Carpenter, J. K., Otto, M. W., Rosenfield, D., Dutcher, C. D., Dowd, S., Lewis, M., Witcraft, S., Pollack, M. H., & Smits, J. A. J. (2019). Effect of D-cycloserine on fear extinction training in adults with social anxiety disorder. *PLoS ONE, 14*(10), e0223729. https://doi.org/10.1371/journal.pone.0223729

Holt, D. J., Coombs, G., Zeidan, M. A., Goff, D. C., & Milad, M. R. (2012). Failure of neural responses to safety cues in schizophrenia. *Archives of General Psychiatry, 69*(9), 893–903. https://doi.org/10.1001/archgenpsychiatry.2011.2310

Hu, K. (2018). Neural activity to threat in ventromedial prefrontal cortex correlates with individual differences in anxiety and reward processing. *Neuropsychologia, 117,* 566–573. https://doi.org/10.1016/j.neuropsychologia.2018.07.004

Jalbrzikowski, M., Larsen, B., Hallquist, M. N., Foran, W., Calabro, F., & Luna, B. (2017). Development of white matter microstructure and intrinsic functional connectivity between the amygdala and ventromedial prefrontal cortex: Associations with anxiety and depression. *Biological Psychiatry, 82*(7), 511–521. https://doi.org/10.1016/j.biopsych.2017.01.008

Johnstone, T., Van Reekum, C. M., Urry, H. L., Kalin, N. H., & Davidson, R. J. (2007). Failure to regulate: Counterproductive recruitment of top-down prefrontal-subcortical circuitry in major depression. *Journal of Neuroscience, 27*(33), 8877–8884. https://doi.org/10.1523/JNEUROSCI.2063-07.2007

Kaiser, R. H., Andrews-Hanna, J. R., Wager, T. D., & Pizzagalli, D. A. (2015). Large-scale network dysfunction in major depressive disorder: A meta-analysis of resting-state functional connectivity. *JAMA Psychiatry, 72*(6), 603–611. https://doi.org/10.1001/jamapsychiatry.2015.0071

Kennedy, S. H., Konarski, J. Z., Segal, Z. V., Lau, M. A., Bieling, P. J., McIntyre, R. S., & Mayberg, H. S. (2007). Differences in brain glucose metabolism between responders to CBT and venlafaxine in a 16-week randomized controlled trial. *American Journal of Psychiatry, 164*(5), 778–788. https://doi.org/10.1176/ajp.2007.164.5.778

Killgore, W. D., Britton, J. C., Schwab, Z. J., Price, L. M., Weiner, M. R., Gold, A. L., Rosso, I. M., Simon, N. M., Pollack, M. H., & Rauch, S. L. (2014). Cortico-limbic responses to masked affective faces across PTSD, panic disorder, and specific phobia. *Depression and Anxiety, 31*(2), 150–159. https://doi.org/10.1002/da.22156

Kim, M. J., Gee, D. G., Loucks, R. A., Davis, F. C., & Whalen, P. J. (2011). Anxiety dissociates dorsal and ventral medial prefrontal cortex functional connectivity with the amygdala at rest. *Cerebral Cortex, 21*(7), 1667–1673. https://doi.org/10.1093/cercor/bhq237

Kito, S., Hasegawa, T., & Koga, Y. (2012). Cerebral blood flow in the ventromedial prefrontal cortex correlates with treatment response to low-frequency right prefrontal repetitive transcranial magnetic stimulation in the treatment of depression. *Psychiatry and Clinical Neurosciences, 66*(2), 138–145. https://doi.org/10.1111/j.1440-1819.2011.02312.x

Klass, A., Glaubitz, B., Tegenthoff, M., & Lissek, S. (2017). D-cycloserine facilitates extinction learning and enhances extinction-related brain activation. *Neurobiology of Learning and Memory, 144*, 235–247. https://doi.org/10.1016/j.nlm.2017.08.003

Koch, S. B., van Zuiden, M., Nawijn, L., Frijling, J. L., Veltman, D. J., & Olff, M. (2016). Aberrant resting-state brain activity in posttraumatic stress disorder: A meta-analysis and systematic review. *Depression and Anxiety, 33*(7), 592–605. https://doi.org/10.1002/da.22478

Koenigs, M., & Grafman, J. (2009). The functional neuroanatomy of depression: Distinct roles for ventromedial and dorsolateral prefrontal cortex. *Behavioural Brain Research, 201*(2), 239–243. https://doi.org/10.1016/j.bbr.2009.03.004

Kohls, G., Schulte-Rüther, M., Nehrkorn, B., Müller, K., Fink, G. R., Kamp-Becker, I., Herpertz-Dahlmann, B., Schultz, R. T., & Konrad, K. (2013). Reward system dysfunction in autism spectrum disorders. *Social Cognitive and Affective Neuroscience, 8*(5), 565–572. https://doi.org/10.1093/scan/nss033

Kral, T. R. A., Schuyler, B. S., Mumford, J. A., Rosenkranz, M. A., Lutz, A., & Davidson, R. J. (2018). Impact of short- and long-term mindfulness meditation training on amygdala reactivity to emotional stimuli. *NeuroImage, 181*, 301–313. https://doi.org/10.1016/j.neuroimage.2018.07.013

Kucyi, A., & Davis, K. D. (2014). Dynamic functional connectivity of the default mode network tracks daydreaming. *NeuroImage, 100*, 471–480. https://doi.org/10.1016/j.neuroimage.2014.06.044

Kühn, S., & Gallinat, J. (2013). Resting-state brain activity in schizophrenia and major depression: A quantitative meta-analysis. *Schizophrenia Bulletin, 39*(2), 358–365. https://doi.org/10.1093/schbul/sbr151

Lebois, L. A., Papies, E. K., Gopinath, K., Cabanban, R., Quigley, K. S., Krishnamurthy, V., Feldman Barrett, L., & Barsalou, L. W. (2015). A shift in perspective: Decentering through mindful attention to imagined stressful events. *Neuropsychologia, 75*, 505–524. https://doi.org/10.1016/j.neuropsychologia.2015.05.030

Lombardo, M. V., Chakrabarti, B., Bullmore, E. T., Sadek, S. A., Pasco, G., Wheelwright, S. J., Suckling, J., MRC AIMS Consortium, & Baron-Cohen, S. (2010). Atypical neural self-representation in autism. *Brain, 133*(2), 611–624. https://doi.org/10.1093/brain/awp306

Long, Z., Du, L., Zhao, J., Wu, S., Zheng, Q., & Lei, X. (2020). Prediction on treatment improvement in depression with resting state connectivity: A coordinate-based meta-analysis. *Journal of Affective Disorders, 276*, 62–68. https://doi.org/10.1016/j.jad.2020.06.072

Macrae, C. N., Moran, J. M., Heatherton, T. F., Banfield, J. F., & Kelley, W. M. (2004). Medial prefrontal activity predicts memory for self. *Cerebral Cortex, 14*(6), 647–654. https://doi.org/10.1093/cercor/bhh025

Mehta, N. D., Haroon, E., Xu, X., Woolwine, B. J., Li, Z., & Felger, J. C. (2018). Inflammation negatively correlates with amygdala-ventromedial prefrontal functional connectivity in association with anxiety in patients with depression: Preliminary results. *Brain, Behavior, and Immunity, 73*, 725–730. https://doi.org/10.1016/j.bbi.2018.07.026

Milad, M. R., Furtak, S. C., Greenberg, J. L., Keshaviah, A., Im, J. J., Falkenstein, M. J., Jenike, M., Rauch, S. L., & Wilhelm, S. (2013). Deficits in conditioned fear extinction in obsessive–compulsive disorder and neurobiological changes in the fear circuit. *JAMA Psychiatry, 70*(6), 608–618; quiz 554. https://doi.org/10.1001/jamapsychiatry.2013.914

Milad, M. R., Wright, C. I., Orr, S. P., Pitman, R. K., Quirk, G. J., & Rauch, S. L. (2007). Recall of fear extinction in humans activates the ventromedial prefrontal cortex and hippocampus in concert. *Biological Psychiatry, 62*(5), 446–454. https://doi.org/10.1016/j.biopsych.2006.10.011

Miller, D. R., Hayes, S. M., Hayes, J. P., Spielberg, J. M., Lafleche, G., & Verfaellie, M. (2017). Default mode network subsystems are differentially disrupted in posttraumatic stress disorder. *Biological*

Psychiatry: Cognitive Neuroscience and Neuroimaging, 2(4), 363–371. https://doi.org/10.1016/j.bpsc.2016.12.006

Mitchell, J. P., Banaji, M. R., & Macrae, C. N. (2005). The link between social cognition and self-referential thought in the medial prefrontal cortex. *Journal of Cognitive Neuroscience, 17*(8), 1306–1315. https://doi.org/10.1162/0898929055002418

Mitchell, J. P., Schirmer, J., Ames, D. L., & Gilbert, D. T. (2011). Medial prefrontal cortex predicts intertemporal choice. *Journal of Cognitive Neuroscience, 23*(4), 857–866. https://doi.org/10.1162/jocn.2010.21479

Morriss, J., Christakou, A., & Van Reekum, C. M. (2015). Intolerance of uncertainty predicts fear extinction in amygdala-ventromedial prefrontal cortical circuitry. *Biology of Mood and Anxiety Disorders, 5,* 4. https://doi.org/10.1186/s13587-015-0019-8

Myers-Schulz, B., & Koenigs, M. (2012). Functional anatomy of ventromedial prefrontal cortex: Implications for mood and anxiety disorders. *Molecular Psychiatry, 17*(2), 132–141. https://doi.org/10.1038/mp.2011.88

Nave, A. M., Tolin, D. F., & Stevens, M. C. (2012). Exposure therapy, d-cycloserine, and functional magnetic resonance imaging in patients with snake phobia: A randomized pilot study. *Journal of Clinical Psychiatry, 73*(9), 1179–1186. https://doi.org/10.4088/JCP.11m07564

Nieuwenhuis, I. L., & Takashima, A. (2011). The role of the ventromedial prefrontal cortex in memory consolidation. *Behavioural brain research, 218*(2), 325–334.

Nicholson, A. A., Friston, K. J., Zeidman, P., Harricharan, S., McKinnon, M. C., Densmore, M., Neufeld, R. W. J., Théberge, J., Corrigan, F., Jetly, R., Spiegel, D., & Lanius, R. A. (2017). Dynamic causal modeling in PTSD and its dissociative subtype: Bottom–up versus top–down processing within fear and emotion regulation circuitry. *Human Brain Mapping, 38*(11), 5551–5561. https://doi.org/10.1002/hbm.23748

Nobler, M. S., Oquendo, M. A., Kegeles, L. S., Malone, K. M., Campbell, C., Sackeim, H. A., & Mann, J. J. (2001). Decreased regional brain metabolism after ECT. *American Journal of Psychiatry, 158*(2), 305–308. https://doi.org/10.1176/appi.ajp.158.2.305

Pagani, M., Di Lorenzo, G., Verardo, A. R., Nicolais, G., Monaco, L., Lauretti, G., Russo, R., Niolu, C., Ammaniti, M., Fernandez, I., & Siracusano, A. (2012). Neurobiological correlates of EMDR monitoring—an EEG study. *PLOS ONE, 7*(9), e45753. https://doi.org/10.1371/journal.pone.0045753

Phelps, E. A., Delgado, M. R., Nearing, K. I., & LeDoux, J. E. (2004). Extinction learning in humans: Role of the amygdala and vmPFC. *Neuron, 43*(6), 897–905. https://doi.org/10.1016/j.neuron.2004.08.042

Pitman, R. K., Rasmusson, A. M., Koenen, K. C., Shin, L. M., Orr, S. P., Gilbertson, M. W., Milad, M. R., & Liberzon, I. (2012). Biological studies of post-traumatic stress disorder. *Nature Reviews. Neuroscience, 13*(11), 769–787. https://doi.org/10.1038/nrn3339

Poerio, G. L., Sormaz, M., Wang, H. T., Margulies, D., Jefferies, E., & Smallwood, J. (2017). The role of the default mode network in component processes underlying the wandering mind. *Social Cognitive and Affective Neuroscience, 12*(7), 1047–1062. https://doi.org/10.1093/scan/nsx041

Rauch, S. L., Shin, L. M., & Phelps, E. A. (2006). Neurocircuitry models of posttraumatic stress disorder and extinction: Human neuroimaging research—Past, present, and future. *Biological Psychiatry, 60*(4), 376–382. https://doi.org/10.1016/j.biopsych.2006.06.004

Reddy, M., Greenberg, B., & Philip, N. (2017). 636. Combining Transcranial Direct Current Stimulation with Virtual Reality Exposure for PTSD. *Biological Psychiatry, 81*(10), S258.

Reddy, A. S., O'Brien, D., Pisat, N., Weichselbaum, C. T., Sakers, K., Lisci, M., Dalal, J. S., & Dougherty, J. D. (2017). A comprehensive analysis of cell type–Specific nuclear RNA from neurons and glia of the brain. *Biological Psychiatry, 81*(3), 252–264. https://doi.org/10.1016/j.biopsych.2016.02.021

Rougemont-Bücking, A., Linnman, C., Zeffiro, T. A., Zeidan, M. A., Lebron-Milad, K., Rodriguez-Romaguera, J., Rauch, S. L., Pitman, R. K., & Milad, M. R. (2011). Altered processing of contextual information during fear extinction in PTSD: An fMRI study. *CNS Neuroscience and Therapeutics, 17*(4), 227–236. https://doi.org/10.1111/j.1755-5949.2010.00152.x

Roy, M. J., Costanzo, M. E., Blair, J. R., & Rizzo, A. A. (2014). Compelling evidence that exposure therapy for PTSD normalizes brain function. *Studies in Health Technology and Informatics, 199,* 61–65.

Roy, M., Shohamy, D., & Wager, T. D. (2012). Ventromedial prefrontal-subcortical systems and the generation of affective meaning. *Trends in Cognitive Sciences, 16*(3), 147–156. https://doi.org/10 .1016/j.tics.2012.01.005

Rubin-Falcone, H., Weber, J., Kishon, R., Ochsner, K., Delaparte, L., Doré, B., Zanderigo, F., Oquendo, M. A., Mann, J. J., & Miller, J. M. (2018). Longitudinal effects of cognitive behavioral therapy for depression on the neural correlates of emotion regulation. *Psychiatry Research. Neuroimaging, 271,* 82–90. https://doi.org/10.1016/j.pscychresns.2017.11.002

Scopinho, A. A., Scopinho, M., Lisboa, S. F., Correa, F. M., Guimarães, F. S., & Joca, S. R. L. (2010). Acute reversible inactivation of the ventral medial prefrontal cortex induces antidepressant-like effects in rats. *Behavioural Brain Research, 214*(2), 437–442. https://doi.org/10.1016/j.bbr.2010.06 .018

Straub, J., Plener, P. L., Sproeber, N., Sprenger, L., Koelch, M. G., Groen, G., & Abler, B. (2015). Neural correlates of successful psychotherapy of depression in adolescents. *Journal of Affective Disorders, 183,* 239–246. https://doi.org/10.1016/j.jad.2015.05.020

VanElzakker, M. B., Staples-Bradley, L. K., & Shin, L. M. (2018). The neurocircuitry of fear and PTSD. In *Sleep and Combat-Related Post Traumatic Stress Disorder* (pp. 111–125). Springer.

Via, E., Fullana, M. A., Goldberg, X., Tinoco-González, D., Martínez-Zalacaín, I., Soriano-Mas, C., Davey, C. G., Menchón, J. M., Straube, B., Kircher, T., Pujol, J., Cardoner, N., & Harrison, B. J. (2018). Ventromedial prefrontal cortex activity and pathological worry in generalised anxiety disorder. *British Journal of Psychiatry, 213*(1), 437–443. https://doi.org/10.1192/bjp.2018.65

Wagner, D. D., Haxby, J. V., & Heatherton, T. F. (2012). The representation of self and person knowledge in the medial prefrontal cortex. *WIREs Cognitive Science, 3*(4), 451–470. https://doi.org/10 .1002/wcs.1183

Will, G. J., Rutledge, R. B., Moutoussis, M., & Dolan, R. J. (2017). Neural and computational processes underlying dynamic changes in self-esteem. *eLife, 6.* https://doi.org/10.7554/eLife.28098

Zald, D. H., Mattson, D. L., & Pardo, J. V. (2002). Brain activity in ventromedial prefrontal cortex correlates with individual differences in negative affect. *Proceedings of the National Academy of Sciences of the United States of America, 99*(4), 2450–2454. https://doi.org/10.1073/pnas.042457199

Zeidan, F., Martucci, K. T., Kraft, R. A., McHaffie, J. G., & Coghill, R. C. (2014). Neural correlates of mindfulness meditation-related anxiety relief. *Social Cognitive and Affective Neuroscience, 9*(6), 751–759. https://doi.org/10.1093/scan/nst041

DORSOLATERAL PREFRONTAL CORTEX REFERENCES

Amat, J., Paul, E., Zarza, C., Watkins, L. R., & Maier, S. F. (2006). Previous experience with behavioral control over stress blocks the behavioral and dorsal raphe nucleus activating effects of later uncontrollable stress: Role of the ventral medial prefrontal cortex. *Journal of Neuroscience, 26*(51), 13264–13272. https://doi.org/10.1523/JNEUROSCI.3630-06.2006

Ansell, E. B., Rando, K., Tuit, K., Guarnaccia, J., & Sinha, R. (2012). Cumulative adversity and smaller gray matter volume in medial prefrontal, anterior cingulate, and insula regions. *Biological Psychiatry, 72*(1), 57–64. https://doi.org/10.1016/j.biopsych.2011.11.022

Arnsten, A. F., Raskind, M. A., Taylor, F. B., & Connor, D. F. (2015). The effects of stress exposure on prefrontal cortex: Translating basic research into successful treatments for post-traumatic stress disorder. *Neurobiology of Stress, 1,* 89–99. https://doi.org/10.1016/j.ynstr.2014.10.002

Asensio, S., Romero, M. J., Palau, C., Sanchez, A., Senabre, I., Morales, J. L., Carcelen, R., & Romero, F. J. (2010). Altered neural response of the appetitive emotional system in cocaine addiction: An fMRI Study. *Addiction Biology, 15*(4), 504–516. https://doi.org/10.1111/j.1369-1600.2010 .00230.x

Auerbach, R. P., Stewart, J. G., Stanton, C. H., Mueller, E. M., & Pizzagalli, D. A. (2015). Emotion-processing biases and resting EEG activity in depressed adolescents. *Depression and Anxiety*, *32*(9), 693–701. https://doi.org/10.1002/da.22381

Aupperle, R. L., Allard, C. B., Grimes, E. M., Simmons, A. N., Flagan, T., Behrooznia, M., Cissell, S. H., Twamley, E. W., Thorp, S. R., Norman, S. B., Paulus, M. P., & Stein, M. B. (2012). Dorsolateral prefrontal cortex activation during emotional anticipation and neuropsychological performance in posttraumatic stress disorder. *Archives of General Psychiatry*, *69*(4), 360–371. https://doi.org/10.1001/archgenpsychiatry.2011.1539

Azizian, A., Nestor, L. J., Payer, D., Monterosso, J. R., Brody, A. L., & London, E. D. (2010). Smoking reduces conflict-related anterior cingulate activity in abstinent cigarette smokers performing a Stroop task. *Neuropsychopharmacology*, *35*(3), 775–782. https://doi.org/10.1038/npp.2009.186

Balderston, N. L., Vytal, K. E., O'Connell, K., Torrisi, S., Letkiewicz, A., Ernst, M., & Grillon, C. (2017). Anxiety patients show reduced working memory related dlPFC activation during safety and threat. *Depression and Anxiety*, *34*(1), 25–36. https://doi.org/10.1002/da.22518

Ballard, I. C., Murty, V. P., Carter, R. M., MacInnes, J. J., Huettel, S. A., & Adcock, R. A. (2011). Dorsolateral prefrontal cortex drives mesolimbic dopaminergic regions to initiate motivated behavior. *Journal of Neuroscience*, *31*(28), 10340–10346. https://doi.org/10.1523/JNEUROSCI.0895-11.2011

Barr, M. S., Farzan, F., Wing, V. C., George, T. P., Fitzgerald, P. B., & Daskalakis, Z. J. (2011). Repetitive transcranial magnetic stimulation and drug addiction. *International Review of Psychiatry*, *23*(5), 454–466. https://doi.org/10.3109/09540261.2011.618827

Bellamoli, E., Manganotti, P., Schwartz, R. P., Rimondo, C., Gomma, M., & Serpelloni, G. (2014). rTMS in the treatment of drug addiction: An update about human studies. *Behavioural Neurology*, *2014*, 815215. https://doi.org/10.1155/2014/815215

Benjamin, D. J., Laibson, D., Mischel, W., Peake, P. K., Shoda, Y., Wellsjo, A. S., & Wilson, N. L. (2020). Predicting mid-life capital formation with pre-school delay of gratification and life-course measures of self-regulation. *Journal of Economic Behavior and Organization*, *179*, 743–756. https://doi.org/10.1016/j.jebo.2019.08.016

Bertsch, K., Krauch, M., Roelofs, K., Cackowski, S., Herpertz, S. C., & Volman, I. (2019). Out of control? Acting out anger is associated with deficient prefrontal emotional action control in male patients with borderline personality disorder. *Neuropharmacology*, *156*, 107463. https://doi.org/10.1016/j.neuropharm.2018.12.010

Bora, E., Fornito, A., Pantelis, C., & Yücel, M. (2012). Gray matter abnormalities in Major Depressive Disorder: A meta-analysis of voxel based morphometry studies. *Journal of Affective Disorders*, *138*(1–2), 9–18. https://doi.org/10.1016/j.jad.2011.03.049

Bora, E., Harrison, B. J., Davey, C. G., Yücel, M., & Pantelis, C. (2012). Meta-analysis of volumetric abnormalities in cortico-striatal-pallidal-thalamic circuits in major depressive disorder. *Psychological Medicine*, *42*(4), 671–681. https://doi.org/10.1017/S0033291711001668

Boukezzi, S., El Khoury-Malhame, M., Auzias, G., Reynaud, E., Rousseau, P. F., Richard, E., Zendjidian, X., Roques, J., Castelli, N., Correard, N., Guyon, V., Gellato, C., Samuelian, J.-C., Cancel, A., Comte, M., Latinus, M., Guedj, E., & Khalfa, S. (2017). Grey matter density changes of structures involved in posttraumatic stress disorder (PTSD) after recovery following Eye Movement Desensitization and Reprocessing (EMDR) therapy. *Psychiatry Research. Neuroimaging*, *266*, 146–152. https://doi.org/10.1016/j.pscychresns.2017.06.009

Bracht, T., Horn, H., Strik, W., Federspiel, A., Schnell, S., Höfle, O., Stegmayer, K., Wiest, R., Dierks, T., Müller, T. J., & Walther, S. (2014). White matter microstructure alterations of the medial forebrain bundle in melancholic depression. *Journal of Affective Disorders*, *155*, 186–193. https://doi.org/10.1016/j.jad.2013.10.048

Brody, A. L., Mandelkern, M. A., London, E. D., Childress, A. R., Lee, G. S., Bota, R. G., Ho, M. L., Saxena, S., Baxter, L. R., Jr., Madsen, D., & Jarvik, M. E. (2002). Brain metabolic changes during cigarette craving. *Archives of General Psychiatry*, *59*(12), 1162–1172. https://doi.org/10.1001/archpsyc.59.12.1162

Brosnan, M. B., & Wiegand, I. (2017). The dorsolateral prefrontal cortex, a dynamic cortical area to enhance top-down attentional control. *Journal of Neuroscience*, *37*(13), 3445–3446. https://doi .org/10.1523/JNEUROSCI.0136-17.2017

Bruce, S. E., Buchholz, K. R., Brown, W. J., Yan, L., Durbin, A., & Sheline, Y. I. (2012). Altered emotional interference processing in the amygdala and insula in women with post-traumatic stress disorder. *NeuroImage: Clinical*, *2*, 43–49. https://doi.org/10.1016/j.nicl.2012.11.003

Brunoni, A. R., Valiengo, L., Baccaro, A., Zanão, T. A., de Oliveira, J. F., Goulart, A., Boggio, P. S., Lotufo, P. A., Benseñor, I. M., & Fregni, F. (2013). The sertraline vs. electrical current therapy for treating depression clinical study: Results from a factorial, randomized, controlled trial. *JAMA Psychiatry*, *70*(4), 383–391. https://doi.org/10.1001/2013.jamapsychiatry.32

Buckholtz, J. W., Asplund, C. L., Dux, P. E., Zald, D. H., Gore, J. C., Jones, O. D., & Marois, R. (2008). The neural correlates of third-party punishment. *Neuron*, *60*(5), 930–940. https://doi.org/10.1016/j .neuron.2008.10.016

Buhle, J. T., Silvers, J. A., Wager, T. D., Lopez, R., Onyemekwu, C., Kober, H., Weber, J., & Ochsner, K. N. (2014). Cognitive reappraisal of emotion: A meta-analysis of human neuroimaging studies. *Cerebral Cortex*, *24*(11), 2981–2990. https://doi.org/10.1093/cercor/bht154

Carter, R. (1999). *Mapping the mind*. University of California Press.

Chang, L. J., Smith, A., Dufwenberg, M., & Sanfey, A. G. (2011). Triangulating the neural, psychological, and economic bases of guilt aversion. *Neuron*, *70*(3), 560–572. https://doi.org/10.1016/j .neuron.2011.02.056

Chanraud, S., Martelli, C., Delain, F., Kostogianni, N., Douaud, G., Aubin, H. J., Reynaud, M., & Martinot, J. L. (2007). Brain morphometry and cognitive performance in detoxified alcohol-dependents with preserved psychosocial functioning. *Neuropsychopharmacology*, *32*(2), 429–438. https://doi.org/10.1038/sj.npp.1301219

Chanraud, S., Pitel, A. L., Rohlfing, T., Pfefferbaum, A., & Sullivan, E. V. (2010). Dual tasking and working memory in alcoholism: Relation to frontocerebellar circuitry. *Neuropsychopharmacology*, *35*(9), 1868–1878. https://doi.org/10.1038/npp.2010.56

Chen, F., Ke, J., Qi, R., Xu, Q., Zhong, Y., Liu, T., Li, J., Zhang, L., & Lu, G. (2018). Increased inhibition of the amygdala by the mPFC may reflect a resilience factor in post-traumatic stress disorder: A resting-state fMRI granger causality analysis. *Frontiers in Psychiatry*, *9*, 516. https://doi.org/10 .3389/fpsyt.2018.00516

Cheng, Y., Xu, J., Arnone, D., Nie, B., Yu, H., Jiang, H., Bai, Y., Luo, C., Campbell, R. A. A., Shan, B., Xu, L., & Xu, X. (2017). Resting-state brain alteration after a single dose of SSRI administration predicts 8-week remission of patients with major depressive disorder. *Psychological Medicine*, *47*(3), 438–450. https://doi.org/10.1017/S0033291716002440

Chiesa, A., & Serretti, A. (2010). A systematic review of neurobiological and clinical features of mindfulness meditations. *Psychological Medicine*, *40*(8), 1239–1252. https://doi.org/10.1017/ S0033291709991747

Cieslik, E. C., Zilles, K., Caspers, S., Roski, C., Kellermann, T. S., Jakobs, O., Lagner, R., Laird, A. R., Fox, P. T., & Eickhoff, S. B. (2013). Is there "one" DLPFC in cognitive action control? Evidence for heterogeneity from co-activation-based parcellation. *Cerebral Cortex*, *23*(11), 2677–2689. https:// doi.org/10.1093/cercor/bhs256

Cirillo, P., Gold, A. K., Nardi, A. E., Ornelas, A. C., Nierenberg, A. A., Camprodon, J., & Kinrys, G. (2019). Transcranial magnetic stimulation in anxiety and trauma-related disorders: A systematic review and meta-analysis. *Brain and Behavior*, *9*(6), e01284. https://doi.org/10.1002/brb3.1284

Clark, L., & Manes, F. (2004). Social and emotional decision-making following frontal lobe injury. *Neurocase*, *10*(5), 398–403. https://doi.org/10.1080/13554790490882799

Coles, A. S., Kozak, K., & George, T. P. (2018). A review of brain stimulation methods to treat substance use disorders. *American Journal on Addictions*, *27*(2), 71–91. https://doi.org/10.1111/ajad.12674

Cooper, S., Robison, A. J., & Mazei-Robison, M. S. (2017). Reward circuitry in addiction. *Neurotherapeutics*, *14*(3), 687–697. https://doi.org/10.1007/s13311-017-0525-z

Curtis, C. E., & D'Esposito, M. (2003). Persistent activity in the prefrontal cortex during working memory. *Trends in Cognitive Sciences*, 7(9), 415–423. https://doi.org/10.1016/s1364-6613(03)00197-9

Dillon, D. G., & Pizzagalli, D. A. (2013). Evidence of successful modulation of brain activation and subjective experience during reappraisal of negative emotion in unmedicated depression. *Psychiatry Research*, 212(2), 99–107. https://doi.org/10.1016/j.pscychresns.2013.01.001

Downar, J., & Daskalakis, Z. J. (2013). New targets for rTMS in depression: A review of convergent evidence. *Brain Stimulation*, 6(3), 231–240. https://doi.org/10.1016/j.brs.2012.08.006

Drobetz, R., Hänggi, J., Maercker, A., Kaufmann, K., Jäncke, L., & Forstmeier, S. (2014). Structural brain correlates of delay of gratification in the elderly. *Behavioral Neuroscience*, 128(2), 134–145. https://doi.org/10.1037/a0036208

Duckworth, A. L., Tsukayama, E., & Kirby, T. A. (2013). Is it really self-control? Examining the predictive power of the delay of gratification task. *Personality and Social Psychology Bulletin*, 39(7), 843–855. https://doi.org/10.1177/0146167213482589

Duman, R. S., Aghajanian, G. K., Sanacora, G., & Krystal, J. H. (2016). Synaptic plasticity and depression: New insights from stress and rapid-acting antidepressants. *Nature Medicine*, 22(3), 238–249. https://doi.org/10.1038/nm.4050

Egner, T., & Hirsch, J. *Nature Neuroscience*. (2005 December). Cognitive control mechanisms resolve conflict through cortical amplification of task-relevant information, *Nature Neuroscience*, 8(12), 1784–1790. https://doi.org/10.1038/nn1594

Fales, C. L., Barch, D. M., Rundle, M. M., Mintun, M. A., Mathews, J., Snyder, A. Z., & Sheline, Y. I. (2009). Antidepressant treatment normalizes hypoactivity in dorsolateral prefrontal cortex during emotional interference processing in major depression. *Journal of Affective Disorders*, 112(1–3), 206–211. https://doi.org/10.1016/j.jad.2008.04.027

Farb, N. A. S., Segal, Z. V., Mayberg, H. S., Bean, J., McKeon, D., Fatima, Z., & Anderson, A. K. (2007). Attending to the present: Mindfulness meditation reveals distinct neural modes of self-reference. *Social Cognitive and Affective Neuroscience*, 2(4), 313–322. https://doi.org/10.1093/scan/nsm030

Fehr, E., & Krajbich, I. (2014). Social preferences and the brain. In *Neuroeconomics* (pp. 193–218). Academic Press.

Fitzgerald, P. B., Oxley, T. J., Laird, A. R., Kulkarni, J., Egan, G. F., & Daskalakis, Z. J. (2006). An analysis of functional neuroimaging studies of dorsolateral prefrontal cortical activity in depression. *Psychiatry Research*, 148(1), 33–45. https://doi.org/10.1016/j.pscychresns.2006.04.006

Fujii, E., Mori, K., Miyazaki, M., Hashimoto, T., Harada, M., & Kagami, S. (2010). Function of the frontal lobe in autistic individuals: A proton magnetic resonance spectroscopic study. *Journal of Medical Investigation*, 57(1–2), 35–44. https://doi.org/10.2152/jmi.57.35

Garland, E. L., Froeliger, B., & Howard, M. O. (2014). Mindfulness training targets neurocognitive mechanisms of addiction at the attention-appraisal-emotion interface. *Frontiers in Psychiatry*, 4, 173. https://doi.org/10.3389/fpsyt.2013.00173

Gärtner, M., Rohde-Liebenau, L., Grimm, S., & Bajbouj, M. (2014). Working memory-related frontal theta activity is decreased under acute stress. *Psychoneuroendocrinology*, 43, 105–113. https://doi.org/10.1016/j.psyneuen.2014.02.009

George, M. S., & Post, R. M. (2011). Daily left prefrontal repetitive transcranial magnetic stimulation for acute treatment of medication-resistant depression. *American Journal of Psychiatry*, 168(4), 356–364. https://doi.org/10.1176/appi.ajp.2010.10060864

Germain, A., Richardson, R., Moul, D. E., Mammen, O., Haas, G., Forman, S. D., Rode, N., Begley, A., & Nofzinger, E. A. (2012). Placebo-controlled comparison of prazosin and cognitive-behavioral treatments for sleep disturbances in US Military Veterans. *Journal of Psychosomatic Research*, 72(2), 89–96. https://doi.org/10.1016/j.jpsychores.2011.11.010

Geuze, E., Vermetten, E., Ruf, M., de Kloet, C. S., & Westenberg, H. G. (2008). Neural correlates of associative learning and memory in veterans with posttraumatic stress disorder. *Journal of Psychiatric Research*, 42(8), 659–669. https://doi.org/10.1016/j.jpsychires.2007.06.007

Goldstein, R. Z., & Volkow, N. D. (2011). Dysfunction of the prefrontal cortex in addiction: Neuroimaging findings and clinical implications. *Nature Reviews Neuroscience, 12*(11), 652–669. https://doi.org/10.1038/nrn3119

Golkar, A., Lonsdorf, T. B., Olsson, A., Lindstrom, K. M., Berrebi, J., Fransson, P., Schalling, M., Ingvar, M., & Öhman, A. (2012). Distinct contributions of the dorsolateral prefrontal and orbitofrontal cortex during emotion regulation. *PLoS ONE, 7*(11), e48107. https://doi.org/10.1371/journal.pone.0048107

Greene, J. D. (2007). Why are VMPFC patients more utilitarian? a dual process theory of moral judgment explains. *Trends in Cognitive Sciences, 11*, 322–323.

Greene, J. D., Sommerville, R. B., Nystrom, L. E., Darley, J. M., & Cohen, J. D. (2001). An fMRI investigation of emotional engagement in moral judgment. *Science, 293*(5537), 2105–2108. https://doi.org/10.1126/science.1062872

Grieve, S. M., Korgaonkar, M. S., Koslow, S. H., Gordon, E., & Williams, L. M. (2013). Widespread reductions in gray matter volume in depression. *NeuroImage: Clinical, 3*, 332–339. https://doi.org/10.1016/j.nicl.2013.08.016

Grüsser, S. M., Wrase, J., Klein, S., Hermann, D., Smolka, M. N., Ruf, M., Weber-Fahr, W., Flor, H., Mann, K., Braus, D. F., & Heinz, A. (2004). Cue-induced activation of the striatum and medial prefrontal cortex is associated with subsequent relapse in abstinent alcoholics. *Psychopharmacology, 175*(3), 296–302. https://doi.org/10.1007/s00213-004-1828-4

Hamilton, J. P., Etkin, A., Furman, D. J., Lemus, M. G., Johnson, R. F., & Gotlib, I. H. (2012). Functional neuroimaging of major depressive disorder: A meta-analysis and new integration of base line activation and neural response data. *American Journal of Psychiatry, 169*(7), 693–703. https://doi.org/10.1176/appi.ajp.2012.11071105

Hare, T. A., Camerer, C. F., & Rangel, A. (2009). Self-control in decision-making involves modulation of the vmPFC valuation system. *Science, 324*(5927), 646–648. https://doi.org/10.1126/science.1168450

Heinz, A., Wrase, J., Kahnt, T., Beck, A., Bromand, Z., Grüsser, S. M., Kienast, T., Smolka, M. N., Flor, H., & Mann, K. (2007). Brain activation elicited by affectively positive stimuli is associated with a lower risk of relapse in detoxified alcoholic subjects. *Alcoholism, Clinical and Experimental Research, 31*(7), 1138–1147. https://doi.org/10.1111/j.1530-0277.2007.00406.x

Helpman, L., Marin, M. F., Papini, S., Zhu, X., Sullivan, G. M., Schneier, F., Neria, M., Shvil, E., Aragon, M. J. M., Markowitz, J. C., Lindquist, M. A., Wager, T. D., Milad, M. R., & Neria, Y. (2016). Neural changes in extinction recall following prolonged exposure treatment for PTSD: A longitudinal fMRI study. *NeuroImage: Clinical, 12*, 715–723. https://doi.org/10.1016/j.nicl.2016.10.007

Herringa, R., Phillips, M., Almeida, J., Insana, S., & Germain, A. (2012). Post-traumatic stress symptoms correlate with smaller subgenual cingulate, caudate, and insula volumes in unmedicated combat veterans. *Psychiatry Research, 203*(2–3), 139–145. https://doi.org/10.1016/j.pscychresns.2012.02.005

Hester, R., Nestor, L., & Garavan, H. (2009). Impaired error awareness and anterior cingulate cortex hypoactivity in chronic cannabis users. *Neuropsychopharmacology, 34*(11), 2450–2458. https://doi.org/10.1038/npp.2009.67

Holmes, S. E., Scheinost, N., DellaGioia, N., Davis, M. T., Matuskey, D., Pietrzak, R. H., Hampson, M., Krystal, J. H., & Esterlis, I. (2018). Cerebellar and prefrontal cortical alterations in PTSD: Structural and functional evidence. *Chronic Stress, 2*, 2. https://doi.org/10.1177/2470547018786390

Holmes, S. E., Scheinost, D., Finnema, S. J., Naganawa, M., Davis, M. T., DellaGioia, N., Nabulsi, N., Matuskey, D., Angarita, G. A., Pietrzak, R. H., Duman, R. S., Sanacora, G., Krystal, J. H., Carson, R. E., & Esterlis, I. (2019). Lower synaptic density is associated with depression severity and network alterations. *Nature Communications, 10*(1), 1529. https://doi.org/10.1038/s41467-019-09562-7

Hölzel, B. K., Ott, U., Hempel, H., Hackl, A., Wolf, K., Stark, R., & Vaitl, D. (2007). Differential engagement of anterior cingulate and adjacent medial frontal cortex in adept meditators and nonmeditators. *Neuroscience Letters, 421*(1), 16–21. https://doi.org/10.1016/j.neulet.2007.04.074

Hou, C., Liu, J., Wang, K., Li, L., Liang, M., He, Z., Liu, Y., Zhang, Y., Li, W., & Jiang, T. (2007). Brain responses to symptom provocation and trauma-related short-term memory recall in coal mining accident survivors with acute severe PTSD. *Brain Research, 1144*, 165–174. https://doi.org/10.1016/j.brainres.2007.01.089

Hunt, L. T., & Behrens, T. E. (2011). Frames of reference in human social decision making. In R. B. Mars, J. Sallet, M. F. S. Rushworth, & N. Yeung (Eds.) *Neural Basis of Motivational and Cognitive Control* (pp. 409–424). MIT Press.

Joormann, J., & Stanton, C. H. (2016). Examining emotion regulation in depression: A review and future directions. *Behaviour Research and Therapy, 86*, 35–49. https://doi.org/10.1016/j.brat.2016.07.007

Kan, R. L. D., Zhang, B. B. B., Zhang, J. J. Q., & Kranz, G. S. (2020). Non-invasive brain stimulation for posttraumatic stress disorder: A systematic review and meta-analysis. *Translational Psychiatry, 10*(1), 168. https://doi.org/10.1038/s41398-020-0851-5

Karsen, E. F., Watts, B. V., & Holtzheimer, P. E. (2014). Review of the effectiveness of transcranial magnetic stimulation for post-traumatic stress disorder. *Brain Stimulation, 7*(2), 151–157. https://doi.org/10.1016/j.brs.2013.10.006

Kennedy, S. H., Evans, K. R., Krüger, S., Mayberg, H. S., Meyer, J. H., McCann, S., Arifuzzman, A. I., Houle, S., & Vaccarino, F. J. (2001). Changes in regional brain glucose metabolism measured with positron emission tomography after paroxetine treatment of major depression. *American Journal of Psychiatry, 158*(6), 899–905. https://doi.org/10.1176/appi.ajp.158.6.899

Kim, P., Evans, G. W., Angstadt, M., Ho, S. S., Sripada, C. S., Swain, J. E., Liberzon, I., & Phan, K. L. (2013). Effects of childhood poverty and chronic stress on emotion regulatory brain function in adulthood. *Proceedings of the National Academy of Sciences of the United States of America, 110*(46), 18442–18447. https://doi.org/10.1073/pnas.1308240110

King, A. P., Block, S. R., Sripada, R. K., Rauch, S., Giardino, N., Favorite, T., Angstadt, M., Kessler, D., Welsh, R., & Liberzon, I. (2016). Altered default mode network (DMN) resting state functional connectivity following a mindfulness-based exposure therapy for posttraumatic stress disorder (PTSD) in combat veterans of Afghanistan and IRAQ. *Depression and Anxiety, 33*(4), 289–299. https://doi.org/10.1002/da.22481

Knoch, D., & Fehr, E. (2007). Resisting the power of temptations: The right prefrontal cortex and self-control. *Annals of the New York Academy of Sciences, 1104*(1), 123–134. https://doi.org/10.1196/annals.1390.004

Knoch, D., Nitsche, M. A., Fischbacher, U., Eisenegger, C., Pascual-Leone, A., & Fehr, E. (2008). Studying the neurobiology of social interaction with transcranial direct current stimulation—The example of punishing unfairness. *Cerebral Cortex, 18*(9), 1987–1990. https://doi.org/10.1093/cercor/bhm237

Knoch, D., Pascual-Leone, A., Meyer, K., Treyer, V., & Fehr, E. (2006). Diminishing reciprocal fairness by disrupting the right prefrontal cortex. *Science, 314*(5800), 829–832. https://doi.org/10.1126/science.1129156

Ko, C.-H., Liu, G.-C., Hsiao, S., Yen, J. Y., Yang, M.-J., Lin, W.-C., Yen, C.-F., & Chen, C. S. (2009). Brain activities associated with gaming urge of online gaming addiction. *Journal of Psychiatric Research, 43*(7), 739–747. https://doi.org/10.1016/j.jpsychires.2008.09.012

Koenen, K. C., Driver, K. L., Oscar-Berman, M., Wolfe, J., Folsom, S., Huang, M. T., & Schlesinger, L. (2001). Measures of prefrontal system dysfunction in posttraumatic stress disorder. *Brain and Cognition, 45*(1), 64–78. https://doi.org/10.1006/brcg.2000.1256

Korgaonkar, M. S., Grieve, S. M., Etkin, A., Koslow, S. H., & Williams, L. M. (2013). Using standardized fMRI protocols to identify patterns of prefrontal circuit dysregulation that are common and specific to cognitive and emotional tasks in major depressive disorder: First wave results from the iSPOT-D study. *Neuropsychopharmacology, 38*(5), 863–871. https://doi.org/10.1038/npp.2012.252

Kozasa, E. H., Radvany, J., Barreiros, M. A., Leite, J. R., & Amaro, E. (2008). Preliminary functional magnetic resonance imaging Stroop task results before and after a Zen meditation retreat. *Psychiatry and Clinical Neurosciences, 62*(3), 366. https://doi.org/10.1111/j.1440-1819.2008.01809.x

Krawczyk, D. C. (2002). Contributions of the prefrontal cortex to the neural basis of human decision making. *Neuroscience and Biobehavioral Reviews*, 26(6), 631–664. https://doi.org/10.1016/s0149 -7634(02)00021-0

Kühn, S., & Gallinat, J. (2013). Gray matter correlates of posttraumatic stress disorder: A quantitative meta-analysis. *Biological Psychiatry*, 73(1), 70–74. https://doi.org/10.1016/j.biopsych.2012.06.029

Kühn, S., Schubert, F., & Gallinat, J. (2010). Reduced thickness of medial orbitofrontal cortex in smokers. *Biological Psychiatry*, 68(11), 1061–1065. https://doi.org/10.1016/j.biopsych.2010.08.004

Li, X., Du, L., Sahlem, G. L., Badran, B. W., Henderson, S., & George, M. S. (2017). Repetitive transcranial magnetic stimulation (rTMS) of the dorsolateral prefrontal cortex reduces resting-state insula activity and modulates functional connectivity of the orbitofrontal cortex in cigarette smokers. *Drug and Alcohol Dependence*, 174, 98–105. https://doi.org/10.1016/j.drugalcdep .2017.02.002

Li, Y., Wang, L., Jia, M., Guo, J., Wang, H., & Wang, M. (2017). The effects of high-frequency rTMS over the left DLPFC on cognitive control in young healthy participants. *PLOS ONE*, 12(6), e0179430. https://doi.org/10.1371/journal.pone.0179430

Lindauer, R. J. L., Booij, J., Habraken, J. B. A., Meijel, E. P. M., Uylings, H. B., Olff M., Carlier I. V. E., den Heeten G. J., van Eck-Smit B. L. F., & Gersons, B. P. (2008). Effects of psychotherapy on regional cerebral blood flow during trauma imagery in patients with post-traumatic stress disorder: A randomized clinical trial. *Psychologie Medicale*, 38(4), 543–554.

Liston, C., Miller, M. M., Goldwater, D. S., Radley, J. J., Rocher, A. B., Hof, P. R., Morrison, J. H., & McEwen, B. S. (2006). Stress-induced alterations in prefrontal cortical dendritic morphology predict selective impairments in perceptual attentional set-shifting. *Journal of Neuroscience*, 26(30), 7870–7874. https://doi.org/10.1523/JNEUROSCI.1184-06.2006

Lupi, M., Martinotti, G., Santacroce, R., Cinosi, E., Carlucci, M., Marini, S., Acciavatti, T., & di Giannantonio, M. (2017). Transcranial direct current stimulation in substance use disorders: A systematic review of scientific literature. *Journal of ECT*, 33(3), 203–209. https://doi.org/10.1097/ YCT.0000000000000401

Ma, Y. (2015). Neuropsychological mechanism underlying antidepressant effect: A systematic meta-analysis. *Molecular Psychiatry*, 20(3), 311–319. https://doi.org/10.1038/mp.2014.24

MacDonald, A. W., Cohen, J. D., Stenger, V. A., & Carter, C. S. (2000). Dissociating the role of the dorsolateral prefrontal and anterior cingulate cortex in cognitive control. *Science, 288*(5472), 1835–1838. https://doi.org/10.1126/science.288.5472.1835

MacNamara, A., Rabinak, C. A., Kennedy, A. E., Fitzgerald, D. A., Liberzon, I., Stein, M. B., & Phan, K. L. (2016). Emotion regulatory brain function and SSRI treatment in PTSD: Neural correlates and predictors of change. *Neuropsychopharmacology*, 41(2), 611–618. https://doi.org/10 .1038/npp.2015.190

Mayberg, H. S. (2009). Targeted electrode-based modulation of neural circuits for depression. *Journal of Clinical Investigation*, 119(4), 717–725. https://doi.org/10.1172/JCI38454

Mayberg, H. S., Brannan, S. K., Tekell, J. L., Silva, J. A., Mahurin, R. K., McGinnis, S., & Jerabek, P. A. (2000). Regional metabolic effects of fluoxetine in major depression: Serial changes and relationship to clinical response. *Biological Psychiatry*, 48(8), 830–843. https://doi.org/10.1016/ s0006-3223(00)01036-2

Metcalfe, J., & Mischel, W. (1999). A hot/cool-system analysis of delay of gratification: Dynamics of willpower. *Psychological Review*, 106(1), 3–19. https://doi.org/10.1037/0033-295x.106.1.3

Milad, M. R., & Quirk, G. J. (2012). Fear extinction as a model for translational neuroscience: Ten years of progress. *Annual Review of Psychology*, 63, 129–151. https://doi.org/10.1146/annurev .psych.121208.131631

Miller, B. L. (1999). *The human frontal lobes*. Guilford Press.

Miller, B. L., & Cummings, J. L. (Eds.). (2017). *The human frontal lobes: Functions and disorders*. Guilford Publications.

Moores, K. A., Clark, C. R., McFarlane, A. C., Brown, G. C., Puce, A., & Taylor, D. J. (2008). Abnormal recruitment of working memory updating networks during maintenance of trauma-neutral information in post-traumatic stress disorder. *Psychiatry Research*, *163*(2), 156–170. https://doi .org/10.1016/j.pscychresns.2007.08.011

Morgan, C. A., Doran, A., Steffian, G., Hazlett, G., & Southwick, S. M. (2006). Stress-induced deficits in working memory and visuo-constructive abilities in Special Operations soldiers. *Biological Psychiatry*, *60*(7), 722–729. https://doi.org/10.1016/j.biopsych.2006.04.021

Moser, D. A., Aue, T., Suardi, F., Kutlikova, H., Cordero, M. I., Rossignol, A. S., . . . & Schechter, D. S. (2015). Violence-related PTSD and neural activation when seeing emotionally charged male–female interactions. *Social cognitive and affective neuroscience*, *10*(5), 645–653.

Murrough, J. W., Abdallah, C. G., Anticevic, A., Collins, K. A., Geha, P., Averill, L. A., Schwartz, J., DeWilde, K. E., Averill, C., Yang, G. J.-W., Wong, E., Tang, C. Y., Krystal, J. H., Iosifescu, D. V., & Charney, D. S. (2016). Reduced global functional connectivity of the medial prefrontal cortex in major depressive disorder. *Human Brain Mapping*, *37*(9), 3214–3223. https://doi.org/10.1002/ hbm.23235

Nakama, H., Garcia, A., O'Brien, K., & Ellis, N. (2014). Case report of a 24-year-old man with resolution of treatment-resistant major depressive disorder and comorbid PTSD using rTMS. *Journal of ECT*, *30*(1), e9–e10. https://doi.org/10.1097/YCT.0b013e182a2705d

Nejati, V., Salehinejad, M. A., & Nitsche, M. A. (2018). Interaction of the left dorsolateral prefrontal cortex (l-DLPFC) and right orbitofrontal cortex (OFC) in hot and cold executive functions: Evidence from transcranial direct current stimulation (tDCS). *Neuroscience*, *369*, 109–123. https://doi .org/10.1016/j.neuroscience.2017.10.042

O'Connor, J. A., & Hemby, S. E. (2007). Elevated GRIA1 mRNA expression in Layer II/III and V pyramidal cells of the DLPFC in schizophrenia. *Schizophrenia Research*, *97*(1–3), 277–288. https://doi .org/10.1016/j.schres.2007.09.022

Olson, E., Kaiser, R., Rauch, S., & Rosso, I. (2018). O24. Altered DLPFC-precuneus connectivity in PTSD: Morphological, clinical, and fear conditioning correlates. *Biological Psychiatry*, *83*(9), S117–S118. https://doi.org/10.1016/j.biopsych.2018.02.310

Philip, N. S., Barredo, J., van't Wout-Frank, M., Tyrka, A. R., Price, L. H., & Carpenter, L. L. (2018). Network mechanisms of clinical response to transcranial magnetic stimulation in posttraumatic stress and major depressive disorders. *Biological Psychiatry*, *83*(3), 263–272.

Prehn, K., Wartenburger, I., Mériau, K., Scheibe, C., Goodenough, O. R., Villringer, A., van der Meer, E., & Heekeren, H. R. (2008). Individual differences in moral judgment competence influence neural correlates of socio-normative judgments. *Social Cognitive and Affective Neuroscience*, *3*(1), 33–46. https://doi.org/10.1093/scan/nsm037

Quirk, G. J., & Mueller, D. (2008). Neural mechanisms of extinction learning and retrieval. *Neuropsychopharmacology*, *33*(1), 56–72. https://doi.org/10.1038/sj.npp.1301555

Rabinak, C. A., MacNamara, A., Kennedy, A. E., Angstadt, M., Stein, M. B., Liberzon, I., & Phan, K. L. (2014). Focal and aberrant prefrontal engagement during emotion regulation in veterans with posttraumatic stress disorder. *Depression and Anxiety*, *31*(10), 851–861. https://doi .org/10.1002/da.22243

Radaelli, D., Sferrazza Papa, G. S., Vai, B., Poletti, S., Smeraldi, E., Colombo, C., & Benedetti, F. (2015). Fronto-limbic disconnection in bipolar disorder. *European Psychiatry*, *30*(1), 82–88. https://doi .org/10.1016/j.eurpsy.2014.04.001

Rajkowska, G., & Goldman-Rakic, P. S. (1995). Cytoarchitectonic definition of prefrontal areas in the normal human cortex: II. Variability in locations of areas, 9 and 46 and relationship to the Talairach Coordinate System. *Cerebral Cortex*, *5*(4), 323–337.

Rajkowska, G., & Stockmeier, C. A. (2013). Astrocyte pathology in major depressive disorder: Insights from human postmortem brain tissue. *Current Drug Targets*, *14*(11), 1225–1236. https://doi.org/10 .2174/13894501113149990156

Robinson, H., Calamia, M., Gläscher, J., Bruss, J., & Tranel, D. (2014). Neuroanatomical correlates of executive functions: A neuropsychological approach using the EXAMINER battery. *Jour-*

nal of the International Neuropsychological Society, 20(1), 52–63. https://doi.org/10.1017/S135561771300060X

Rosenbloom, M. H., Schmahmann, J. D., & Price, B. H. (2012). The functional neuroanatomy of decision-making. *Journal of Neuropsychiatry and Clinical Neurosciences, 24*(3), 266–277. https://doi.org/10.1176/appi.neuropsych.11060139

Roy, M. J., Francis, J., Friedlander, J., Banks-Williams, L., Lande, R. G., Taylor, P., Blair, J., McLellan, J., Law, W., Tarpley, V., Patt, I., Yu, H., Mallinger, A., Difede, J., Rizzo, A., & Rothbaum, B. (2010). Improvement in cerebral function with treatment of posttraumatic stress disorder. *Annals of the New York Academy of Sciences, 1208,* 142–149. https://doi.org/10.1111/j.1749-6632.2010.05689.x

Salehinejad, M. A., Ghanavai, E., Rostami, R., & Nejati, V. (2017). Cognitive control dysfunction in emotion dysregulation and psychopathology of major depression (MD): Evidence from transcranial brain stimulation of the dorsolateral prefrontal cortex (DLPFC). *Journal of Affective Disorders, 210,* 241–248. https://doi.org/10.1016/j.jad.2016.12.036

Salo, R., Ursu, S., Buonocore, M. H., Leamon, M. H., & Carter, C. (2009). Impaired prefrontal cortical function and disrupted adaptive cognitive control in methamphetamine abusers: A functional magnetic resonance imaging study. *Biological Psychiatry, 65*(8), 706–709. https://doi.org/10.1016/j.biopsych.2008.11.026

Scheinost, D., Holmes, S. E., DellaGioia, N., Schleifer, C., Matuskey, D., Abdallah, C. G., Hampson, M., Krystal, J. H., Anticevic, A., & Esterlis, I. (2018). Multimodal investigation of network level effects using intrinsic functional connectivity, anatomical covariance, and structure-to-function correlations in unmedicated major depressive disorder. *Neuropsychopharmacology, 43*(5), 1119–1127. https://doi.org/10.1038/npp.2017.229

Schlam, T. R., Wilson, N. L., Shoda, Y., Mischel, W., & Ayduk, O. (2013). Preschoolers' delay of gratification predicts their body mass 30 years later. *Journal of Pediatrics, 162*(1), 90–93. https://doi.org/10.1016/j.jpeds.2012.06.049

Schwartz, D. L., Mitchell, A. D., Lahna, D. L., Luber, H. S., Huckans, M. S., Mitchell, S. H., & Hoffman, W. F. (2010). Global and local morphometric differences in recently abstinent methamphetamine-dependent individuals. *NeuroImage, 50*(4), 1392–1401. https://doi.org/10.1016/j.neuroimage.2010.01.056

Segrave, R. A., Arnold, S., Hoy, K., & Fitzgerald, P. B. (2014). Concurrent cognitive control training augments the antidepressant efficacy of tDCS: A pilot study. *Brain Stimulation, 7*(2), 325–331. https://doi.org/10.1016/j.brs.2013.12.008

Selemon, L. D., Young, K. A., Cruz, D. A., & Williamson, D. E. (2019). Frontal lobe circuitry in posttraumatic stress disorder. *Chronic Stress, 3,* 3. https://doi.org/10.1177/2470547019850166

Seminowicz, D. A., Shpaner, M., Keaser, M. L., Krauthamer, G. M., Mantegna, J., Dumas, J. A., Newhouse, P. A., Filippi, C. G., Keefe, F. J., & Naylor, M. R. (2013). Cognitive-behavioral therapy increases prefrontal cortex gray matter in patients with chronic pain. *Journal of Pain, 14*(12), 1573–1584. https://doi.org/10.1016/j.jpain.2013.07.020

Shackman, A. J., McMenamin, B. W., Maxwell, J. S., Greischar, L. L., & Davidson, R. J. (2009). Right dorsolateral prefrontal cortical activity and behavioral inhibition. *Psychological Science, 20*(12), 1500-1506. https://doi.org/10.1111/j.1467-9280.2009.02476.x

Shou, H., Yang, Z., Satterthwaite, T. D., Cook, P. A., Bruce, S. E., Shinohara, R. T., Rosenberg, B., & Sheline, Y. I. (2017). Cognitive behavioral therapy increases amygdala connectivity with the cognitive control network in both MDD and PTSD. *NeuroImage: Clinical, 14,* 464–470. https://doi.org/10.1016/j.nicl.2017.01.030

Sim, M. E., Lyoo, I. K., Streeter, C. C., Covell, J., Sarid-Segal, O., Ciraulo, D. A., Kim, M. J., Kaufman, M. J., Yurgelun-Todd, D. A., & Renshaw, P. F. (2007). Cerebellar gray matter volume correlates with duration of cocaine use in cocaine-dependent subjects. *Neuropsychopharmacology, 32*(10), 2229–2237. https://doi.org/10.1038/sj.npp.1301346

Simons, J. S., Henson, R. N., Gilbert, S. J., & Fletcher, P. C. (2008). Separable forms of reality monitoring supported by anterior prefrontal cortex. *Journal of Cognitive Neuroscience, 20*(3), 447–457. https://doi.org/10.1162/jocn.2008.20036

Smith, E. H., Horga, G., Yates, M. J., Mikell, C. B., Banks, G. P., Pathak, Y. J., Schevon, C. A., McKhann, G. M., II., Hayden, B. Y., Botvininck, M. M., & Sheth, S. A. (2019). Widespread temporal coding of cognitive control in the human prefrontal cortex. *Nature Neuroscience, 22*(11), 1883–1891. https://doi.org/10.1038/s41593-019-0494-0

Sosic-Vasic, Z., Abler, B., Grön, G., Plener, P., & Straub, J. (2017). Effects of a brief cognitive behavioural therapy group intervention on baseline brain perfusion in adolescents with major depressive disorder. *NeuroReport, 28*(6), 348–353. https://doi.org/10.1097/WNR.0000000000000770

Stojek, M. M., McSweeney, L. B., & Rauch, S. A. M. (2018). Neuroscience informed prolonged exposure practice: Increasing efficiency and efficacy through mechanisms. *Frontiers in Behavioral Neuroscience, 12*, 281. https://doi.org/10.3389/fnbeh.2018.00281

Stuss, D. T., & Knight, R. T. (Eds.). (2013). *Principles of frontal lobe function.* Oxford University Press.

Suzuki, S., Mell, M. M., O'Malley, S. S., Krystal, J. H., Anticevic, A., & Kober, H. (2020). Regulation of craving and negative emotion in alcohol use disorder. *Biological Psychiatry. Cognitive Neuroscience and Neuroimaging, 5*(2), 239–250. https://doi.org/10.1016/j.bpsc.2019.10.005

Tang, Y. Y., Tang, R., & Posner, M. I. (2013). Brief meditation training induces smoking reduction. *Proceedings of the National Academy of Sciences of the United States of America, 110*(34), 13971–13975. https://doi.org/10.1073/pnas.1311887110

Taylor, F. B., Lowe, K., Thompson, C., McFall, M. M., Peskind, E. R., Kanter, E. D., Allison, N., Williams, J., Martin, P., & Raskind, M. A. (2006). Daytime prazosin reduces psychological distress to trauma specific cues in civilian trauma posttraumatic stress disorder. *Biological Psychiatry, 59*(7), 577–581. https://doi.org/10.1016/j.biopsych.2005.09.023

Taylor, F. B., Martin, P., Thompson, C., Williams, J., Mellman, T. A., Gross, C., Peskind, E., & Raskind, M. A. (2008). Prazosin effects on objective sleep measures and clinical symptoms in civilian trauma posttraumatic stress disorder: A placebo-controlled study. *Biological Psychiatry, 63*(6), 629–632. https://doi.org/10.1016/j.biopsych.2007.07.001

Tian, F., Yennu, A., Smith-Osborne, A., Gonzalez-Lima, F., North, C. S., & Liu, H. (2014). Prefrontal responses to digit span memory phases in patients with post-traumatic stress disorder (PTSD): A functional near infrared spectroscopy study. *NeuroImage: Clinical, 4*, 808–819. https://doi.org/10.1016/j.nicl.2014.05.005

Tik, M., Hoffmann, A., Sladky, R., Tomova, L., Hummer, A., Navarro de Lara, L. N., Bukowski, H., Pripfl, J., Biswal, B., Lamm, C., & Windischberger, C. (2017). Towards understanding rTMS mechanism of action: Stimulation of the DLPFC causes network-specific increase in functional connectivity. *NeuroImage, 162*, 289–296. https://doi.org/10.1016/j.neuroimage.2017.09.022

Van Den Bos, W., Van Dijk, E., Westenberg, M., Rombouts, S. A. R. B., & Crone, E. A. (2011). Changing brains, changing perspectives: The neurocognitive development of reciprocity. *Psychological Science, 22*(1), 60–70. https://doi.org/10.1177/0956797610391102

VanElzakker, M. B., Dahlgren, M. K., Davis, F. C., Dubois, S., & Shin, L. M. (2014). From Pavlov to PTSD: The extinction of conditioned fear in rodents, humans, and anxiety disorders. *Neurobiology of Learning and Memory, 113*, 3–18. https://doi.org/10.1016/j.nlm.2013.11.014

van Lange, P. A. M., Rockenbach, B., & Yamagishi, T. (Eds.) (2014). *Social dilemmas: New perspectives on reward and punishment.* Oxford University press. https://doi.org/10.1093/acprof:oso/9780199300730.003.0009

van't Wout-Frank, M., Shea, M. T., Larson, V. C., Greenberg, B. D., & Philip, N. S. (2019). Combined transcranial direct current stimulation with virtual reality exposure for posttraumatic stress disorder: Feasibility and pilot results. *Brain Stimulation, 12*(1), 41–43. https://doi.org/10.1016/j.brs.2018.09.011

Vinci, C., Peltier, M., Waldo, K., Kinsaul, J., Shah, S., Coffey, S. F., & Copeland, A. L. (2016). Examination of trait impulsivity on the response to a brief mindfulness intervention among college student drinkers. *Psychiatry Research*, 242, 365–374. https://doi.org/10.1016/j.psychres.2016.04.115

Vrtička, P., Bondolfi, G., Sander, D., & Vuilleumier, P. (2012). The neural substrates of social emotion perception and regulation are modulated by adult attachment style. *Social Neuroscience*, 7(5), 473–493. https://doi.org/10.1080/17470919.2011.647410

Wang, K., Wei, D., Yang, J., Xie, P., Hao, X., & Qiu, J. (2015). Individual differences in rumination in healthy and depressive samples: Association with brain structure, functional connectivity and depression. *Psychological Medicine*, 45(14), 2999–3008. https://doi.org/10.1017/S0033291715000938

Wang, L., Wang, L., Manning, K., & Steffens, D. (2020). Weakened role of ventromedial and dorsolateral prefrontal cortex in regulating amygdala activity in LATE-LIFE depression – a dynamic causal modelling study on resting state FMRI. *The American Journal of Geriatric Psychiatry*, 28(4), S135. https://doi.org/10.1016/j.jagp.2020.01.167

Wang, S., Kong, F., Zhou, M., Chen, T., Yang, X., Chen, G., & Gong, Q. (2017). Brain structure linking delay discounting and academic performance. *Human Brain Mapping*, 38(8), 3917–3926. https://doi.org/10.1002/hbm.23638

Witkiewitz, K., Lustyk, M. K. B., & Bowen, S. (2013). Retraining the addicted brain: A review of hypothesized neurobiological mechanisms of mindfulness-based relapse prevention. *Psychology of Addictive Behaviors*, 27(2), 351–365. https://doi.org/10.1037/a0029258

Wobrock, T., Falkai, P., Schneider-Axmann, T., Frommann, N., Wölwer, W., & Gaebel, W. (2009). Effects of abstinence on brain morphology in alcoholism: A MRI study. *European Archives of Psychiatry and Clinical Neuroscience*, 259(3), 143–150. https://doi.org/10.1007/s00406-008-0846-3

Yalachkov, Y., Kaiser, J., & Naumer, M. J. (2009). Brain regions related to tool use and action knowledge reflect nicotine dependence. *Journal of Neuroscience*, 29(15), 4922–4929. https://doi.org/10.1523/JNEUROSCI.4891-08.2009

Yan, T., Xie, Q., Zheng, Z., Zou, K., & Wang, L. (2017). Different frequency repetitive transcranial magnetic stimulation (rTMS) for posttraumatic stress disorder (PTSD): A systematic review and meta-analysis. *Journal of Psychiatric Research*, 89, 125–135. https://doi.org/10.1016/j.jpsychires.2017.02.021

Yang, H., de Jong, J. W., Tak, Y., Peck, J., Bateup, H. S., & Lammel, S. (2018). Nucleus accumbens subnuclei regulate motivated behavior via direct inhibition and disinhibition of VTA dopamine subpopulations. *Neuron*, 97(2), 434–449.e4. https://doi.org/10.1016/j.neuron.2017.12.022

Yang, Z., Oathes, D. J., Linn, K. A., Bruce, S. E., Satterthwaite, T. D., Cook, P. A., Satchell, E. K., Shou, H., & Sheline, Y. I. (2018). Cognitive behavioral therapy is associated with enhanced cognitive control network activity in major depression and posttraumatic stress disorder. *Biological Psychiatry:Cognitive Neuroscience and Neuroimaging*, 3(4), 311–319. https://doi.org/10.1016/j.bpsc.2017.12.006

Yuan, Y., Zhu, Z., Shi, J., Zou, Z., Yuan, F., Liu, Y., Lee, T. M. C., & Weng, X. (2009). Gray matter density negatively correlates with duration of heroin use in young lifetime heroin-dependent individuals. *Brain and Cognition*, 71(3), 223–228. https://doi.org/10.1016/j.bandc.2009.08.014

Zrenner, B., Zrenner, C., Gordon, P. C., Belardinelli, P., McDermott, E. J., Soekadar, S. R., Fallgatter, A. J., Ziemann, U., & Müller-Dahlhaus, F. (2020). Brain oscillation-synchronized stimulation of the left dorsolateral prefrontal cortex in depression using real-time EEG-triggered TMS. *Brain Stimulation*, 13(1), 197–205. https://doi.org/10.1016/j.brs.2019.10.007

INDEX

prosocial behavior(s)
    dorsolateral PFC in, 122
psychiatric medications
    in anxiety disorders management, 28
    in depression management, 101
    in PTSD management, 127
    in trauma management, 127
psychological stressor(s)
    PVT effects of, 11
psychopathy
    ventromedial PFC in, 117–18
psychosis(es)
    brain regions impacted by, 145, 146t–49t
psychotherapy
    in depression management, 116
    in PTSD management, 126–27
    in trauma management, 126–27
PTSD (post-traumatic stress disorder). *see also*
        under trauma
    ACC in, 91–95
    ACC–related presentation of, 93
    ACC–related treatment implications for, 93–95,
        97–98
    amygdala hijacking and, 92
    amygdala in, 29, 92
    anterior insula activity in, 59
    brain regions impacted by, 145, 146t–49t
    CBT for, 30, 94–95
    dorsolateral PFC activation in, 123–24
    dorsolateral PFC gray matter in, 125
    dorsolateral PFC hypoactivation in, 124–25
    dorsolateral PFC in, 123–28
    dorsolateral PFC–related presentation of,
        125–26
    dorsolateral PFC–related treatment implica-
        tions for, 126
    dorsolateral PFC underactivation in, 124
    dorsolateral PFC volume in, 125
    EMDR for, 10–11, 109, 127
    emotion dysregulation and, 108
    exposure-based therapies for, 94–95, 109, 127
    features of, 91
    frontal lobe dysfunction in, 124
    hippocampus in, 44–46
    insula activation in, 58
    insula hypoactivation in, 58
    "neural profile" of, 92
    numbing symptoms of, 83
    posterior insula and, 57–58
    psychiatric medications for, 127

    psychotherapy for, 126–27
    re-experiencing symptoms of, 8–10, 125–26
    self-regulation difficulties with, 92
    SSRIs for, 127
    thalamus and, 8–11
    TMS for, 128
    ventromedial PFC connectivity in, 107
    ventromedial PFC hypoactivation in, 107, 109
    ventromedial PFC in, 106–9
    ventromedial PFC–related presentation of, 108
    ventromedial PFC–related treatment implica-
        tions for, 108–9
PVT. *see* paraventricular nucleus of thalamus
        (PVT)

rACC. *see* rostral anterior cingulate cortex
        (ACC)
rage
    amygdala volume and, 18
reality testing
    dorsolateral PFC underactivation impact on,
        126
reasoning
    emotional, 111
recent memory(ies)
    remote memories vs., 105
re-experiencing symptoms
    PTSD–related, 8–10, 125–26
Reil, J.C., 51
reinforcement
    left amygdala in, 18
    nucleus accumbens in, 74
relay station of brain
    thalamus as, 52
remote memory(ies)
    recent memories vs., 105
repetitive transcranial magnetic stimulation
        (rTMS)
    in anxiety management, 84
    in attenuating insula function in addiction, 69
retrograde amnesia, 38
reward
    nucleus accumbens in, 82
    thalamus in, 13–15
reward expectation
    nucleus accumbens in, 71
reward pathway
    nucleus accumbens in, 71, 73f
right amygdala
    in negative emotions, 18

ABOUT THE AUTHOR

Originally trained as a neuroscientist, **Jennifer Sweeton, Ph.D.**, is a clinical and forensic psychologist, Amazon #1 best-selling author, and internationally-recognized expert on trauma and neuroscience. Dr. Sweeton completed doctoral training at the Stanford University School of Medicine, Palo Alto University, and the National Center for PTSD. Additionally, she holds a master's degree in affective neuroscience from Stanford University. Dr. Sweeton owns a group private practice, and co-owns OnlineCECredits. com, a nationwide continuing education company. She holds an adjunct faculty appointment at the University of Kansas School of Medicine, and is a former President of the Greater Kansas City Psychological Association.